The
·MILLER HOWE·
Cookbook

Over 200 recipes from John Tovey's famous Lake District restaurant

JOHN TOVEY

Photographs by Trevor Richards
Food by Robert Lyons

EBURY PRESS
LONDON

Published in 1992 by Ebury Press
an imprint of the Random Century Group
Random Century House
20 Vauxhall Bridge Road
London SW1X 2SA

Third impression 1992

British Library Cataloguing in Publication Data

Tovey, John, 1933
    The Miller Howe Cookbook: over 200 recipes
    from the famous Lake District restaurant
    1. Cookery. International
    I. Title
    641.5   TX725.A1

ISBN 0 09 177061 0

Designed by Bob Vickers
Illustrated by Paul Saunders
Photographs by Trevor Richards
Styling by Isabella Forbes
Food preparation for photography by Robert Lyons
Props loaned by the General Trading Company

Typeset in Monophoto Bembo by
Vision Typesetting, Manchester
Printed and bound in Great Britain by
Butler and Tanner Ltd, Frome

·Contents·

· Illustrations ·

· How and Why ·
I Came to Cooking

Ever since my childhood days, getting under the feet and in the way of my North Country maternal grandmother, I have loved food, and my figure has always clearly revealed this. 'Fatty' was my nickname at infant and junior schools; it graduated to 'Fatso' at the grammar school where, to make more pocket money and to enjoy enormous free school dinners (pocketing the weekly dinner money doled out to me at home), I worked each lunchtime on the Hobart dishwashing machine.

To escape an otherwise unhappy childhood, I forged my father's signature on a job application form and became a junior clerical officer (I was only sixteen) with the then government of Rhodesia. I sailed to Cape Town on the *Winchester Castle* in June 1949, and my post-war eyes opened wide at the sight of the spreads afforded us for three full meals daily. I was first in the early-morning queue for pre-breakfast coffee and croissants on the main deck; first for hot mid-morning consommé with rusks; and for afternoon tea, I went round three times in between gentle strolls round the deck (travelling steerage we were only allowed on *half* the deck); and my appetite for the midnight feasts was limitless! Union Castle made very little out of my fifty-one pound single fare Southampton to Cape Town with two weeks' board and lodging thrown in!

I landed in Cape Town penniless, went berserk in the OK bazaars of Adderley Street with my five pounds advance subsistence allowance for the sixty-hour rail journey up to Salisbury, and had to seek more money at Bulawayo to pay my way on the last night of the horrendous journey on the slow steam train. So much so that, as we got in to Salisbury on Sunday morning, my neck was one mass of boils and I was the original Michelin man waddling off the train with my three suitcases! The nightmarish buggy ride at lunchtime from Salisbury out to the government hostel at Mount Hampden on dirt roads with clay dust blowing in everywhere was soon forgotten when I espied the hostel lunch menu. Starters, soups, fish, three main courses and four puds – and in those days, two starters, one soup, one fish, three main courses and four puds was the normal eating pattern at each mealtime! Queuing up on the Monday morning in the offices of the Public Services Commission for my eventual appointment found me fainting flat on my face and, when interviewed by the government doctor, I was given my first rollicking for sheer obesity.

I was despatched off to the Ministry of Defence as a junior clerk in their machine-accounting office situated in the King George VI Barracks right opposite the Sergeants' Mess. As my first task was related to Army pay and travelling expenses I soon found my way round getting goodies to eat in return for quickly settled claims! I eventually found myself up in Nyasaland as private secretary-cum-accountant to the general manager of the Native Labour Supply Commission. This was fun as every three months I had to go on trips which took me up into Tanganyika, Portuguese East Africa, Northern Rhodesia and Bechuanaland doing stock-takings and sorting out problems as well as, on numerous occasions, preceding my boss in order to arrange cocktail and dinner parties. No mean feat, I assure you, arriving at the back of beyond attempting to sort out with the travelling cook boy and *dhobi* how to purchase foodstuffs and get them cooked on wood-burning stoves and served by the light of kerosene lamps, avoiding the endless moths, mice, rats and compound dogs.

Perhaps that is where my affinity with curry developed! Rancid butter was made palatable with garlic and lemon juice, finely shredded cabbage substituted for lettuce, the taste of potassium permanganate crystals was diminished by heavy use of dried herbs and spices, and vinegars were always a *must* with literally every meat dish. Carefully nurtured cream taken along for the buggy rides of 180 miles or so over bumpy dirt roads was invariably 'off' on arrival, so boozy flummeries had to be concocted for puds. Canned food predominated. Heinz tomato soup was enhanced with grated cheese and lots of croûtons, thick slices of canned bully beef were fried in (often weevil-full) slices of bread dipped in eggs, canned stews were enriched with bottles of Guinness, canned salmon was made into fishcakes (once considered *the* in thing at smart colonial dinner parties when served with parsley sauce, until I discovered the cook using very green grass from the cow pastures as a substitute!), and to end a meal one was very much the society hostess if canned peach halves were flambéd with lots of booze. In fact booze was essential in most dishes, either to get the party going or to pacify the rumbling, groaning stomach.

In my personal life in Nyasaland, I was offered the choice of hostel living or bachelor quarters. I settled for the latter and soon established a reputation for a good table. Always being a workaholic, I was up at the crack of dawn and into Limbe to visit the early market: buying fresh fish from the lake, attempting to get the first of the meat kill from the slaughterhouse before the heat of the sun provided an all-over coating of big black flies, and haggling over bundles of vegetables. For a time I kept chickens and rabbits on my smallholding but eventually conceded defeat to their theft by the endless 'wild animals of the night' (they were mostly two-legged)!

When on leave from a stint in the newly formed Ghana, I fell in love with an old Victorian theatre in the north of England and threw my lot in with that! What halcyon days they were. Three of us living off the smell of an oil rag, continually keeping creditors at bay, at the theatre playing to nigh empty houses, but managing to keep our bellies full by going round the outside market each Wednesday and Friday as it was closing, and looking pathetic to get the cheapest cuts of meat. The very small, but extremely loyal, band of weekly rep-goers, besides buying their seats (top price 2/9 in the dress circle), often brought some of their own home-made produce for the dwindling company, and so during this period we laughed a lot and I learned a lot – about food and life.

But as the pennies ran out, so the necessity for one of us to make a proper living became more and more obvious. I needed a live-in job with no expenses, so that I could save as much money as possible. One cold dismal December day, when the audience of twenty-eight old-age pensioners in for a shilling each on their Thursday night special were particularly noisy and belligerent during the performance, I plucked up courage and phoned the manager of the Old England Hotel in Bowness. By sheer perseverance I got him on the phone to bombard him with a load of garbage about him needing an efficient private secretary, someone to take the administrative burden off his shoulders . . . and at least he granted me an interview. This went very well, actually, as the thought of a dogsbody obviously appealed to Mr Campbell (particularly at the large weekly live-in wage of six pounds a week in 1960).

I was given the job, but as I was making a happy exit, his last-minute remark was: 'You will have to have black tails and pin-striped trousers, Tovey', to which I replied simply, 'But of course'. Being so penniless I had had to hitch to Bowness and then back in time for the evening performance so the prospect of raising thirty quid for a suit was a worry. However, necessity is the mother of invention and I pawned an 8 mm cine camera from my colonial days for a fiver, spent three crisp notes on a thirty-pound club cheque, and the other two on a slap-up high tea in the only upmarket café in the town. I managed to get the local tailor to make the suit *to measure* in time for my starting work on 2 January!

I shall never forget my entrance into the 'front office' of the Old England because of its large, warm coal fire, beautifully highly polished desks, thick red carpet, and – more important still – a pushbell to the next-door stillroom for morning coffee and afternoon teas served by the lounge waiter! Lunch in the stewards' room was a joy, and dinner heaven. On the second day, however, Mr Campbell asked me if I would like to take over the front office as I seemed to be coping remarkably well with his office needs, and by Thursday he had asked me to think about becoming a trainee manager. I considered it for all of five seconds and replied enthusiastically in the affirmative.

Now in those days a trainee manager was usually a flat-footed penguin who had been sent to a low-down, bottom-of-the-pile public school and had failed at everything, so was despatched into catering. Being none of these I was the exception rather than the rule but soon found myself filling in when staff in other departments absented themselves. One afternoon it would be the silver/plate room and the next morning the stillroom, and, on many evenings, the floors. All this *as well* as being private secretary and in charge of the front office!

I adored every single minute, and it was the best training anybody could have had as I learned by my mistakes at the same time as I learned all the tricks of the trade. No such things then as government training schemes and hotel and catering industrial training boards. You were pushed in at the deep end by the side of Nelly and George and learned their own ways, like it or not. It soon became obvious to me that this was a great profession. During the busy high season (when there was an acute shortage of beds) I saw how a ten shilling note procured a bedroom from the head receptionist in an otherwise *full house*; how lock-up garages could be secured for half a crown from a smarmy Uriah Heep head porter when all had been allocated months previously; and how a crisp pound note would always secure the best window table available from the horrifyingly stern head waiter!

In those days the hotel was the flagship of the Old Trust House regime and was run incredibly smoothly, with old-fashioned service, and had regular patrons who returned year after year for the same weeks, often accompanied by their own servants. Silver service for all meals; sheets changed daily with rooms being serviced in the morning, titivated during the service of afternoon tea and then serviced again during dinner. All this was done with a so-called management team of Mr Campbell and myself (with one control clerk, who put the fear of God in us all as she daily stomped down the corridor with yesterday's manual tab in order to show us the few bob missed from guests' bills)! Then the hotel, when full, slept 148 guests with a complement of 46 staff at the most pandering to their every whim; nowadays the same hotel can sleep 160 guests, and there are upward of 75 staff as well as a management team of 7.

In 1963 I was offered the management of the Hydro in Windermere, a large, rambling, gothic 'coaching' hotel (not the romantic kind, but one which specialised in overnight coach parties). My first season was horrendous as everybody seemed to have been trained in the previous century, and I didn't know how I could motivate them. However, just at the end of the season, the chef was killed in a car crash, which put me on my mettle and, upon securing the head chef from the Old England, I started a short uphill battle to pull the place up by its short and curlies. By the winter season of 1965 we were coping with every single local function possible and turning in nearly 100 per cent occupancy nightly. As for meals, it was the norm to do 150 breakfasts, 500 luncheons followed quite closely by 250 high teas, and then 150 dinners. The owners were marvellous as they let me have a lot of rope and encouraged me in my difficult demands, and we built up a splendid team . . .

Around 1968, however, when another two establishments were put under my rule, the gilding began to dull and I wanted a challenge. The staff, too, were a little fed up with the 'factory' we were running. We decided to use a small and hideous dining-room, seating only twenty-eight, as a new evening restaurant called 'Tonight at 8.30'. This would serve a set meal at a set time to a set number of guests, and we would change the menu weekly. I invented the menus, did the waiting – and, for the first time, did some creative cooking. The chef did the main courses, but I was responsible mainly for the starters and desserts. Apart from Saturday nights, it never really took off financially, but *The Good Food Guide* in its first year gave it a high award, and I knew thereafter that cooking and food were very much for me.

I had by then met the accomplished food writer, Margaret Costa (is there a finer cookbook than her *Four Seasons Cookery Book*?), who gave me every possible encouragement and, in the end, simply said, 'If you want to cook, bloody well learn to do so and stop living in cloud-cuckoo land.' What wonderful words of advice. At the same time I was egged on by the two finest professionals in the north – Francis Coulson and Brian Sack of Sharrow Bay with whom I had become very friendly, and whom I held in awe. I quit my lucrative general managership position, spent three gruelling weeks with Susan Eckstein at the Marylebone Road Cordon Bleu School, and persuaded Sharrow to take me on. That was the first failure in my life and one that has caused me endless sleepless nights since because, for a time, I lost my job and, more important still, their friendship.

I was in one hell of a depression and actually felt nigh suicidal, but suddenly the

Westmorland Gazette had Miller Howe on offer for what was then a horrendous amount of money. I phoned a very long-standing friend, who immediately came up, bought the house the same day, and five weeks later I opened it as a hotel having obtained change of use, a licence, carpeted, curtained, furnished and installed a reasonable kitchen. The opening night – 1 July 1971 – was glorious as regards weather, but sheer, unmitigated hell behind the scenes. I only had three staff and so I was rushing out on to the terrace taking drink orders and serving, keeping an eye on what was in and on the stove, and eventually herding the thirty-two guests into the small dining room.

The first dinner was

FRENCH ONION TART

TOMATO AND TARRAGON SOUP

BAKED SAVOURY FILLET OF SOLE

STUFFED BREAST OF LOCAL CHICKEN
with a selection of four vegetables

APPLE PIE WITH CREAM

As I dished up, served and cleared each course, so I took a swig of the cooking brandy to get me through, oblivious to the fact that the meal started and ended with a pastry! When they were all having coffee in the lounges I suddenly realised that we, the staff, hadn't been fed. There was nothing left for us, so I despatched someone up to the village for fish and chips. Just as we were about to eat I realised I hadn't made out any bills for the diners, nor had I any change or a float!

Practically every single day I telephoned Margaret Costa (who had just successfully opened Lacy's Restaurant in London) and she told me what to do and what not to do. I soon took on extra staff and by the third week we were doing *two* sittings on Saturdays, but when I look back on those menus my heart sinks! We managed on those Saturday evenings to serve over sixty guests (they literally queued outside for second sitting like the old-fashioned cinema days) and all that despite only having *one* sink in the kitchen for pots, pans, dishes, plates, glasses, cutlery and hands! There were two and a half of us in the kitchen, and three out front, but we still coped. Now on two-sitting Saturdays, when we cook for over ninety, there are six in the kitchen – with five sinks and a huge dishwashing machine – and nine or ten front of house!

Margaret Costa sent many of her cookery writer friends up to Miller Howe. Derek Cooper of 'The Food Programme' and his wife Janet came that summer and were won over, followed by Dennis Curtis, cookery editor of the *Sunday Telegraph* magazine. But a newspaper strike meant their copy couldn't hit the news-stands . . . until mid October when the *Guardian* came out one day with a headline 'Beside the lake beneath the trees I discovered Miller Howe', followed by an eulogising piece by Derek Cooper. The phone started then to ring in earnest and kept us busy until early January when we closed.

To bring pennies in during November, I had been persuaded to run two-day cookery classes for locals, and even today some of those participants come up to me in the street and say, 'Do you remember those fun cooking days – you've gone quite far since then, haven't you?' . . . and I have, thanks to wonderful support from wonderful friends and, more important still, a wonderful staff.

For the first two seasons, I lived in the cellar next to the boiler room and had a Bendix washing machine as a bedside table. First thing in the morning when my Teasmade woke me I would put last night's napkins into the Bendix and waddle upstairs to have a good wash in the kitchen and get ready for the housekeeper coming on duty. Morning coffee, lunch and afternoon teas were served then as well as dinner, and I never seemed to get away from the stove or sink. During the terrible winter of 1971–2 (when the miners were on strike and electricity was only available for eight-hour periods daily), we managed to build a forty-seater, two-tier, plate-glass dining-room, add bathrooms to three bedrooms and splendid French windows and balconies to six rooms as well as construct a sun lounge – all in the period of a five-week closure. Try to do that nowadays!

The Good Food Guide was extremely enthusiastic about us, and so were the food critics who came in a steady stream, and with whom Miller Howe has still kept in touch and remained close acquaintances. But the core of Miller Howe is basically the loyal staff, some of whom have been here now for ten, twelve, fourteen and fifteen years. They are the ones who have stood the flash of my tongue and flare of occasional temper when things haven't gone right, who have put up with my shortcomings, endured my moods, and helped put the place on the gastronomic map worldwide.

For, in 1974, we started working some of the closed winter weeks with the help of British Airways. Talk about a travelling circus! New York, Boston, Toronto, Philadelphia, Houston, Dallas, San Francisco, Miami have all experienced our 'Festival of British Country House Cooking' in an attempt to dispel the myth that British cooking consists only of tough overcooked beef and soggy cabbage. And we have cooked too in Muscat, Dubai, Tokyo, Osaka, Fukuoka, Johannesburg, Cape Town and Durban. We have now got the annual tour down to a fine art, but it is hellish hard work, I assure you!

A team of six staff has to get down to Heathrow with six suitcases and four large heavy trunks filled with food, pots, pans, dishes and equipment. We have to fly off overseas and face a barrage of questions from the customs and then immigration; when we get to a new venue, we get our gear in, check the pre-ordered stores, and a dummy run in the ovens is the order of the first day. The programme thereafter is an opening night to which the local food press and travel agents are invited, and a further five nightly dinners for the public as well as cooking demonstrations, TV interviews and press receptions. We have to pack up late on a Saturday night and travel on to the next city on Sunday and start the whole thing all over again! It's rather like an old-fashioned variety touring company with smart planes replacing the old steam trains and Boston Airport becoming the Crewe of its day! But this sophisticated soft-sell does produce bums in beds here at Miller Howe, and is a positive boost to tourism even if demanding on time and tempers.

Often people come to me during the current spring and autumn residential cookery courses at the hotel and quietly ask, 'I want to come into this business, what can you tell me?' I often feel sorely tempted to utter one syllable, 'Don't', but then I have to think of how I became motivated and eventually successful, and how all heartaches disappear with the sheer magic of still having to put on a show each evening. And running a hotel and restaurant should be simply that – pure entertainment for the guests. Behind the scenes there may occasionally be a tragedy, sometimes a farce – but it must always be *entertainment*.

· Entertaining at Home · the Miller Howe Way

My years in the theatre led me to liken entertaining – in *Entertaining with Tovey* – to a theatrical performance, and I still think this is an effective simile. You as host/ess are putting on a performance, and in order that that performance will go without a hitch, you need ability, confidence, a good script, props and scenery and, above all, good stage management.

Ability, confidence and a good script – the menu – are the first prerequisites. All my recipes are fairly simple to follow – if not, occasionally, in concept – and by practising them on the family first before presenting them more splendidly to guests, you will gain that irreplaceable confidence. Many of the recipes, too, are presented in such a way that once you have mastered a *basic* recipe you can ring the changes almost eternally. If you work your way through the basic cream soup section, for instance, I'm sure you will be able to serve a different soup at each dinner party throughout a year at least! Advance preparation, part of the stage management that is so vital for any performance, also gives confidence, and a great number of my recipes can be prepared the morning or day before a dinner. This allows you to concentrate on other aspects of the evening's entertainment, for, never forget it, *you* are meant to enjoy the occasion too!

I hope that the following notes, culled both from my Miller Howe experiences and from those as a home entertainer, will help.

BASIC EQUIPMENT

The props for a performance are important, and you will already have equipped yourself with the majority that you need. However, I'll just outline a few of the things *I* consider necessary.

The only pieces of electrical equipment I use and feel do help me to take short-cuts and improve my cooking are a Kenwood Chef Excel, Kenwood Food Processor, and Kenwood electric hand-beater; a juice extractor and two toasters, one taking two slices, and a semi-commercial one which will do four slices very quickly when entertaining. I have had all these for at least four years, they are always in constant use (if not in the kitchen, invariably in the boot of the car or a trunk in the trailer to assist me with cooking demonstrations throughout the country), and I simply have never had to call a service engineer out or have anything done to them.

For the person just setting up house I would recommend an initial investment in the Chef Excel, as this will take a great load of work out of cooking routines. The machine comes with many handy gadgets at a relatively bargain price. But if times are really hard, watch out for sales and go for an electric hand-beater which won't break anyone's bank. Although one can so easily be tarred with the brush of commercialism, I feel I can hold my head high as the kitchen gadgets and equipment I mention suit me down to the ground. And please remember that what I say works for me both at home and in my professional capacity, so I'm divulging such information in the hope of making cooking and entertaining easier for you eventually.

For years and years my heart and soul were always in cooking by gas, but now I can't cook at home without my Sovereign Tricity with its advanced halogen hob. This must surely be a breakthrough for electricity as, at the turn of the knob, I have instant red-hot heat, and by a simple twist in the opposite direction, low, low heat, ideal for simmering and reconstituting gelatine. Because of the overall spread of heat over the four hobs – when all are in use – it is relatively easy to have six saucepans in action even if one is simply 'holding' a sauce and another a vegetable. When cold the top is so easy to clean and more important, to *keep* clean. The well insulated ovens allow bread to prove in the top one while the temperature of the lower rapidly builds up for the bread to bake when risen. I could go on but . . .

I also always find a use, when entertaining, for a deep fryer. This will allow you to serve an extra veg which can be cooked at the last minute while you are, literally, arranging the main course on the plates. There are many varieties on the market. Always use a good, healthy, light oil, and change it fairly frequently.

Other necessities for the kitchen are, for me, at least two medium frying pans, saucepans of various sizes – up to 6 pints (3.5 litres) in capacity for starting off stocks – and a double boiler, although you can improvise with a Christmas pudding-type bowl over a pan of simmering water. A good, long rolling pin is needed by pastry makers, and knives – large, small, serrated, plain but, above all, sharp – are vital; get some good palette knives too, at least 12 inches (30 cm), as this length is vital for many kitchen operations.

Long-handled plain and perforated metal spoons, and wooden spoons are necessary too. The latter should be examined carefully as they should – *must* – have a half-moon back which can push a substance evenly on to the side of a pan or bowl; many modern and inexpensive wooden spoons are virtually cut out of planks, so are straight, and hopeless for the purpose. Get a set of measuring spoons, as well as a set of gill, half-gill and quarter-gill measures (often in grotty antique shops). These are the equivalent of $\frac{1}{4}$ pint or 5 fl oz (150 ml), and so on downwards.

Sieves are important, and I have a variety of sizes. They're in both metal and plastic, because some hot things will not go through plastic, some foods react with metal, and I keep one small metal one especially for gelatine. Flour and sugar shakers I find useful as well, mainly for baking. To shake from a flour shaker is more efficient than simply throwing a handful of flour on to your work surface, but do make sure the holes are of a sensible size, and that the screw top is firm and won't fly off when being shaken. A sugar shaker isn't so necessary, but if it holds a vanilla pod immersed in the sugar, it will make an immense difference to the top of cooked custards and farmhouse pies as well as to biscuits and cakes. Initially a fresh vanilla pod will make you gasp with horror at the cost, but it lasts ages and is infinitely superior to the vanilla essence sold in small bottles.

A sturdy stainless-steel, four-sided grater will long outlive an inferior weak tin one. Amongst the substances it will grate are root vegetables, cheese, orange rind and nutmeg.

Trays of all kinds are used in my kitchen – white plastic for storing, metal for baking, and wire mesh for cooling. The most useful baking trays have non-stick coatings and come in a variety of sizes, some with narrow lips, some without. I still, almost always, however, cover them with good greaseproof paper. The patty trays with depressions are useful too – for small Yorkshire puddings and for putting individual cupcake cases in. And you can also get very small ones in which to make canapé-sized containers. Baking or roasting tins too are essential, in various sizes, to cope with your different needs (a basic bain-marie, for instance).

For many 'baking' recipes, I use a Le Creuset terrine dish – not just for terrines – and of course good loaf tins of 1 lb (450 g) and 2 lb (900 g) are the best for my wholemeal bread and many loaf cakes. My local suppliers, Lakeland Plastics of Windermere, run an excellent mail order service, having brought modern techniques to old-fashioned methods. They offer expandable loaf/cake tins, square cake tins with easy to remove insides, round, spring-sided, loose-bottomed cake tins and fluted loose-bottomed flan tins – all of which I can't do without!

They also offer plastic bowls with round bottoms – so much easier to use than straight-sided stainless steel bowls with a 45 degree angle base, and they're far lighter to handle. They indulge lazy bakers like me even further by selling ready-cut greaseproof paper circles with which to line their cake tins. If you demur at this, do buy *good* Bakewell; cheap greaseproof is a bad investment and causes an enormous amount of frustration. They sell good rubber spatulas with which to get every scrap of mixture out of a bowl, sensible oven thermometers – *vital* for baking, even if your oven has the most sensitive temperature control – and good storage containers for freezer, fridge or cupboard. I urge you to send for their catalogue and have a whole new world opened up for you!

The best Christmas stocking gift ever given me was a clip-on-apron alarm timer, because, try as I may, I am the world's worst at forgetting about things in the oven or on the hob. It's all very well setting an ordinary timer, but then I wander off down to the conservatory and become engrossed in watering the plants, or I do some tapestry or drawing . . .

Finally, good thick oven gloves are always handy by the stove, and to save your work surfaces, you should always have to hand a couple of trivets. My heart still stops at the thought of one of my MGM Christmas numbers at a friend's house. While trying to juggle with six saucepans plus a frying pan on a four-plate hob, I badly burned the magnificent white work surface.

SHOPPING

I find shopping can be one of two things, fun or frustration, and obviously it should always be the former for us. The secret, when shopping for entertaining, is simply prior organization. Even a few moments spent beforehand going through the shopping needs for that particular day or occasion is time well spent – and it's a help on the purse too, more often than not. Make a detailed list of your requirements, but keep an idea in your head of what you are planning to cook so that, if the ingredient is not available, you can adapt. This is easier than you might think – but it doesn't, sadly, work every time.

Do not, however, stint on the quality of raw ingredients. Everything must be fresh, in good condition, prepared properly, etc. The most worthwhile shopping 'tip' is to get to know your butcher and greengrocer – chosen because he/she is good, interested and knowledgeable – and give in return lots of good, interested and knowledgeable encouragement and patronage.

Don't go for second-best, either, with other goods and foods. Several basic ingredients can vary enormously in quality and I hope the following notes will be of some use.

• *Cheese* •

Cheese is a food made from the pressed curds of milk and, basically speaking, these fermented curds fall into two categories: the soft cheeses such as Brie and the hard cheeses such as Cheddar.

The cheese I would always recommend for cooking is a good Cheddar, which should be of a golden hue, smooth and fairly hard. If it's rubbery or flaky it is either immature or badly made, so avoid.

It's a tremendous source of protein, 2 oz (50 g) containing double the amount of most meats. Despite this, cheese is extremely good for carbohydrate watchers – there is none – but not so good for those who are calorie counting! A monthly treat for me at home is the delivery of the Paxton & Whitfield cheeses of the month from their excellent club. All arrive in prime condition, and this is a very joyous way of shopping!

Throughout the book when cheese other than Cheddar has been mentioned in recipes, I mean an excellent, full fat cream cheese which should have about 60–65 per cent fat content.

Even after you have bought your piece of cheese – often hacked off an enormous whole – it will continue to ripen, so storage is of paramount importance. I tend to store most of my cheeses in a plastic box in the bottom drawer of the fridge where it is the least cool. Cream and creamy cheeses I put in individual polythene bags and leave lots of air around the portions before tying. A good Cheddar I wrap in an old tea towel wrung out in salt water and then in foil. However I then make sure that, before using the cheese, I allow it time out of the fridge to come round to room temperature.

Any end bits of *any* cheeses I simply grate and store in a screw-top 1 lb (450 g) preserving jar in the fridge, and this comes in very handy for sauces, quiches or adding to a salad. Waste not, want not!

• *Chocolate* •

I clearly recall doing a chat show in the States once when I rabbited on about this delicious commodity to be interrupted by the interviewer looking at my sagging paunch and double chin. 'But chocolate is bad for you!' she screamed hysterically. 'I don't care,' replied I, 'as life for me without chocolate is life without joy.' After the show was over we went up to the staff canteen where, for devilment, I ordered a large hot chocolate to accompany a wedge of 'Mother's Made Apple Tart' with a blob of chocolate ice cream on the side. They were unspeakable commercial rubbish, and so I could see in some small way why she had formulated such a strong opinion on the subject. (Mind you, she was as skinny as Twiggy, as tense as a violin string, and as dull as dishwater!)

Nowadays the older of the food writers bemoan the fact that there is no true cooking chocolate available. At Miller Howe, however, we buy the Swiss Dohler chocolate which is superb. At home I settle for Bournville Plain and, when feeling particularly extravagant, I use the Terry's chocolate oranges. But, whatever you do, don't be taken in by slabs of cheap cooking chocolate or drops. The results will often taste of chocolate laxative, and could have the same result! Similarly, don't ever replace chocolate in a recipe with cocoa powder – the taste will not be the same (and *never* replace cocoa with drinking chocolate).

Do take care when cooking with chocolate. Never ever simply put it straight into a saucepan over direct heat without any liquid; it will split horribly, you will have to throw it away, and have a very dirty pan to wash to boot. Always break the chocolate up into small pieces (or, if you have cold hands, it can be grated), and put into your double boiler or a bowl over simmering water, along with the recommended liquid (usually, in my case, of an alcoholic nature).

Did you know that chocolate contains a small amount of the alkaloid, theobromine, which resembles caffeine and is therefore a stimulant? This can also have a connection with migraines – doesn't affect me, thank goodness!

• *Eggs* •

My food bible states simply that eggs are a 'spheroidal body produced by the females of birds containing the germ of a new bird surrounded by a rough shell'. Now I tell you, here and now, they mean much more to me than that, for they are a wondrous source of joy: they can be eaten raw (particularly good for a hangover), boiled, poached or fried, scrambled with a little cream, and they have a thousand other uses in cooking. Can you imagine life without them?

Eggs, of course, have lately been criticised because the yolk is so full of the fats and cholesterol that are bad for you – but I don't care. What I *do* care about though is the recent legislation by the bureaucratic bunglers of the EEC who have laid down all sorts of ridiculous rules of what an egg should be in terms of quality and weight, and insist on a statement of where they were *packed* – nothing about where they originated!

For me eggs are and always will be fresh, free-range, farm – small, medium or large – end of story. I want eggs from hens that have roamed their domain scratching the very surface of the earth to seek out bugs, insects, herbs and all sorts of goodies to give their produce an orangey gold yolk and perky white. And the only way that you can find out your own source is to scratch around similarly, and when you find a dealer, grocer, supermarket, neighbour or farmer who will give you what *you* want, sign him up at once on a long-term contract!

Bobby Lyons, the head chef at Miller Howe, now has a nearby smallholding to which he has given every single minute of his spare time these last two years. Chickens abound, being chased by their two cockerels; a goat keeps the 'bush' at bay; and cats climb trees and play hide and seek in the bulrushes of the flowing stream. On the occasional Sunday, he stops by at my house en route to work to deliver six or eight newly laid (rather dirty) eggs, which encourages me to get up early on my day off in order to simply boil them and eat with enormous pleasure and soldiers of well buttered toast.

My grandmother used to test her eggs for freshness by simply allowing them to sink in a large bowl of very cold water. Because hers were *truly* free-range – collected from the woods and lanes in the ration-ruled war days –the occasional old egg would rise to the top filled with its gases. But I can't remember when last I broke a bad egg into a mixing bowl – can you?

Most recipes are based on an old-fashioned medium standard egg which weighed, give or take a bit, 2 oz (50 g) out of the shell. However, the hen doesn't know this, and if the weight is critical – as in meringues (see page 204) – you'd be better weighing them after cracking. And I think personally that all cooking is the better for *room* temperature eggs – other than meringues again, when I prefer to use egg whites straight from the fridge.

To separate eggs, I find it easiest to simply crack them on their sides against a sharp edge, and to swish the yolk from half to half of the egg shell, allowing the white to drop into a bowl below. Some people are scared of doing this though, so you can use a saucer. Crack the egg open on to this, then, encasing the yolk in an upturned egg cup, slide the white off into your bowl. Couldn't be simpler!

• *Garlic* •

Those averse to this member of the lily family miss so much, although the experience of one reader of mine is salutary. One morning through the second post came a dingy brown envelope bearing no stamp whatsoever (and a demand from the postman for 25p excess). It was addressed simply to 'TOVEY, MILLER HOWE', and said: 'I had old valued friends round for dinner the other evening and the whole affair was ruined by your cheese and herb pâté. The friends left before I had time to serve the pudding (one of my old favourites, not one of yours), and my husband hasn't spoken to me since. You should check your recipes.'

Fine way, thought I, to start the day, but I got on to telephone enquiries and managed to track the lady and her number down. At coffee break I took courage and placed a call. When the phone was answered by the lady in question, I said, 'John Tovey here' (in my most sugary of voices resulting in the widest of ugly smiles which caused great mirth to the two secretaries), 'and I am so sorry about your dilemma. I would like to help and see what went wrong.'

I told her I made the cheese and herb pâté every week of my life, but it became obvious that she had basically done what the recipe stated. What was equally obvious was that it was the end taste that was horrible, so I asked her if she knew what three cloves of garlic were. The strong reply came through the phone like dynamite down a mine shaft but I repeated the question. A whole garlic bulb is made of ten to twelve individual cloves, but Madam had laboriously skinned and pounded away at three whole *bulbs* (over thirty cloves), and of course the result must have been hellish. And as to her husband not talking to her, I doubt if he could open his mouth! And where had she been all those years cooking away without garlic?

Back to garlic. Always considered an excellent medicinal herb (in the earliest times it was considered excellent as an internal antiseptic), there is only one thing to remember when buying garlic – feel it. If it is large and firm, buy, if soft, damp or crumbling and shrunken, avoid it like the plague. Garlic powder and salts are never a substitute, as their heavy proportion of preservatives distort the original flavour.

When preparing cloves of garlic, simply top and tail and remove the skin (put them all into the stock pot), and then split down the middle lengthwise to ascertain if there is a green fibrous middle. If so, discard as it is very bitter. Then, using runny or soft salt and the edge of a knife, simply press away to a lovely, delicious paste. When cooking with this, add to your normal base of onions as late as possible as it can burn rather easily.

• *Herbs* •

Happily more and more supermarkets and stores are featuring fresh herbs as the norm on their greengrocery counters, and more and more smallholders are developing herb-growing as part of their business. Quite apart from enhancing practically any main course of fish, meat or poultry, herbs are so good for you.

As the season drew to a close, I used to chop as many different herbs as possible and freeze them in ice-cube trays with water and used to think that, defrosted and added to a dish, they were excellent. Then a friend told me that it was better to simply drench them with fresh lemon juice and store them in the fridge. So now, during the summer, I accumulate my old-fashioned ink bottles with the screw tops (yes, I do still use a real fountain pen for personal letters), and put them through the dishwasher once or twice. Then, in October, I chop chives, mint, tarragon, basil and marjoram, put them into separate bottles and then pour on real lemon juice to merely dampen them. I have also used wine vinegar with the mint and tarragon and felt happy with the result.

It is terribly easy to have a small herb plot or a window box planted with fresh herbs, but I must admit I am the worst person possible where plants and gardening are concerned. Some people I know will plant a brick and a house will grow, but practically anything I attempt to plant soon withers away. However, three years ago, I was given a long window box which I installed on a low wall outside the back door and things have managed to flourish. I nip out and gently cut off what I require, and most have reappeared the next year.

If you do have to resort to dried herbs, buy as little as possible as often as possible and store in airtight containers. Be quite ruthless about throwing out old stale dried herbs as they will simply taste of wood chippings when used in cooking (use them as mulch for your pot plants or for your window box of *fresh* herbs).

• *Spices* •

Like dried herbs, ground spices should be bought in very small quantities as often as possible and should always be kept in secure airtight containers as they very soon lose their pungency when exposed to air.

Coriander, juniper berries, nutmeg and peppercorns I always buy whole, and grate or pound as and when necessary. In fact in my kitchen I have a second pepper mill which contains whole coriander seeds, and I find it gives that little oomph to grilled meats (even thick rashers of bacon), or vegetables. Nutmeg is one of my favourites, and I grate it on to a lot of goodies. It's wonderful on a large beaker of milk sweetened with honey and given a bit of spice with a measure of cooking brandy, and I always sleep better when this is administered to me when suffering from a cold or 'flu.

As far as peppercorns are concerned, there are three – black, white and green. A few years ago pink peppercorns appeared on the market, which even I used on many occasions – but the experts now inform us they came from poison ivies! You can, of course, go without a pepper mill in your kitchen, and buy the ready ground stuff, but you will be missing out on the true flavours.

Although I am not a lover of saffron (reminds me of the chloroform forced on my nose as a five-year-old when having an operation), I think I should warn you of the many imitations sold cheaply and called saffron. It is the most expensive spice in the world as it is produced from a limited supply of dried crocus stigmas, and nearly a quarter of a million flowers produce just over 2 lb (900 g) of *pure* saffron!

Curry powder is a mixture of many spices, and I suppose we all have tucked away in our store cupboard a can or packet of curry powder bought ages ago from the supermarket and which when used disappoints with its lack of flavour. You are always far better off experimenting in your own kitchen to get your own personal blend that suits your palate. Or you could buy excellent commercial curry pastes.

The basic spices for your own mixture can be chosen from things like coriander, cumin, nutmeg, allspice, cinnamon, ginger, pepper, aniseed, fennel, mace, cardamon, cloves, fenugreek, mustard seed and turmeric. These are all *spicy*, and it is only when dried chillies are added that a curry powder mixture acquires heat. Always add this sparingly.

I find my electric coffee grinder ideal for mixing my blend but because the small lid is plastic I always have to soak it several times and wash it well before using it for coffee beans. Mind you, on one occasion necessity meant that the beans had to go in an hour or so after a curry mix had been made. Eyes lit up, eyebrows were raised, and immediately everybody asked, 'What coffee is this, I can't detect the flavour?' Neither could I, but it was drinkable and very different!

On my sole visit to India a few years ago, the only disappointment was, in fact, the curries. Innocuous, bland and watered-down stews was our undivided opinion on each occasion, and I suddenly realised that we were probably being served what our forefathers thought were good curries in the days of the Raj. Heaven forbid! But I was enchanted by the outdoor markets of many Indian villages. The women took an incredible length of time to purchase their minuscule amounts of spices: haggling, sniffing, chattering, oohing and aahing away.

When preparing curries, it is essential to heat the fat first, fry off the basic onions and garlic, and *then* fry the curry powder or paste.

——PREPARING FOR A DINNER——PARTY

The arrangement of a table for a dinner party is like designing the sets for a play in the theatre. It is here that all the celebration and conviviality of your performance will take place, and it must look good. (The rest of the house will, of course, be warm, well lit, spick and span, with everything to cater to the comfort of your guests!)

At Miller Howe, we use linen tablecloths and napkins, and, despite the small size of the tables, manage to fit on to them the cutlery for a five-course dinner, two sets of glasses, a side plate per person, a wine cooler, a tiny flower arrangement, a bottle of water, and a dish of butter. In the early days, I used Meissen blue china at Miller Howe which cost an arm and a leg, and the line was eventually discontinued. I was saved by a delightful sales rep. from Wedgwood who popped her smiling face round the office door one day, and we have been mutual fans ever since! I went for her absolutely plain white china with a thin dark brown rim with the letters MH in a circle of leaves, which, we soon realised, was a wonderful base for the food – the picture the food made had nothing to compete with! The liner plates at Miller Howe are garishly 'printed' in a warm sepia with the view out of the dining-room windows and have proved to be collectors' pieces (and we ring the changes with early morning tea services, breakfast and afternoon tea).

At home, however, I like to be a little more adventurous. I too use white plates, but I am continually seeking out antique or junk shops on my travels in which I buy beautiful old plates in batches of six, eight or twelve. These provide a contrast, and often a good dinner-party discussion as I enlarge upon the bargain (or otherwise)! I sort these all out the day before my dinner party so that I have a very clear idea of what I am going to serve in or on, and double check that they are sparkling (I have a funny-peculiar dishwasher that, for some unknown reason, will suddenly completely miss one plate or glass).

As for the table itself, make sure it is of the right size for the numbers you have invited – that should actually be the other way round, in that you shouldn't invite more people than can *comfortably* fit round your table. At home I can seat six very comfortably round an oval glass-topped dining table in the main dining room, and eight at a white garden table in the conservatory (or, if the weather is good – only once in 1986 – outside the conservatory on the patio). The glass dining-table top can be removed and a specially built table-tennis like table top can be clamped on to the base which then will seat from eight to twelve. I'm never very comfortable with this actually because on one occasion, one very large guest leaned his whole weight on his elbows and nearly shot the other end of the table in the air! When entertaining friends and close acquaintances, I normally stick to six round the table and then everybody can hear well what everybody has to say and it doesn't develop into a shouting match. It's also very much easier to *cook* at home for six people.

So, for normal homely good entertaining, I invariably lay the table the day before and get one job out of the way. Place mats are used on the smaller tables, but when we pull out the stops and have to seat eight to twelve it is a huge tablecloth of end-of-roll material bought at Ulverston Market. At the moment I have one large cloth covered with hydrangeas, and with this I display plain brown napkins (once again from roll-end material), and can swap around to use hydrangea napkins and a plain brown cloth. The only snag is the cloths do tend to run a bit as I haven't had them hemmed (hardly worth the bother), only cut with pinking shears. The napkins, however, which are more closely inspected by guests, have been hemmed by my obliging housekeeper. The cloth and napkins should be clean and ironed, the cloth *on* the table for best effect, before you start to lay up the table.

I am a stickler for highly polished silver and I have a huge container of silver dip (it keeps for ages). I pour this into a smaller ice cream container and throw in the cutlery for a couple of minutes, immediately remove it and put into hot soapy water. I rinse with very hot clean water, and dry at once. And when laying the table, get into the habit of always holding the cutlery in one hand encased in a clean tea towel, enabling you to give a last-minute polish with the other as you lay the item down on the table.

I have four individual silver salt containers – two of which I fill with coarse sea salt, two with fine – and if the weather is at all damp I cover them with bits of cling film. Check, of course, that your pepper mills are full and in working order. I like the relatively inexpensive perspex ones available nowadays which come in various sizes, but *don't* just have one on the table as you will spend most of your time passing it round and the dinner will become like a new parlour game!

Although I have spent many years now watching Derek Bridges 'do' the flower side of our popular 'Food and Flowers for the Four Seasons' demonstration, he could upstage me any day on floral arrangements (but then he's still a lousy cook, relying on a lovely adoring wife and talented daughter). His *Flower Arrangers' Bible* is simply superb and gives a host of ideas, from the most simple to the most extravagant, for dinner-table and other flower arrangements. However modest my own attempts, in comparison, I always like to have a small low centre arrangement of flowers on the table – low so that you can see the guests on the other side of the table. Occasionally I might place candles in it, but I usually have two large candles on the table in silver holders which my grandmother left me. A tip here is always to put your candles in the freezer for several hours before your dinner (wicks covered with foil), and then they don't drip when lit. Quite often I scatter *objets d'art* round the table to break up the spaces (this is where I go a trifle OTT perhaps): I use very small cherub statues, wine glasses filled with semi-precious stones, pieces of coloured glass and bits of silver.

The day before, glasses are put on the table upside down, but they are not given a final polishing until the afternoon before the dinner party. This is done by simply getting a jug of boiling water, holding the glasses over the steam, and quickly giving them a rub to produce a crystal sparkling effect. I even go to the trouble of setting the coffee tray the day before – this can be covered with a clean tea towel.

———— *BEHIND THE SCENES*————

I am continually using the phrase 'stage management' when trying to explain to people the art of entertaining without panic, and if that phrase conveys little to you let me simply say that the whole operation can be summed up in one word, *organisation*. Your dinner party should be a good theatrical performance and so it must be brilliantly stage-managed or organized from beginning to end, and this is where advance preparation and thought are essential.

Quietly, the day before, go through the actual service of the meal and decide *where* to serve and plate (and of course what to serve on and with). If you are going to use little dishes on a serving plate for one course, see that this liner plate is doyleyed (and a fern head or sprig of conifer with a simple flower will be effective), and that they are stacked conveniently. Make sure you always have plenty of work space available for the actual serving of the main course, along with spoons to help serve. There's no use having everything cooked and ready, to find there is no cutlery available for dishing up! And make sure, once you've finished cooking, that there's space for those inevitable dirties, the most important consideration of all. Have ready a large ice cream container in which you can dump all the dirty cutlery, blades and prongs down, in hot soapy water when the time comes. And do remember to have the relevant plates heating in the oven or chilling in the fridge.

I always go for plate service – as we do at Miller Howe – and plonk everything down in front of folk rather than have tureens and dishes of vegetables being passed to and fro getting cold. When plating, have a clear picture in your mind of what you wish to see on the plate, taking colours and shapes into account: don't put cabbage, mashed potato and cauliflower side by side when you are also serving French beans and glazed carrots – the latter two will break up the display nicely. Always have a sauce jug warming as some guests might prefer additional sauce or gravy and this can be passed round when everybody starts.

It's now, when the meal has started, that the true 'organisation' starts – clearing away the dirties at the same time as serving the next course. The problem should almost be given as much attention as the original menu! Sometimes there is sufficient time to allow a little washing up to be done as the meal proceeds; and some are fortunate enough to have efficient dishwashing machines (and enough plates) into which they can immediately clear everything away.

In my next kitchen I plan to have a double stainless steel sink with very large sloping rimmed draining boards large enough to take two plastic plate holders with, connected to the taps, a shower spray. I will simply submerge the dirty plates (cleared of excess garbage into a large, close-at-hand ice cream container) in hot soapy water, transfer to hot clean water and then stack in the plastic holders and shower clean hot water over them to remove any traces of detergent. With experience I have found that using very hot water (and thick rubber gloves) means that as I clear the next course, so the first-course plates are practically dry.

What is important, though, is that you are methodical as you clear, and if you're not going to wash up there and then, get into the habit of piling the cleared plates up on top of each other in an orderly fashion. Otherwise you will run out of space in your kitchen and next day when the party spirits have worn off, you will ask, 'What the hell was I doing last night having that lot round for dinner?'

Helpful guests (the kind we all like) are normally only too pleased to pass you their perfectly empty plates and cutlery while you sit down still enjoying the conversation, and what you do is this. Using your own plate as a base, remove the cutlery and hold this in one hand while you put another plate and cutlery on top of yours. Assuming you are a normal left-hand fork, right-hand knife person, leave the fork in position on this second plate and slide the knife underneath it at an angle, and then place your own fork and knife in a similar way. Remove this top plate with the cutlery on it and take the next dirty plate and cutlery. Repeat this process until you have a pile of six or eight dirty plates neatly stacked with all the cutlery on the top plate. When you go through to the kitchen you can grab all the knives in your work hand and put them and the forks easily into the prepared container, and the plates into the sink.

After clearing the main-course plates, if you are only going to serve a pud thereafter, remember to remove the side plates too. If you get into the habit of doing this when the family dine daily you will soon see how professional it looks and how much easier it is than removing two plates at a time and traipsing back and forth to the kitchen.

Some time during the meal make sure you go into the lounge where you had drinks to clear away the dirty glasses and ashtrays (try to have spare clean ones rather than mess about washing and drying the dirty ones), plump up the cushions, check the heating and put out the coffee tray. Fortunately my friends leave at a civilised hour mostly, but if yours don't and you've had enough, simply pull out the plugs, cease the supply of drinks and coffee, and sit there smiling sweetly, willing them to go!

If you have something in abundance in the garden, give it to your guests when they actually depart. At Brantlea there is a large rose garden which, for a few months, is prolific in buds and so often a couple of these are wrapped in foil. A little jar of something like home-made marmalade or a preserve would be a nice parting gift as well.

If you have been neat and methodical about the clearing and stacking of dishes, don't attempt to wash them after the guests leave. Clear the table, though, check the ashtrays and fire, put out the lights and go to bed with a Thermos flask of a pre-made rich, hot and boozy milk drink. Have a good old natter about what went right – leaving what went wrong for the morning or next evening when you have to come home to face the washing up and eat the leftovers!

—DRINKS FOR ENTERTAINING—

Drinks are obviously terribly important when one is entertaining but at the same time they can be a nightmare. The perfect host (if there is such a person or thing) should be able to produce at a moment's notice anything from a straightforward gin and tonic to a tequila delight without flickering an eyelash. I am sorry to say I am unable to do this as I find entertaining quite enough of an effort already if I want my guests to relax and thoroughly enjoy themselves. I am definitely one for taking short-cuts and cutting corners where possible; so drinks for me simply involve one for all and all for one. No 'What would you like?' as they arrive, but simply a welcoming smile, firm handshake or hug and kiss, and a glass thrust into their hands with my eyes imploring them to *drink*.

Some hosts feel the party is only a success if their guests are well on the way to being merry as quickly as possible, and dish up the most potent concoctions. I clearly recall one party where this happened, but I spotted the density of the spirit in the 'summer drink' so held off, to find fellow guests behaving quite foolishly as we went in to lunch, very badly towards the end of the meal and, I strongly suspect, quite ill on the way home. Our host had insisted that the 'kick' was provided by a liberal dash of Tabasco; I found out later it was pure gut-rot cane spirit mixed with some extremely coarse Eau de Vie de Marc!

This doesn't mean I don't like the occasional spirit-based drink – I do. Some Sundays I feel my body craves the stuff, so I will laboriously make a Bloody Mary or have a gin and tonic with a squirt of fresh lime juice and a touch of Angostura Bitters. *One* will set me up for the day. And of course, as you know, I use a modicum of spirits in my cooking – brandy, Scotch, Irish whiskey, Pernod and a selection of liqueurs.

My very favourite of these latter at the moment, by the way, is something called Frangelico. I was introduced to it about nine years ago, when I was being interviewed by the society gossip columnists of an American West Coast, highly-thought-of, daily newspaper. I was at the end of a gruelling four-week 'cooks' tour' working with British Airways and the British Tourist Authority, and I vividly remember half-way through lunch thinking how effete they were and how utterly empty: picking at their food, nit-picking about people, continually trying to see if there were other people in the restaurant whom they knew or whom they *should* know and pay court to, spending most of their time telling me of all the famous restaurants they had dined at (complimentary, of course), and the fabulous hotels they had stayed in (on the house, naturally)! The interview with me was never printed as I switched off and must have been the dullest person they had ever met – *but*, at the end of the meal they insisted they had a glass of a chilled, unheard-of liqueur to go with their raspberries, and I joined them. Thus I owe to them my liking, nay desire, for Frangelico, an Italian liqueur created from wild hazelnuts, herbs and berries nurtured in the warmth of the Mediterranean sunshine (at least that is how the publicity blurb goes). It is so, so good, and comes in a bottle shaped like a cowled monk with a rope around his waist.

Always serve it chilled – with raspberries or other summer fruits – and it also goes down very well with the sticky toffee pudding or the caramelised apple hazelnut cake (see page 199), as well as lending new flavour to an old favourite such as bavarois.

But, on the whole, it is wine and wine cocktails that I like most and would offer my guests as they arrived; I find them the easiest to serve, and the best digested by happy guests. The classic wine cocktail is, of course, Kir or Kir Royale, but so often this turns out to be rather sweet and sickly instead of dry and refreshing because too much blackcurrant liqueur is used. (In fact Minims in Paris have the audacity to serve this made with a very inferior blackcurrant *cordial*.) I usually take out of my bottle of dry white or sparkling wine under one glass of liquid and replace this with the blackcurrant liqueur, Cassis, and very gently invert the bottle several times to allow it to mix right through the wine. This means you simply pour from the bottle straight into the glasses which makes things so much easier.

• *Wines* •

I am not into homeopathic medicine at all but once, when staying at a 'fat farm', I gave full marks to the resident doctor who gave a lecture on 'a healthful approach to life'. Quite seriously he announced that wine was one of the oldest and finest medicines in the world. My ears pricked up, I went from a slouched to an upright position, and my brain started to tick – in spite of being on a nigh starvation diet for five days and completely devoid of booze for the same period!

When I go into the fat farm (should be annually) I can quite easily give up all food and be content (if not altogether happy) with my early-morning cup of fresh lemon juice, my mid-morning cup of vegetable tea, lunch of one apple, peach or pear, herb tea without sugar or milk in the afternoon and then half a melon at night – but I do get very slight withdrawal symptoms being off the booze. So much so that the last time I went into a health hydro for ten days I deliberately took in a large bottle of duty-free cognac and hid it in the lavatory cistern; each night as the sun went down I had a large tumbler full and kept my sanity, and my wicked imbibing never seemed to show up in any tests! Also, before my visit to India some years ago, I was told by one of those know-alls that the part I was visiting would be dry, and the only way I could get booze in would be to have a doctor's declaration that I was a registered alcoholic. A letter of sorts I did procure and on arrival in Delhi my partner said I would have to go through immigration alone with my bag of booze and my letter. This immediately gave me the ruddy shakes – I'm a lousy liar – but at least the shakes made me look as if I were for real! However, I then discovered that the area was *not* dry – and was charged a hefty airport duty!

To get back to this homeopathic doctor. . . . He argued most earnestly and convincingly (not that I needed convincing) that good quality wine is one of the finest sources of nutrition, but should be seen as a 'supporting' medicine – and so it has been supporting me ever since. He went on to say that by actually studying the climate and soil conditions where various wines are grown, taking into account the mineral salts and analysing their oxidisation, you can find out what percentage of phosphorus, sugar, fat, sulphur etc is in the various wines. And, apparently no matter what is wrong with you, there is a wine that can help – not *cure*, but help. And how much nicer to open a bottle and drink it along with food than opening a bottle of medicine and, grimacing, swallowing a tablespoon or so.

From my shorthand notes I see I wrote that for anxiety one should drink at least two glasses of claret (Médoc) each meal as it is rich in phosphorus; for cholesterol, one should alternately drink Muscadet and wines from the Côtes de Provence, because the former is acidic and low in sugar, and the wines from Provence 'encourage the flow of organic wastes'. For fatigue, Burgundies from the Côte de Beaune are recommended as they are rich in tannin and iron in its soluble form, and for sufferers of gout Sancerre is the answer because of its alkaline properties which dissolve the oxalic acids. Such a pity they are not available on the National Health!

Having learned and kept this very much in my mind I have always drunk wine daily, and at fifty-four am fat, flabby and flatulent – but *fun*. All this settling of conscience nonsense apart, the wine that you drink should surely be one that suits your purse and your palate, and as no two people's palates (or indeed purses) are similar it is a tricky subject to give guidelines on.

Initially everybody is rather overawed by the whole mystique of wine buffs and their throw-away daft descriptions. I clearly remember going to one of my first wine tastings and becoming increasingly bewildered by the utterances from the experts, who seemed to vie with each other for the greater or dafter eulogy. When, on one occasion, I was asked what I thought the wine tasted of, I was confronted with very disapproving faces when I loudly declaimed 'brown boot polish'. But it honestly did and to this day when I smell this particular wine I still think of brown boot polish.

At a literary lunch once at Miller Howe, I was overcome with horror when a respected wine correspondent (and one whom I still avidly follow) caused much consternation among the well-heeled, blue-rinsed, twin-setted, real pearly audience when she actually said during her coffee-time speech, 'Wine isn't for drinking, it's meant to be knowledgeably sniffed, swirled round one's mouth and spat out'! I just *had* to bounce in immediately and say, 'What the hell are you on about, I'm here to *sell* the stuff, get people to swallow it to warm the cockles of their hearts, and to go home happy. Can you imagine seventy-odd diners sniffing, swirling and then spitting!'

But I do now see what was meant. To get to *know* a wine you must look at it closely in your very clean glass, give it a good old sniff before getting a drop into your mouth and swilling it around to aerate it, and then (preferably only at a wine tasting) spitting it out. But it goes against my North-Country image to spit good stuff out so I seldom go to posh wine tastings, and when I do I simply settle for a small glass of the four or five that take my fancy and let them swoosh down my gullet into my belly. In fact when buying for the hotel each year I always ask the suppliers to let me have *two* bottles of each wine they would like to be seen on the list. One the staff and I open with our supper and if – and only if – most people like it, I take the other bottle home and drink it by myself. If I feel clear-headed and fine next morning, it will be on the list; if I have a dicky night and get up befuddled, it won't.

Normally, at the beginning, most people are attracted to the sweeter wines, and I clearly remember discovering the joys of La Flora Blanche on my very first leave from Rhodesia way back in the early fifties. Going into Bertorelli's for lunch (as host for the very first time), I immediately ordered (dismissing the offer of the wine list) La Belle Hélène (I told you I wasn't good at French). The motherly waitress said, 'That's a sweet,' and I replied, 'Of course, I know,' and she produced one pear with ice cream on chocolate sauce and three glasses. From that day on I have respected most sommeliers! Thereafter either the young Beaujolais or Bulgarian sweetish reds become appealing and slowly one learns to appreciate the subtleties of the grape. Basically you should be totally honest with yourself and let your own tastebuds work and your belly send up its own messages about the wine.

Nowadays we are lucky in having so many good wines available from many of the large nationwide supermarkets, and the weekly wine writers in the nationals are very much down to earth most of the time. I follow the Friday page in the *Guardian* and have seldom been disappointed by the recommendations there: finding a wine writer that is more to your taste than another is rather like finding the particular crossword that you can do!

There was a time, many years ago, when Sancerre was always a must for me with its distinctive gooseberry, flinty flavour, and delightful greeny tint. Nowadays show me a real traditional fine Sancerre, and I will be truly surprised.

Good Riojas take a lot of beating . . . but a lot of finding too. The current Marqués de Grinon 1982 aged in oak is a favourite of mine at the moment. California wines are delicious but with the rate of exchange not particularly good value for money, unless you seek out those from the Clos du Bois.

But I have recently discovered the joys of New Zealand and Australian wines, and what bargains they are! I go for the Chardonnay and Sauvignon grapes from both countries – the latter resembling the Sancerres I remember of old, and the former coming close to a very fine, old-fashioned white Burgundy. The 1985 Chardonnay from the Hill Smith Estate of the Barossa Valley in Australia is a firm favourite. Of the reds the Cabernet Sauvignon and the Merlots from both these countries hold their own by their European counterparts.

But it is the New Zealands that are coming through strong and clear, with outstanding value. Margaret Harvey of Harvey Fine Wines in London has opened my eyes to many small estates. The Sauvignon Blanc 1986 from the Esk Valley in Hawkes Bay is fantastic, and so is the slightly sweeter Semillon Sauvignon Blanc from the Mission Estate, and their 1985 Merlot is deliciously smooth. The Fumé Blanc 1986 from the Waimaku Estate in the Matua Valley goes down a treat and any of the Delegat wines will prove extremely reliable. Simply get their wine list and try some, and your bias will be blown out of the door very quickly, I feel quite sure.

· Miller Howe ·
Breakfasts

Breakfasts at Miller Howe are leisurely affairs, even if we do end service a bit early for some. (You're meant to walk the fells when up in the Lake District, not lie in bed all day!) They start at the bottom of the main staircase with a glass of Buck's Fizz – an equal mix of fresh orange juice and champagne – and you can drink more fresh orange juice when you sit down (we go through six to eight cases of oranges each week). Cereals, up to six, are next – at home, you could serve a muesli of your own concoction – or a selection of fresh grapefruit, figs, or other stewed fruit. You could also opt for my rib-sticking porridge, the oats for which I soak overnight with all milk, then serve with cream, butter, whisky and demerara sugar – none of that Scots spartanness and salt for me!

For the main part of the meal – the cooked (and fattening) bit, you can usually choose between smoked haddock, kippers, kidneys, eggs however you fancy them, or the by now quite famous Hearty Lakeland Platter. (Called by the 1985 *Good Food Guide*, the 'fry-up to end all fry-ups', it's really a 'bake-up'!) Hot baps and toast are the climax, along with farm butter and home-made marmalades and honey (well, the latter's not quite home-made, but wins all the prizes in the local shows), and coffee or tea.

It's what everyone looks forward to and expects when they're on holiday and staying in a hotel – but, of course, at home it could be a bit much to reproduce every day. But why not serve it as a special Sunday brunch for family or for friends – an unusual variation on the entertaining theme. I do this quite often on my days off at home, and an 11 o'clock start allows me both a lie-in and a read of the papers before the pleasures start. The secret – as always – lies in advance preparation, and most of the recipes can be made up to a certain extent the day or evening before.

I've included a few familiar recipes, plus a few less familiar, trying to think of ways in which to titillate the Sunday morning appetite. Instead of a poached haddock dish, you could serve warm slices of smoked haddock quiche (see page 54); and instead of a bowl of figs you could offer a more unusual combination of fresh figs and smoked chicken. You can serve as many courses as you like – my Victorian breakfast in *Entertaining with Tovey* had six courses, not counting the liquids involved (some alcoholic) – or as few as you have the energy to prepare. Do try, however, to have a fruity starter of some sort – even if only a juice – plus one cooked course, and some delicious rolls or bread, butter and preserve . . .

Muesli

A good home-made muesli is unbeatable, in terms of both taste and health. Buy a cereal base – barley, oats, rye or whole or cracked wheat (with perhaps some bran or wheatgerm) – from the health-food shop, or some of the larger, better supermarkets. Mix into this in a large bowl a variety of interesting additions, the more the merrier and tastier. Use nuts (almonds, hazelnuts, walnuts), seeds (poppy, sesame, sunflower) and dried fruit. Don't just limit yourself to sultanas, raisins or currants: chop up some prunes, apples, peaches, pears or apricots, all available dried now, and full of goodness. Try adding some dried banana flakes, some desiccated coconut, or some toasted pine kernels.

Once you have made your own individual mixture, you can store it in an airtight container, ready for use each morning. Serve it with fresh chopped fruit, with natural yoghurt or top of the milk, and some soft brown sugar. It makes a satisfying and healthy start to a breakfast or brunch.

Scrambled Eggs

People *must* wait for scrambled eggs, not the other way round, and however organised I think I am, whether at Miller Howe, down at Brantlea or on the Farm, timing is tricky – particularly as some people take ages over their first breakfast course, while others seem to clear their plates very quickly. Eggs take only about 2–3 minutes to scramble, so time the cooking very carefully. Normally I would allow two large eggs per person, but if the main part of the breakfast – or indeed any meal – is to be scrambled eggs, go up to three and serve them with some of the additions below. If allowing three eggs use a full $\frac{1}{2}$ oz (15 g) butter per person.

A thick-bottomed saucepan is essential, and I also use a small, stainless steel wire whisk and my electric hand-beater.

Per person

just under $\frac{1}{2}$ oz (15 g) butter	salt
2 large eggs	1 tablespoon double cream
freshly ground black pepper	

Warm the butter very gently over a fairly low heat, as in no way do you want it to burn. In a large round-sided bowl beat the eggs with a generous touch of freshly ground black pepper and a pinch of salt. Pour into the pan and turn up the heat just a little, bearing in mind that if the base of the saucepan gets too hot your egg mix will simply cook rigid to resemble an omelette. Whisk away with your wire whisk all the time.

Once the egg begins to cook – especially if there is the slightest fear that your guests might be a trifle late – take the pan off the stove and pour the eggs back into the mixing bowl. Fluff them up with the electric hand-beater. Add a little of the double cream, beat it in, and then return to the saucepan and carry on cooking. As the mixture is nearly right – slightly soft and runny, *never* dry – return to the bowl, beat in a little more double cream and then pop back on the heat for a moment.

*A magnificent — and fairly modest, for me — table setting for eight
in the dining room at Brantlea. To complement the brown cloth on the table,
we used green napkins, green candles and my green dragon plates — and
the yellow flowers sing with colour. The wine is already decanted,
the candles are lit, where are the guests . . .?*

*Me on the terrace at Miller Howe with some of the staff —
without whom neither I nor the hotel could operate!*

Just before spooning out on to your warmed plates, you could mix in some chopped chives or other herbs, or garnish with an enormous sprig of deep-fried parsley (see page 98); the colour looks attractive and the crunchy texture is an added richness. If you want the eggs to be more substantial, some cubes of smoked salmon (go easy on the salt at the beginning of cooking) could be mixed in; garnish with some American red salmon caviar roe and some triangle croûtons (see page 97). You could also serve scrambled eggs with grilled or baked bacon rolls, with butter-fried mushroom caps, with chunks of smoked trout, or in or on a pastry base or container of some sort. Anything you fancy, really.

—— Creamed Smoked Haddock with —— Puff Pastry

Smoked haddock is another fish popular at breakfast time, and although many in the north like it simply poached in seasoned milk, I prefer it flaked into a cheese sauce and served with a puff pastry vol-au-vent. Do be careful to get a good Finnan haddock rather than those which are bright yellow (that's all colouring). Most elements of this dish can be prepared in advance.

Serves 4–6

½ recipe quantity rough puff pastry (see page 57)
2 lb (900 g) smoked Finnan haddock, each cut into four
1½ pints (900 ml) milk
a few fresh parsley stalks
2 onion rings

8 peppercorns
1¾ oz (45–50 g) butter
1½ oz (40 g) plain flour, sieved
4 oz (100 g) Cheddar cheese, finely grated
melted butter, for glazing

Roll the pastry out to ⅛ inch (3 mm) thickness and cut into circles of 3½ inches (9 cm) with a fluted cutter. Chill well, prick as described on page 59, then bake in a preheated oven at 450°F/230°C/Gas 8 for about 15 minutes. Do check to see that the pastry is not browning too much. Remove from the oven when cooked and split the circles in half, discarding any greasy uncooked layers. Leave on one side to cool. These circles could be prepared in advance (the evening before, say).

Place the haddock in a baking dish in one layer, and add enough milk to cover, along with the parsley stalks, onion rings and peppercorns. Bake slowly in the oven preheated to 300°F/150°C/Gas 2 for about 20 minutes. Pour the fishy milk through a sieve into a measuring jug. Flake the fish into a bowl, removing all bones and skin.

To make the sauce, melt the butter in a small pan, add the flour and beat well. Add slowly, beating constantly, 1 pint (600 ml) of the flavoured milk, and simmer until you have a good white sauce. Add the cheese and allow to melt, mixing in well. Fold the flaked fish into the sauce. This can be prepared the day before.

When you are ready to serve, warm the fish through in a double boiler for about 20 minutes, and the puff pastry circles for about 5 minutes in an oven at 350°F/180°C/Gas 4. Fill the pastry at the last moment with the creamed haddock mixture and brush the lid with a spot of melted butter. Garnish if you like with a couple of wedges of tomato and a sprig of parsley.

Steamed Kippers

Kippers – the most popular variety of smoked herring – are available whole or filleted. They are usually grilled for breakfast, but oh how the smell permeates everything for days afterwards. Sometimes they're 'jugged' – simply immersed in boiling water in a jug for about 10 minutes. I like to poach kippers (fillets usually) in seasoned milk until they simply warm through – the smoking means they are already virtually cooked, but when pandering to a slimming whim I steam them.

Place a large sieve over a pan of simmering water. Lay the kipper(s) in the sieve, place over the simmering water, and season with freshly ground black pepper. Cover the bowl and sieve with foil and leave for about 8 minutes.

Serve them on hot plates garnished simply with alternate slices of cucumber and very, very thinly sliced lemon.

Hearty Lakeland Platter

This is the most popular cooked dish on the Miller Howe breakfast menu, and although it sounds enormous it isn't really – helpings of each individual ingredient are small. And if you think a hearty platter is complicated – think again. If you follow my simple instructions, you'll find it a doddle! Offer a glass of burgundy if serving as part of a brunch – delicious!

Per person

butter	$\frac{1}{2}$ tomato
1 small sausage (or chunk of Cumberland sausage)	salt
	sugar
1 rasher good back bacon	freshly ground black pepper
1 triangle crustless bread	a few slices of par-boiled potato
1 slice apple	1 egg
2 medium mushrooms	

Preheat the oven to 350°F/180°C/Gas 4. Butter a couple of baking trays very generously.

Prick the sausages, rind the bacon, and soak the bread triangles in melted butter. Core, peel and slice an apple or apples, and trim the mushrooms of their stalks, topping the caps with a small knob of butter. Brush the tomato halves with melted butter and season with salt, sugar and freshly ground black pepper.

From this stage, the whole process will take 30 minutes, so you can alert family or guests. Individual items are placed on the baking trays in order of cooking time.

Sausages	– about 30 minutes
Bacon	– about 15 minutes
Fried bread ⎫	
Apple slice ⎬	– about 10 minutes
Mushrooms ⎭	
Tomato	– about 5 minutes

While these are baking in the oven, fry the potato slices in butter and, at the last minute, cook the eggs according to taste: fried for up to four guests, scrambled for six or more. Don't forget to put plates in to heat.

Sliced Cold Chicken
with Aïoli and Fresh Fig

Although I love fresh roast chicken done in various ways for a main course (see page 142), I also like to serve it cold at a homely breakfast after I have had scrambled eggs with American red salmon caviar roe!

You could also serve *more* slices of chicken – prepared in the same way – but without the aïoli. Arrange in slices as in the photograph opposite page 48, and cut the fig flower into more wedges. Sit it on some segments of pink grapefruit, garnish with chives, parsley and lettuce, and slip a slice of hard-boiled egg into the fig.

Per person

2 slices chicken breast
2 slices chicken leg meat
home-made mayonnaise (see page 134)
French dressing (see page 136)

1 black fig, skinned if you like
home-made aïoli (see page 136)
parsley or watercress

I slice the breasts of chicken very thinly indeed to give me lovely slivers of white meat and then slice the darker legs a trifle thicker. The latter I paint with some mayonnaise, and the thin breast slices I paint with some French dressing. From the top end of the fig, cut through three-quarters of the way into four wedges (resembling a Union Jack) and then ease each section open.

In the centre of your plate pipe a large twirl of aïoli. Plonk the fig 'flower' on top of the aïoli and build up the chicken slices around it, alternating the breast and leg. Garnish with the watercress or parsley. This not only looks good, but is quite filling and satisfying, especially if accompanied by some wholemeal bread.

Wholemeal Bread

Bread is something most people aspire to make, but it is also something about which many have cold feet and hot flushes! It is the art of kneading (and it *is* an art) that they're frightened of, and this is indeed quite tricky to master initially. But this bread needs *no kneading whatsoever*, and can, in fact, be made by the kids. There are various slight variations in the ingredients (at the end of the recipe), that can make it even more interesting. It can also be doubled to make four 1 lb (450 g) loaves or two 2 lb (900 g) loaves.

Makes 2 × 1 lb (450 g) loaves

1 lb (450 g) wholemeal flour
a generous pinch of sea salt
2 tablespoons black treacle
$\frac{1}{8}$ pint (75 ml) warm water from the tap (the temperature you would bath the baby in)

1 oz (25 g) fresh baker's yeast (see below)
$\frac{1}{2}$ pint (300 ml) warm water

• *Yeast* •

I always say, rightly or wrongly, that *fresh* yeast ought to be used as it leaves no pedantic yeast flavour when baked, and more often than not gives a better texture to your bread. Yeast is a living substance and is immediately killed when it is put into the hot oven. What confuses me, however (and I am sure knowledgeable home economists will rush to put pen to paper to bombard me with insulting or enlightening letters), is that yeast can be *frozen*, and can survive this!

When each year we fly around the world with British Airways we always take several kilos of frozen fresh yeast to help us make the rich rolls served nightly. We never have any problems with it although I do find that you require 25 per cent *more* yeast than most recipes state, when using frozen. So, if it is tricky finding a constant supply of fresh yeast, buy a quantity at a time and weigh it out in $1\frac{1}{4}$ oz (30–32 g) portions which should then be well wrapped in twirls of cling film and frozen. When you wish to use it simply grate the hard piece on your stainless steel grater and follow the recipe!

Fresh yeast does not like draughts, nor does it blossom in cold places, so you must find a warm spot in your kitchen. At home I find if I put the main bottom oven of my electric cooker on, the upper oven will warm up sufficiently for working the yeast, but the airing cupboard or a warm corner of the kitchen totally devoid of draughts will suffice.

• *Method* •

Lightly butter the requisite number of loaf tins, and have ready two bowls. Place the flour with the salt into the larger bowl and warm through in the oven with a pilot light on, or in the aforementioned airing cupboard. Put the treacle and the first lot of water into the second bowl, and crumble the fresh yeast on top. Leave this in a warm place for up to 10 minutes until the yeast has developed and formed a head (like a good glass of cask Guinness).

Add the second lot of warm water to this yeast mixture, and turn the whole caboodle into the bowl of warmed flour. Using a long-handled spoon, simply combine the gooey ingredients with the dry to make a 'dough', and then divide this up between your lightly buttered loaf tins. Press down quite severely and leave once again in that cosseting closet or warm place for about 20–30 minutes to double in size. Preheat the oven to 400°F/200°C/Gas 6.

Put the tins into the prepared oven and cook for 40 minutes. Turn out on to a cooling tray and leave to cool, having tapped the loaves with your knuckles to make sure they give off that lovely hollow drum sound. If you want the outside of the loaves to be rather soft, cover immediately with a dampened tea towel; if you like the crusts to be crusty, leave uncovered. Wait until the loaves are quite cold before you slice and butter them; the slices are not soft and delicate but rather strong and chewy. The bread keeps for up to 10 days in a bread tin, up to 20 days if wrapped in greaseproof paper and foil and stored in the fridge; and it freezes beautifully.

• *Wholemeal Bread Variations* •

Instead of using all wholemeal flour, you could use 8 oz (225 g) strong plain flour plus 8 oz (225 g) wheatmeal or wholemeal flour.

Instead of using black treacle, you could use the same quantity of runny honey.

You could also add one or two of the following when mixing the yeast liquid into the flour:

2 oz (50 g) sultanas or raisins
2 oz (50 g) carrot, coarsely grated
2 oz (50 g) apple or fennel bulb, finely chopped
a pinch of allspice or curry powder

2 oz (50 g) dried banana flakes, roughly chopped
4 oz (100 g) hazelnuts, walnuts or pecan nuts, roughly chopped

The First Course
· *STARTERS* ·

We always try to make starters at Miller Howe look and taste spectacular – starters, after all, are the diner's first introduction to the evening's pleasures to come. There's no reason at all why you shouldn't adopt the same attitude at home. At Miller Howe we dim the lights so that Lake Windermere is revealed in all its splendour, but you could light lots of candles and turn off the overhead lights in your dining room for much the same effect.

It is easiest to serve a cold starter – most of the work involved can have been done in advance (a necessity when entertaining) – but obviously if the main course and pudding are to be cold, a hot starter will be welcome, and will not be too much trouble. Thus, many of the recipes in the following section are cold, although there are a number that need last-minute cooking or heating through (but nothing too elaborately time-consuming).

Some of the recipes you will have encountered before, such as my old favourites, the cheese and herb pâté and mushroom pâté, for instance, but after all these years, they still seem to be winners. There's *so* much you can do with them – as there is indeed with the pastries: people still enthusiastically welcome slices of quiche, pastry bases or containers holding nuggets of delectable fillings. . . . But there are also plenty of new ideas.

There are a few starter rules which you will probably all be aware of already. Do try to make your starter a contrast in colours, flavours and textures to the other courses: don't for instance, serve a pastry starter and a pastry dessert in one meal (although I did this once, see page 13). Do remember that this starter course is a *prelude* to a meal, whether it consists of two, three or five courses – thus it must be fairly light so that your guests have still got room for all the joys to come! And do consider the idea I suggest in the canapé section, that a selection of bits and pieces can be served *before* the guests sit down, as the beginning of a more informal meal.

Cheese and Herb Pâté

This, as I'm sure you all know by now, is one of my very favourite – and most useful – recipes. It's here in the starter section because there are so many starters that can be concocted from one single recipe mixing, but cheese and herb pâté can be used in a myriad other ways in other courses. It's a delicious spread for sandwiches, cold or toasted, and for the base of canapés; a cold garnishing twirl of cheese and herb pâté enlivens baked potatoes or other plain cooked vegetables; it's handy in cold terrines; it can be used as a stuffing for fish or a chicken breast, or for spreading between flesh and skin of a roasting chicken; and it can be baked *with* many vegetables such as cabbage, chicory and courgettes. I outline below some ways in which it can be used for starters and, because it's so useful in so many ways, I urge you to make some and keep it always available in your fridge (it doesn't freeze all that well).

5 oz (150 g) butter
1 lb (450 g) cream cheese
3 garlic cloves, crushed with a little salt

1 tablespoon each of finely chopped chervil, parsley and chives (or any fresh herbs available that take your fancy)

Melt the butter very slowly in a saucepan. Using an electric hand-beater, mix the other ingredients together in a large bowl, making sure that the herbs are evenly distributed.

When the butter has cooled a little, pour it slowly and gradually into the cream cheese mixture. Fold in carefully – it could curdle – and when all has been absorbed, spoon the pâté into a bowl or loaf tin (or item to be stuffed). Leave to cool thoroughly and set. Store in the fridge.

• Cheese and Herb Pâté Starters •

If you allow the pâté to set in a loaf tin, you could slice it – about $\frac{1}{4}$ inch (6 mm) thick – and serve it on top of a carefully composed and dressed salad. Watercress is a good companion with walnuts and orange segments, and a tomato and orange salad is particularly delicious.

The pâté can be piped before it is left to set. This is the way in which you can use it to fill many things: puff pastry cornets or milles-feuilles; choux puffs, eclairs or swans; pancakes, plain or wheatmeal; and a twirl in an avocado half is tasty and visually attractive.

While still soft, the pâté can be spooned or piped into vegetable casings. Small tomatoes with a cheese and herb pâté filling can be served as canapés; the larger, Continental ones can be chilled and then sliced into colourful, greeny-white and red rings. Green or red peppers can be similarly stuffed, chilled and then sliced. Try slotting a couple of walnuts into each pepper, as in the photograph of a lunch box opposite page 145. Cucumber 'boats' are good, too, filled with the pâté. The pâté can also be used as a tasty 'glue' to keep things upright on a plate, or together as in the pyramid of mushrooms on page 66.

Mushroom Pâté

Although of a different nature and consistency from cheese and herb pâté, mushroom pâté has almost as many, if not more, uses in starters and other courses. Starter ideas are below, but this savoury reduction of mushrooms can be used on canapés and in toasted sandwiches; as a topping for pizzas, baked potatoes, baked fish and scrambled eggs; and as a stuffing for vegetables and chicken breasts. Let down with some good chicken stock, mushroom pâté makes a quick and delicious soup (a spoonful can also be used as a soup garnish); and a white sauce is transformed into a mushroom sauce by adding a few ounces.

Those of you who bought *Entertaining with Tovey* may be excused for thinking it an extravagant recipe. All the proof-readers missed the fact that only *1 pint* of red wine should be used – not the 2 pints as stated.

4 oz (100 g) butter
8 oz (225 g) onions, peeled and minced
2 lb (900 g) mushrooms, trimmed and
 minced

a generous pinch of sea salt
freshly ground black pepper
1 pint (600 ml) red wine

Melt the butter gently in a large pan, then add the onions. Simmer for about 10 minutes, then add the mushrooms, salt and pepper. Stir well, and add the red wine. Leave to bubble over a very low heat for 2–3 hours, stirring occasionally. During this time, the wine will gradually evaporate, leaving the mushroom and onion mixture fairly dry. When the correct consistency, remove from the heat and leave to get cold. Store in the fridge – or it freezes extremely well.

• Mushroom Pâté Starters •

Like cheese and herb pâté, this pâté can be used as a filling for a variety of things, pastry particularly. For a pastry tartlet filling (see page 52), mix the mushroom pâté with a reduced Marsala-flavoured cream sauce (see page 128). Or spoon at the last minute into a puff pastry cornet or use as one of the layers in a mille-feuilles.

Stuff small to medium tomatoes with mushroom pâté and serve on a cucumber and orange salad.

Take the dough out of stale dinner cobs and deep-fry the remaining 'shells' (or dip them in melted butter and bake). Fill with mushroom pâté and serve hot or cold.

Duck Liver Pâté

This is a new version of my original Miller Howe duck liver pâté, using the delicious duck fat left over from roasting instead of butter, and adding the juice and rind of an orange to give extra tang.

Do remember that a chicken liver pâté can be made in exactly the same way – but use butter instead of duck fat, and brandy instead of Marsala or sherry.

Makes about 1½ lb (675 g) pâté

8 oz (225 g) belly pork
4 oz (100 g) duck fat (strained off roast duck, see page 148)
1 medium onion, peeled and chopped
1 lb (450 g) duck livers, cleaned
¼ pint (150 ml) Marsala or sherry
2 garlic cloves, peeled and finely crushed

juice and finely grated rind of 1 orange
1 level tablespoon chopped fresh marjoram
freshly ground black pepper

Preheat the oven to 425°F/220°C/Gas 7 and roast the belly pork for an hour. Remove from the oven and leave to cool. When cold, take the meat off the bone and cut it up into small pieces.

Melt the duck fat in a saucepan and fry the chopped onion until golden brown. Add the cleaned duck livers, the Marsala or sherry, garlic, orange rind and juice, marjoram and pepper. Simmer for 15 minutes.

Allow to cool, then combine with the diced belly pork. Process finely in a liquidiser or processor, then pass through a sieve into a clean bowl (or individual pots, see below). Chill until ready to use.

• *Duck Liver Pâté Starters* •

If you have any small individual brown earthenware pots, the pâté looks nice simply levelled off in these, served with a parsley sprig on the top and accompanied by a couple of fresh orange segments.

Like the other two basic Miller Howe starter pâtés, this one can be used as a stuffing for a multitude of containers – small tomatoes; red peppers (try slotting some brandy-soaked dried morels in the middle of the pâté); in well-cooked choux pastry cases, puff pastry cornets or savoury pastry tartlets. It looks particularly effective in a potato basket (see page 60) surrounded by very thinly sliced radishes and topped with a sprig of fresh herb – or, better still, a herb flower.

The pâté can easily be piped, so it can be made into twirls to be served on top of a tomato and orange herbed salad, garnished with parsley and radish slices. Or your pâté twirls can be considerably more elaborate. Have ready the required number of individual 3 inch (7.5 cm) ramekins. Make up a Marsala or port aspic (see page 138), doubling the basic quantity for more than four ramekins. Pour a little aspic into the base of each ramekin and chill to set. Pipe in a good twirl of duck pâté and then, just as the bulk of the aspic is beginning to set, pour in, around and over the twirl. Leave to set completely, when you will have a twirl entirely encased in a rich and gleaming compact jelly.

Serve turned out of the ramekins (dip into hot water briefly) on tomato and orange salad on individual plates – or, as in the photograph between pages 48 and 49, on a bed of aspic, surrounded by sliced strawberries and cucumber and tiny parsley sprigs, and topped with a slice of hard-boiled egg and an olive rabbit (see page 102).

Game Terrine

This mixture can be cooked as a terrine in a dish, wrapped in bacon, or used as a filling for a game pie, using the savoury pastry on page 50. Please note that preparation has to start *2 days* in advance of cooking.

Fills a 14 × 3 × 3 inch (35 × 7.5 × 7.5 cm) terrine

1 lb (450 g) breast of duck, mallard, pigeon or pheasant, cut into strips, and marinated for 2 days in 6 tablespoons port

8 oz (225 g) breast of chicken, cut into strips, and marinated for 2 days in 2 tablespoons cooking brandy

2 tablespoons sultanas, soaked for 2 days in 2 tablespoons sherry

14 oz (400 g) smoked bacon, rinded (for lining terrine only)

8 oz (225 g) pork fat

6 oz (175 g) belly pork meat

6 oz (175 g) lean uncooked ham

2 eggs

$\frac{1}{4}$ pint (150 ml) double cream

4 oz (100 g) whole pistachio nuts, skinned

salt

freshly ground black pepper

4 tablespoons finely chopped parsley

After soaking the duck, chicken and sultanas for 2 days, in port, brandy and sherry respectively, drain them, retaining any liquids. Stretch the bacon rashers with a small knife on your work board, and use to line the terrine dish, overlapping each rasher and allowing enough hanging over the edge to fold over the top eventually. Preheat the oven to 350°F/180°C/Gas 4.

In the food processor, mix and process the pork fat, belly pork meat and ham with the eggs and double cream, adding the liquids from the marinated breasts and sultanas (if any). Turn into a bowl and fold in the nuts, sultanas and salt and pepper to taste. Coat the strips of breast, both game and chicken, with the chopped parsley.

Line the base of the bacon-lined terrine with some of the processed mixture and press down into this some of the strips of coated breasts. Cover with more processed mixture, top with breast strips, and carry on until you have used up both lots of ingredients, ending with the processed mixture.

Bring up the ends of the bacon rashers over the top of the terrine to cover it completely. Cover with foil and then with the lid. Place in the preheated oven and bake for 1$\frac{3}{4}$ hours. Allow to cool, and then remove the terrine from the dish. Wrap in a double thickness of foil and leave for 48 hours before slicing.

Savoury Chicken Liver Gâteau

Serves 12–16

8–9 back bacon rashers, rinded
1 oz (25 g) butter
2 oz (50 g) onions, peeled and finely
    chopped
3 garlic cloves, crushed with 1 teaspoon
    salt
8 oz (225 g) chicken livers, marinated
    overnight in ¼ pint (150 ml) port
2 tablespoons olive oil
1 lb (450 g) boned chicken breast, cubed
    and marinated overnight in ¼ pint
    (150 ml) brandy

2 eggs
2 tablespoons finely chopped mixed
    fresh herbs
2 oz (50 g) walnuts, coarsely chopped
1 tablespoon walnut oil
½ nutmeg, finely grated
rind of 2 oranges, finely grated
12 cocktail gherkins, finely diced
    (optional)

To serve
tomato provençale (see page 132)
aïoli (see page 136)

Line a 10 inch (25 cm) loose-bottomed, round, spring-sided cake tin with the bacon rashers. I haven't discovered the ideal geometrical way in which to do this, but it is easiest to start with the thin end of one rasher at a slight angle up the side of the tin with the thick end going along the base towards the middle. Next to this put a thick end up the outside wall letting the thin end go into the middle etc. It doesn't work out entirely evenly, and you usually end up with a bare half-moon piece, but this is easily covered with an extra bit of bacon. Preheat the oven to 350°F/180°C/Gas 4.

Melt the butter in a pan and cook the onion and crushed garlic until nice and golden. Strain the chicken livers (putting booze into the food processor), and fry these with the onion mixture. When they're sealed, put liver and onion in the food processor, scraping all the bits out of the pan. Heat the olive oil in the same pan and strain off the cubed breast of chicken (putting marinade again into the food processor). Seal the chicken in the hot oil, then add to the food processor. Whizz everything round on high speed, adding the eggs one at a time and then the fresh herbs. Turn out into a bowl.

Meanwhile fry the chopped walnuts in the walnut oil and add the finely grated nutmeg and orange rind. (The very finely diced cocktail gherkins make the dish a little sweeter if you want to add them.) Fold walnuts etc into the mixture and spread over the bacon-lined tin. Cut a double thickness of greaseproof paper into a circle to lay on top, and then cover with a double thickness of foil. Put into a roasting tray and pour in enough boiling water to come 1 inch (2.5 cm) up the side of your round tin. Bake in the preheated oven for 45 minutes. Take out and leave covered for 10 minutes, then remove from tin.

Serve warm, cut into wedges, with some warmed tomato provençale and twirls of aïoli. You can decorate it prior to cutting, as we have done – extravagantly! – in the photograph between pages 48 and 49: use twirls of aïoli topped with cranberries, and radiating circles of orange and pink grapefruit segments, and some tomato provençale in the middle.

Vegetable Terrine

This colourful and tasty terrine should be made the day before you want to serve it. Cook in the normal terrine mould which measures approximately $14 \times 3 \times 3$ inches ($35 \times 7.5 \times 7.5$ cm). Slowly and carefully slice, using a long, sharp, serrated knife, and serve on a simple sauce of fresh tomatoes and a little basil.

Serves 15–20

8 large lettuce leaves
8 small radiccio leaves
salt
6 oz (175 g) French beans, topped and tailed
4 oz (100 g) carrots, cut into strips the size of your little finger
2 leeks, white end only, peeled, of just over ½ inch (12 mm) in diameter and about 6 inches (15 cm) in length
2 oz (50 g) baby sweetcorn, thin ends removed

3 oz (75 g) red pepper, cut into thin strips
3 oz (75 g) courgettes, cut into strips the size of your little finger
12 oz (350 g) boned chicken breast, cubed
3 eggs
¼ pint (150 ml) double cream
1 tablespoon chopped mixed fresh herbs
freshly ground black pepper
2 teaspoons caster sugar

Prepare all the vegetables first. Remove any thick stalks from the lettuce and radiccio leaves, and then simply and quickly blanch them in boiling salted water. Remove them immediately and put in cold water. They will curl up tightly but when cold they are relatively easy to unroll. Use them to line the sides of the ungreased terrine – lettuce all over first, followed by the radiccio – remembering to allow a little to hang over the sides as this will eventually cover the top.

All the remaining vegetables must be blanched in simmering salted water as well, and the timings below are vital. Submerge the vegetables separately in the saucepan inside a metal strainer, cook for the specified time, then immediately refresh under cold running water. Leave to one side.

French beans	2 minutes	baby sweetcorn	1 minute
carrots	2 minutes	red pepper	1 minute
leeks	4 minutes	courgettes	1 minute

Put the cubed chicken breast into your food processor with one of the eggs and whizz round on high speed. Add the other two eggs, one at a time, then dribble in the double cream and add the fresh herbs. Season to taste with salt and pepper.

Sprinkle a teaspoon of sugar over the leaf-lined terrine, and then spread a little of the chicken mixture into the base (a spatula is ideal for this job). Using half of the cold cooked French beans, arrange them in close rows lengthwise in the chicken mixture, and then put in a little more chicken. Push the carrot strips lengthwise in close rows down into this. Add more chicken, then down the middle of this place the two leeks, end to end, the whole length of the terrine. Arrange the baby sweetcorns on either side along the length of the terrine. More chicken yet again, followed by close rows of the red pepper strips, chicken, then courgettes, chicken, then the remainder of the French beans, arranged as before. Top with the balance of the chicken, sprinkle on the other teaspoon of sugar, and fold over the lettuce and radiccio leaves to cover the outside. Place a double layer of greaseproof paper on the top and then the lid.

Put the terrine in a roasting tray and pour in enough boiling water to come half-way up the sides of the terrine. Bake in the preheated oven for 45 minutes. Remove the terrine from the roasting tray and leave to cool. When cold, chill lightly.

Hot Mousses

Each time one of these is served at Miller Howe, guests seem to regard them with a degree of awe. In my very first book, they were called simply 'savoury creams', but we serve revised versions of them at least twice a week now, renaming them 'hot mousses' – although I understand they're more classically known as mousselines.

There are several advantages in presenting hot mousses as a dinner-party starter. Firstly, they're delicious, but they're also very simple to make – if you carefully study and follow my points. And, perhaps best of all, they can be more or less finished off on the morning of your party, put to rest in the fridge, and then cooked at the last minute (although they're never quite so light in texture).

We almost invariably make them with fish, but over the years, I have found chicken or turkey breasts, well marinated offcuts of veal and pork and even chicken or duck livers can be used. Whatever you do use, you will find they are easier to make, simpler to turn out, and will stand firmly upright on the guest's plate if they are actually baked *in* something – a thin fillet of sole or some smoked salmon around the inside of the well-buttered seasoned container for a fish mousse, or a thickish slice of rinded smoked bacon if using chicken, veal or pork. You can even make a 'container' of blanched lettuce or spinach leaves.

Hot mousses are best cooked in individual 3 inch (7.5 cm) wide ramekins which are 1½–2 inches (4–5 cm) deep. But don't rush to buy some of these as sturdy teacups will suffice (in fact, initially the handles are useful as they enable you to turn the cooked dish out more easily). The one thing you *do* need is a food processor – they can't be prepared properly with anything else.

The following recipe is for the basic mousse mixture; see below that for some interesting ways in which to add flavour and texture. If making a fish mousse allow a little extra fish in thinner wider strips, for the lining. If making meat mousses use some bacon for the lining, and don't forget to marinate the diced meat in something delicious – yoghurt is probably the simplest – for at least 24 hours before starting the preparation. Serve with a hollandaise sauce – flavoured if you like for interest (see page 126).

Serves 6

12 oz (350 g) basic fish or marinated meat	3 eggs
salt	butter
freshly ground black pepper	$\frac{3}{4}$ pint (450 ml) double cream

The day before you wish to serve the dish, skin and bone the fish and cut it into 2 inch (5 cm) square pieces. If making a meat mousse, start 2 days beforehand, to allow for marination. Put the pieces of fish or meat into the food processor with the sharp metal blade, season with salt and pepper, and whizz round on high speed. Add the eggs, one at a time, stopping the machine and wiping down the walls of the bowl or goblet after each individual egg has been added and whisked for a minute or so.

When well amalgamated, remove the mixture from the bowl, put into a storage container and leave for 24 hours in the fridge to chill. After this time it will be slightly stiff and gelatinous. At this stage too you can butter and season your containers well, and line them as required. Preheat the oven to 375°F/190°C/ Gas 5.

Return the mixture to the food processor and slowly trickle in the double cream with the machine on medium speed. It is absolutely no use pouring it in like the Victoria Falls – it should be more like a gentle Highland stream trickling away in a long hot summer . . .! Use your common sense here because, if you beat too fast and too long, the mixture will heat and possibly curdle; when I demonstrate this dish, for instance, I tend to use the pulse point on the machine. With this you can retain control.

If you are a dab hand at using a piping bag, it is best to fill your containers using a star nozzle, but if you find this tricky, simply spoon the mixture into the containers – but *do not* attempt to force it down. Lightly cover them with cling film if you want to store (for up to 8 hours in the fridge), or immediately place into a roasting tin. Pour in enough *boiling* water to come about three-quarters up their sides. Place in the preheated oven and bake for about 30–35 minutes.

I usually remove the ramekins from the roasting tin and cover them immediately with foil, allowing them to rest for 3–4 minutes while I make an accompanying hollandaise (see page 126). This is put on to the plate first, and the turned-out hot mousse is then placed in the middle.

You will soon get the knack of turning the hot mousses out (particularly if you have used cups). You may need to run a knife quickly around the inside between cream and container. Using my right hand, I invert the mousse on to my left and then turn it over on top of the sauce. Serve immediately.

• *Hot Mousse Additions* •

Pleasant contrasts in texture can be achieved by using any of the following suggestions.

Sole is by far the lightest fish to use for a hot mousse, but it is possible to have a mixture of equal parts of sole and salmon or, better still visually, two separate mixings, piping the sole around the outside and then the salmon up the middle.

A piping of mushroom pâté through the middle of each ramekin like a maypole gives added flavour and interest to both fish or meat hot mousses.

Whole prawns or shrimps can be folded into a fish mixture, as can cubes of marinated salmon or gravadlax (see page 119).

Hot meat mousses can actually have bits of uncooked diced liver folded in, or well-cooked drained bacon along with finely diced uncooked vegetables.

Generous amounts of fresh herbs can be folded into chicken mousses – or toasted macadamia nuts provide a delightful crunch to the otherwise rich soft texture.

Savoury Pepper, Cucumber, Egg and Cheese Mousse

This cold mousse makes a delightful and colourful starter for a summer dinner party.

Fills 6 × 3 inch (7.5 cm) ramekins

½ oz (15 g) powdered gelatine
5 tablespoons white wine
6 oz (175 g) cream cheese
¼ pint (150 ml) double cream, lightly beaten
1 tablespoon caster sugar
a pinch of grated nutmeg

5 hard-boiled eggs, shelled and roughly chopped
2 oz (50 g) Cheddar cheese, grated
1 red pepper, cleaned and finely diced
½ cucumber, seeds removed and finely chopped

Prepare the gelatine in the white wine as outlined on page 191.

Beat the cream cheese and fold in the double cream with the sugar and nutmeg. Fold in the chopped hard-boiled eggs, grated cheese, red pepper and cucumber and mix well. Stir in the reconstituted gelatine. Pour into six ramekins or other moulds and leave to set. Turn out (by running a knife round the edges and then dipping moulds in hot water) on to a savoury salad (see page 110) on individual plates.

—— MILLER HOWE PASTRIES ——

If there were one particular aspect of cooking that frustrates eager-beaver chefs-to-be it would – I feel sure – be pastry making. Time after time during my travels, when I've been giving talks or demonstrations, or judging various competitions, people have said, 'I can't make pastry for love nor money', to which I invariably reply, 'You needn't make it for either – simply make it for yourself for fun.' For there is no mystique about pastry, it is simply another culinary technique to be tackled and learned.

Whenever quiches, farmhouse pies or puff pastry cornets are served either at Miller Howe or at home, the favourable comments flood back and I begin to feel a bit of a fraud. For not only do I find pastry making sheer simplicity, I actually revel in it! I love mixing it, rolling it, shaping it, find the smell of it cooking heavenly – and the eating sensational!

For those of you who already make Miller Howe pastry, don't immediately think you can skip these pages, as the recipes have been changed over the years. These changes haven't come about because people have tried or have managed to influence my approach to cooking (you will note the butter content is just the same!), but because I have carried on experimenting, testing, tasting: the texture of the farmhouse pastry is the better for the oats, the savoury is enhanced by the curry powder and wholemeal flour, and the rough puff pastry . . . well, that's my particular favourite, and it always works!

• A Few General Rules •

The following apply to each of the three pastry recipes – savoury, rough puff and farmhouse (the latter is in the desserts section, on page 184) – and please always bear them in mind each and every time you start the process of pastry making. But each pastry has its own quirks as well, and the recipe itself describes these in greater detail. Choux pastry, of course, is quite a different matter, and I have outlined *its* rules alongside the recipe.

1. The first 'rule' is that in no way can you decide mid-morning to have a quiche for lunch or pie for supper as the three pastries *must* be made at least the day before use, and indeed will store happily in the fridge or freezer. To illustrate the effectiveness of freezing pastry, I'll tell a little story about one of our demonstrating trips. A few years ago five of the staff and I did a nigh round-the-world tour with British Airways, flying the flag for the British Isles and British food. As we planned the itinerary eyebrows began to be raised at the sheer volume of foodstuffs which would need to be taken on this travelling cooks' circus; we eventually played to capacity audiences in Johannesburg, Durban, Cape Town, Tokyo, Osaka, Fukuoka and Kyoto, followed by San Francisco, Dallas, Houston and New York. As the food pundits had already, by then, accredited me with the title of Master Pastry Maker, I had, naturally, to cash in on this, so the chosen meals were to commence with a quiche and end with a farmhouse pie (not *really* ideal, to have two pastry courses). Forty-two

Cold chicken slices dressed with mayonnaise and French dressing
and garnished with a fig 'flower' make a substantial breakfast.
Try it with aïoli too, and butter your toast with a
Miller Howe swan.

One of the ways in which to serve duck liver pâté as a starter.
● *Encase a twirl of pâté in aspic, decorate the plate as you fancy,* ●
and top it with an olive rabbit!

*An unusual way in which to cook chicken liver pâté as a starter
— as a gâteau, wrapped in bacon. Serve it warm in wedges with tomato provençale
and decorated with twirls of aïoli.*

At Miller Howe we would offer seasonal salads – of anything and everything! – as an appetising starter.

evenings with eighty people per session meant that 420 quiches and apple and orange pies had to be planned (each quiche or pie divides into eight portions). So, frantically, the staff at Miller Howe made 450 lb (202 kg) each of savoury and farmhouse pastries, filling the freezers from bottom to top. All this had to be loaded into freezer containers, then into metal theatrical trunks, before being placed in the holds of the majestic BA 747s. (Incidentally, British Airways was marvellous, as were the customs authorities in each country.)

At each venue the relevant amounts of pastry were transferred from freezer containers to the fridge, brought round, cooked and then served to what turned out to be very appreciative and admiring audiences. The last quiche and pie brought to the tables of the bejewelled guests at the Pierre Hotel in New York were as good as those served in the heat of Johannesburg on the first night of our grand tour!

So, prepare your pastry ahead of time, allowing it a good rest before use. In fact, each of the recipes can be doubled up which means that you can have one enormous pastry-making session, use some, and freeze the rest for use at another time. (One advantage of this for me – a *very* mucky worker – is that I only have to *clean up* once!)

2. The second 'rule' concerns that old adage about needing cold hands, cold heart and a marble slab for the performance. (It's pastry that you're making, say I, not attending a post mortem or wake!) I think that the warmer the kitchen, the quicker it is to make the basic dough – but not *too* hot, of course. Soft butter, for instance, is an absolute must: when you press your thumb into it, the thumbprint stays.

3. A light heart and hands certainly help too. I can formally say here and now, in no way is it any use attempting to make pastry when you have slept in, burnt the toast, spilt the milk, shut the cat's tail in the door or given your spouse a piece of your mind. To make good pastry, you simply have to be really relaxed and in a lighthearted mood.

4. Always weigh and measure out accurately – if you're slapdash, the results will never be as good as they should be. I've spent *years* working out the perfect proportions for you.

5. Always sieve your flour (except wholemeal) even if you have bought it that morning. Hold the sieve some way above the bowl, as this allows air to permeate the flour – and leads to a lighter pastry.

6. Never squeeze pastry into perfectly shaped balls for storing. Many misguided pastry makers feel some sudden inner urge to make the most perfect of round balls and spend quite a few minutes squeezing, rolling and manhandling until they have a perfectly round shape of dough like a ball the kids might take to the beach. This is *quite* wrong, and light hands at the bringing-together stage are vital. Each little extra squeeze you give the dough knocks out a little of all that air and love you've just spent ages putting *into* the pastry.

7. Once you have formed your basic dough – whether rough puff, savoury or farmhouse – put it into the fridge to chill overnight. This is vital.

8. Never attempt to work a chilled pastry until it is 'restored' to its original soft texture. When pastry is ready to be put in the fridge and freezer, pause for a moment or two and use your sensitive touch to implant firmly on your memory the actual texture. The pastry must *never ever* be rolled until it is at this

texture again once it has been brought out to room temperature. Time and time again good cooks fall down because they are insensitive, and in too much of a rush. They force their pastry to stretch itself out on the base of the tin or dish and then are upset – nay, distressed – when the cooked result is a shrunken disaster. If you are of the hard-to-learn type, go and sit down *now* in a corner and write out fifty times, 'I must not roll my pastry until it is soft like plasticine', and memorise these words of wisdom well and truly.

9. Once the pastry is back to its plasticine texture, roll to the proper thickness and shape, and fit into or on to a mould, or cut as desired. Now you must chill it *again*. This allows the gluten in the flour to relax after all the stretching and rolling, and cold air in the pastry will expand more than warm air, giving you a better rise. Leave for at least 30 minutes, and take straight from the fridge to the preheated oven.

10. The final 'rule' – and this applies to each and every pastry, choux and others included – is to have the oven at the *correct* temperature. Have it heating up for quite a time before you are ready to put the pastry in, just to make sure that it is hot enough.

• *Baking Blind* •

This applies only to pastry for quiches and fruit pies – therefore to the savoury and farmhouse pastries – and I strongly recommend that it should be done. Baking a pastry base without a filling ensures that the base is quite dry and firm before any fruit or custards are introduced. The first thing to do is to preheat the oven to 325°F/160°C/Gas 3.

The pastry base will be very firm after its chilling in the fridge or freezer, so it is a relatively simple task to place a piece of foil all over it. Press it down firmly over the base and up around the sides and, most importantly, *over* the top edges. The foil should finish up firmly gripping the outside rim of the flan or quiche tin – vital in order to avoid a burned pastry rim. Scatter dried macaroni, lentils, split peas, rice or, better still, ceramic baking beans, over the foil, so that the base is completely covered.

Bake for 30 minutes (longer if the pastry came from the freezer), and then take out and remove the foil and beans. The pastry should be fairly dry, but if you think it could do with another 5–10 minutes, put it back in the oven without the foil and beans, turn off the oven and let it dry out even further. This ensures that your pastry will never ever be soggy.

Savoury Pastry

This new savoury pastry has the same proportions as the one I gave in *Entertaining with Tovey*, but the wholemeal flour lends texture and health, the extra egg yolks lend richness, and the curry powder gives a unique flavour. It makes three 10 inch (25 cm) quiches, or sixteen individual 3 inch (7.5 cm) baby quiches or tartlets. If you are using the pastry for a sweet dish – frangipanes, for instance – I expect you already realise that you ought to omit the curry powder (and use icing sugar instead)!

8 oz (225 g) wholemeal flour and 8 oz (225 g) plain white flour, or 1 lb (450 g) plain white flour, sieved
a pinch of salt

2 level tablespoons curry powder of choice
10 oz (275 g) soft butter
4 egg yolks, lightly beaten

Mix the two flours together well with the salt and curry powder, and place on your work surface. Make a well in the middle so that an oval section of work surface is relatively free of flour. Into this centre area, pat down the soft butter, making sure you form firm fingerprint indentations as these will allow the egg yolks to stay *on* the butter when you put them on – as you do now – instead of running off and into the flour.

Using your middle three finger ends, dab away at an angle of 90 degrees – from directly above – until the egg yolks and butter are combined. It doesn't matter if a little flour is mixed in at this stage. You're wanting to get a sort of scrambled egg texture, and it will take about 8 minutes of dabbing. With the help of a palette knife, lift the flour up from the four sides and on to the top of the butter/egg mixture to form a rough house-brick shape. For those of you who continually bemoan the fact that you can't make pastry as you are too heavy-handed, this is the pastry for you! You never have to use your hands, as the palette knife does all the work for you.

Now is when you start to bring it all together. Once the flour is on top of the butter, you start cutting *through* the mixture. Always cut quickly, and at an angle of 90 degrees (see the bottom drawing on page 51). From time to time, scrape the knife along the board, underneath the mixture, turning it over so that the butter is evenly distributed through the flour. Be quite vigorous and firm when cutting through – you should hear the edge of the palette knife make a positive contact with the work surface – always at 90 degrees, never 45.

Gradually the mixture will form larger and larger crumbs as it amalgamates, and when it starts to look like a shortbread mixture, stop. Divide into three equal parts and, oh so gently, bring each part into a rough ball shape – do *not* squeeze (see note 6 and read it well). Put the balls into individual polythene bags and leave to chill overnight – or freeze one or more if you want to make less than three quiches at a time.

• *Rolling and Baking Savoury Pastry* •

Allow the pastry to regain the texture it had before chilling. If making a quiche, place the base of a loose-bottomed, metal flan tin on your work surface and flour *around* it, not *on* it. Place the ball of pastry in the centre of the base then, *very* gently, persuade it down in order to start the flattening-out process. Holding a long floured rolling pin at both ends, work lightly (never *press*) from the centre, easing the pastry out over the edges of the base. Don't go too far, only enough for this excess pastry to be high enough for the walls of the quiche. With a palette knife, carefully fold these flaps back over the base, and put the base into its ring. Use your thumbs to ease the flaps back up, and around the sides of the flan ring. Run the rolling pin over the top to cut off excess there, and use this to make little snakes to reinforce the edges of the base – usually the principal trouble spot. Put the finished case back into the fridge to chill, for at least 30 minutes.

When well chilled, set the oven at 325°F/160°C/Gas 3, and line the pastry case in the flan ring with foil and baking beans (see note on baking blind on page 50). Bake for 30 minutes, turn off the oven and remove the foil and beans. If you don't think the pastry is quite dry enough, put the case back into the turned-off oven for another 5–10 minutes.

If you are making savoury tartlets, do so in exactly the same way as above. Allow pastry balls to return to room temperature, roll them out to a thickness of $\frac{1}{8}$ inch (3 mm), and cut into 3 inch (7.5 cm) rounds with a fluted cutter. Fit into appropriately sized tartlet trays and chill for 30 minutes. Bake blind exactly as above, but for 15–20 minutes only.

Savoury Quiches and Tartlets

It's those people who find pastry making difficult who think quiches will be beyond them. But once you've mastered the savoury pastry above, and have the proportions of the custard right, any quiche can become second nature to you, and you can ring endless variations on the basic theme for a multitude of delicious and eye-catching starters. For savoury quiches and tartlets can hold almost anything – and they can be an ideal and tasty way of using up leftovers. The original quiche lorraine, of course, contained onions, eggs and bacon only; you will see from the chart on page 54 that I have allowed myself – and you – considerably more licence.

For each 10 inch (25 cm) pastry case

2 eggs
1 egg yolk
a pinch of salt

freshly ground black pepper
a pinch of grated nutmeg
½ pint (300 ml) double cream

Simply beat all the above together and use in conjunction with one of the suggested fillings below. You *can* lightly precook some of the vegetables for quiche fillings, but I prefer the slight crunchiness of vegetables which were raw initially.

All quiches are cooked in a preheated oven at 375°F/190°C/Gas 5 for 35 minutes. It is often tricky, well nigh impossible, however, to get all the custard into the quiche without spilling some as you wend your way with it to the oven. So what I normally do is put two-thirds of the custard in over the filling, and before transferring to the oven place a double thickness of foil on the shelf below. This acts as a conductor of heat and catches any custard should the quiche leak, saving you the trouble of having to clean a black-blobbed oven base. Leave the quiche in for about 10 minutes and then open the oven door.

Slide the shelf with the quiche on a little way out – practise this on a blind run or else you could find yourself with a shelf that tips up and slides your quiche out of the oven on to the floor (this happened to me on one demonstration recently). Using a small, long-handled soup/sauce ladle, dole out the balance of the custard into the quiche. In this way, your quiche will always come out slightly puffy above the pastry rim rather than sunk below the sides.

Serve quiches after they have cooled a little, but are still quite warm. Cut into eight portions and serve each slice with a savoury salad garnish (see page 110). (Cold quiches can make ideal packed lunch or picnic fodder.)

Savoury tartlets can be made as mini quiches as described above; you merely have to choose smaller principal ingredients, or chop them smaller, and then divide them and the custard between the sixteen cases. Serve warm as a starter, two per person perhaps, along with a savoury salad garnish.

The cooked small bases can also be left to become cold, then filled with a variety of cold fillings – cheese and herb pâté, mushroom pâté or the duck pâté for instance (see pages 39–41). In fact, a magnificent if substantial starter is three very small tartlets per person, each filled with one of the pâtés. Try other fillings or mixtures of fillings – a chutney with some cheese and herb pâté, some of the creamed haddock on page 33, or any of the fillings for choux pastry puffs (see page 56) or toppings for canapés (see page 74).

• *Quiches and Fillings* •

Principal Ingredient	Amount	Comments and Possible Variations
Asparagus, trimmed	12 oz (350 g)	4 tablespoons pine kernels
Bacon, rinded, chopped and baked crisp	1 lb (450 g)	1–2 onions, chopped and lightly fried in bacon fat
Broad Beans, skinned	14 oz (400 g)	ground or whole hazelnuts
Broccoli, trimmed	12 oz (350 g)	1. 2 tablespoons Cheddar cheese, grated
	9 oz (250 g)	2. 3 oz (75 g) crispy bacon bits (see page 99)
Cauliflower florets	12 oz (350 g)	1. a couple of tablespoons piccalilli or other chutney, and 8 olives
		2. 2 oz (50 g) Cheddar cheese, grated
Courgettes, sliced and fanned	9 oz (250 g)	2 tablespoons sunflower seeds
Crab, white meat only	12 oz (350 g)	replace 2 tablespoons cream in custard with dry sherry
Fennel, diced	8 oz (225 g)	2 tablespoons Pernod in custard
French Beans, chopped, 1 inch (2.5 cm) long	12 oz (350 g)	1 diced red pepper
Jerusalem Artichokes, peeled and sliced	10 oz (275 g)	4 water chestnuts, chopped
Leeks, sliced, poached in ½ pint (300 ml) white wine and drained	12 oz (350 g)	4 tablespoons chopped walnuts
Mushrooms, trimmed and sliced, and sautéd in 1 oz (25 g) butter and 1 tablespoon olive oil	1 lb (450 g)	*Or*, simply mix 4 generous tablespoons mushroom pâté (see page 40) into custard
Onions, finely chopped, sautéd in 1 oz (25 g) butter and 1 tablespoon olive oil	12 oz (350 g)	a little custard baked in flan first, then onions, then remaining custard
Peppers, diced	10 oz (275 g)	2 tablespoons flaked almonds
Prawns, well defrosted	1 lb (450 g) packet	3 tablespoons flaked almonds
Runner Beans, sliced	12 oz (350 g)	1 diced red pepper
Smoked Haddock, flaked	12 oz (350 g)	1. ½ teaspoon English mustard and 2 oz (50 g) Cheddar cheese, finely grated
	6 oz (175 g)	2. 3 oz (75 g) each of fennel bulb and red pepper, diced
Smoked Oysters, drained	8 oz (225 g) can	4 oz (100 g) each of red pepper and celery, finely diced
Smoked Salmon, soaked for 6 hours in ¼ pint (150 ml) milk	12 oz (350 g)	1. 4 oz (100 g) Jerusalem artichokes, peeled and finely diced
	9 oz (250 g)	2. 3 oz (75 g) water chestnuts, chopped
Smoked Trout, flaked	9 oz (250 g)	3 oz (75 g) mushroom pâté (see page 40)
Sweetcorn Kernels	10 oz (275 g)	2 tablespoons mustard
Tomatoes, peeled, seeded and chopped	12 oz (350 g)	6 oz (175 g) Emmenthal cheese, grated, anchovy fillets, black olives

Choux Pastry

This surely must be the easiest of pastries to master and make. And it doesn't have to be made the day before like the others.

I used to be most meticulous with an old recipe, insisting on $3\frac{3}{4}$ oz (scant 100 g) flour – which, if you didn't have old-fashioned weighing scales, was a bind to measure out. One day, however, a nice person on one of the cookery courses at Miller Howe came up to me and said, 'You know, it is just as good if you simply use 4 oz of the flour.' This I tried out, and had to agree. It has to be *strong* flour, though, now easily available at most supermarkets. Also, if you have a set of gill measures (see page 16), these make it easy to measure out the water: you need 1 gill and $\frac{1}{2}$ gill.

$7\frac{1}{2}$ fl oz (215 ml) water
$2\frac{1}{2}$ oz (65 g) soft butter, broken into pieces
4 oz (100 g) *strong* plain flour, well sieved (at least twice)

a pinch of salt
3 eggs, beaten

Preheat your oven to 400°F/200°C/Gas 6, and have ready some baking trays lined with dampened greaseproof paper. Prepare also a piping bag with a $\frac{1}{4}$ inch (6 mm) plain nozzle.

Put the water and butter pieces into a saucepan and heat gently. This mixture *must not boil*, for if it does, some of the water will evaporate and you will not have sufficient liquid to take up your flour. Once the butter has melted turn the heat up to high and as soon as the mixture starts bubbling away evenly, put the flour and salt in all at once (pour from a small plate or a sheet of greaseproof paper). Using a good rounded wooden spoon, bash the living daylights out of it to form a dough – this takes about a minute at the most.

I then like to let this mixture cool a little before I start adding the beaten eggs. I do this in the Kenwood using the K beater, but you can do it – more laboriously, of course – by hand. Take care too, because if you add the eggs too quickly, your mixture will not be the same. Add the beaten egg only a little at a time, with the beater on the lowest speed, and never add any more until all the egg has been absorbed by the roux base. The mixture will turn from a dull stodge to a shiny, creamy, dropping, batter consistency. When all the egg has been beaten in, beat the mixture on a high speed for a minute.

Spoon the dough into the piping bag and pipe out your puffs, eclairs, or profiteroles, leaving plenty of space around each. As soon as you place them in the preheated oven, turn it up immediately to 425°F/220°C/Gas 7. The pastry shapes will take from 20–30 minutes to cook, depending on size, but they should be very brown and firm. (Undercooked choux pastry is hideous to eat as it's all stodgy and gooey.) If you have made large eclairs or puffs you should slit them slightly when cooked with a sharp knife and return to the turned-off oven to dry out completely. A good cooked choux should, in my opinion, drop on to the table like a ton of bricks with a resounding crack. This means that, however gooey and sticky your filling, the pastry will remain crisp and crunchy. But that is only my opinion. . . .

• *Choux Pastry Starters* •

Choux pastry, of course, can be used to make delicious desserts – see my pyramid of profiteroles in the photograph opposite page 161 – but here we'll concentrate on the savoury.

Gougères – or my version of them – can be made in patty tins. Pipe the pastry in, over the bottom, then with a wet thumb work the mixture up the sides so that you have quite a well defined 'nest'. This mixing should give you about 20–25 gougères. Bake at 425°F/220°C/Gas 7 for 20 minutes. Scoop out most of the middle, leaving a thin crisp cup case which you can fill with a variety of fillings. As usual, fill at the very last minute to avoid sogginess.

Choux puffs or balls are simply piped on to the dampened greaseproof paper – small (about 30) for canapés, or larger (20 or under) for starters, filled with Cheese and Herb Paté and topped with melted Bovril. Bake at the usual heat for 15–20 minutes, depending on size, until well risen, golden and crisp. Pierce the sides to allow steam to escape and return to the oven for a minute or two to dry out further.

Although eclairs are more generally associated with whipped cream and a chocolate topping, they too can be used as a starter. The mixing will make about twelve 4 inch (10 cm) eclairs – and they should be baked for 20 minutes and slit at the sides.

I used to make savoury swans with choux pastry. These are fun. Pipe out eight oval body shapes and eight S shapes for the necks. Bake the bodies for 20 minutes, the necks for only 7 minutes. Dry the bodies out well by piercing, then cut a slice off the top of each. Cut these in half for the wings. Fill the body cavity with cheese and herb pâté or a flavoured cream (see pages 39 and 129), and anchor the wings and necks in at the appropriate places.

• *Choux Pastry Fillings* •

Use any of the pâtés – the mushroom, cheese and herb, duck (see pages 39–41), or creamed haddock (see page 33). Use a savoury mousse as a filling, or a cream cheese, avocado and tomato mixture. Or simply make a basic, very thick white sauce and mix in first some grated cheese or tomato purée. Thereafter mix in any of the following:

> peas with sliced mushrooms and diced red peppers
> chopped celery, apple, pineapple and ham
> chopped chestnuts and spring onions, grated carrot and turkey or chicken bits
> scrambled eggs with chives and smoked fish pieces
> minced cooked spinach with grated celeriac, chopped pear and lots of grated nutmeg
> very finely sliced runner beans with, if you are lucky enough to get them, those whole baby cherry tomatoes which explode when popped into your mouth
> Dijon mustard with chopped tongue and fresh cherries
> any leftover curried meats with toasted peanuts and desiccated coconut
> leftover fish with tomato provençale (see page 132) and fried garlic cloves

grated parsnip, turnip and carrot go well with shelled peas and a touch of
   mustard for vegetarians
bits of salmon with halved seeded grapes and chopped fennel

Rough Puff Pastry

I have demonstrated this pastry many times – in theatres, restaurants, in cookery
schools and on television – and my audiences never cease to be amazed at how
quickly it can be made. The time taken to make most puff pastries sends many
cooks rushing to the frozen pastry sections in the supermarkets, but I think once
you've tried this, you'll never want to use other than home-made again. It can be
made up in about 10 minutes (well, once you're a dab hand at it), and it can even be
prepared in a warmish kitchen.

I give you the ingredients for a 1 lb (450 g) mixing, but what *I* normally do is
prepare *two separate* 1 lb (450 g) mixings in *two separate* bowls at the same time.
There's *so* much one can make with the pastry, and the slight rest one dough has
while the other is being worked on gives a slightly better result. So although the
ingredients are for *one* mixing, my instructions tell you how to do *two* at a time.
And, one final benefit of preparing two mixings: as it is all rather messy
(particularly when flopping the paintbrush from side to side to remove surplus
flour), the kitchen needs cleaning only once instead of twice!

Double these if you like (see above)

1 lb (450 g) strong plain flour
a generous pinch of salt
8 oz (225 g) soft margarine, broken up
   into $\frac{1}{2}$ oz (15 g) pieces

8 oz (225 g) soft American lard or
   shortening, broken up into $\frac{1}{2}$ oz (15 g)
   pieces
1 tablespoon lemon juice made up to $\frac{1}{2}$
   pint (300 ml) with very cold water

Sieve the two measured quantities of flour plus salt into the two bowls. Put the
pieces of margarine and lard into the bowls and shake to coat the fat with flour.
Make a well in the centre of each bowl and pour in the measured liquids. Mix
roughly together with a palette knife – they'll look floury and lumpy, but don't
worry.

Flour your working surface or pastry board lightly but well, and turn out the
dough from one bowl, scraping off anything stuck to the sides. Shape this roughly
so that it resembles a house brick, with the short end of the brick nearest you.

Holding the rolling pin at both ends (don't use those shorter ones with handles),
delicately tap the brick in the middle and at the top and bottom of the brick. Then,
starting at the rolling pin impression nearest you, give the rolling pin a good push
and a slight downward pressure. Do not *press* down, but make sharp, soft
movements away from you – *always* away from you – until the pastry slowly and
gradually is persuaded out to a rectangle measuring roughly 16×5 inches
(40×12 cm). If it looks slightly egg-shaped, a hard tap with the lengthy rolling pin
will soon give you a good rectangle with four 90° corners.

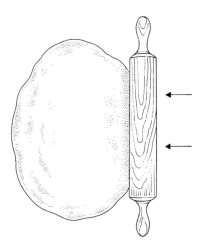

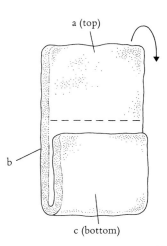

To make sides straight, push rolling
pin, holding at both ends, along surface
into pastry. This is to be done at all
sides to straighten into a rectangle.

Place the bottom third over the middle
third, then the top third over the other
two thirds.

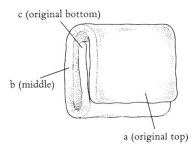

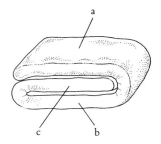

Once the folds have been made, tap
with rolling pin to seal at the three
open edges.

Turn from 6 to 9 o'clock.

Fold this rectangle into three equal parts, bringing the bottom third up over the middle third, and then the top third down on to the other two thirds. To trap the air between these layers, tap down lightly with the rolling pin on to the open sides at left and right, and in front of you. Give the dough a quarter turn – turn it from 6 to 9 o'clock – and put to one side.

Repeat the process with the second mixing of dough, and leave to rest in turn while you carry on with the first.

The pastry will now be smoother in consistency and thus slightly easier to handle. Repeat the tapping, turning, rolling, folding and resting process three more times with each dough, generously flouring your board or work surface between each rolling so that the dough does not stick. When folding, you may find there is a surplus of flour – so just brush it off with a clean 6 inch (15 cm) paintbrush! On the fourth and final rolling, the dough may be a little resistant, so don't *force* it into the 16 × 5 inch (40 × 12 cm) shape.

Pop both doughs into separate polythene bags, chill one and freeze the other (if that's what you want to do).

• *Baking Rough Puff Pastry* •

Never start to roll this pastry until it comes back to a workable consistency after taking it from fridge or freezer (see note 8 on page 49). Allow it about 20–30 minutes in a warm kitchen from the fridge, about 2 hours from the freezer.

Flour your working surface or board and your rolling pin well. Turn the slab of pastry so that the C shape of the folded-over bottom third (from the last folding) is nearest you, then roll out to about $\frac{1}{8}$ inch (3 mm) thickness. Cut out your shapes (see below), place them on slightly dampened baking trays, and put back into the fridge to chill – for about 30 minutes. Preheat the oven to 450°F/230°C/Gas 8.

When you want to cook, remove the trays from the fridge and put a piece of well buttered greaseproof paper on top of the pastry, buttered side down. Prick through the paper and pastry with a sharp pointed knife, then cover the pastry and paper with a double thickness of foil (this ensures an even rise). Put immediately into the hot oven and leave for 15 minutes. As you might be cooking large squares of pastry or small vol-au-vents, it's difficult to be more precise about timing (although cornets will need longer, about 30 minutes, because of the overlapping layers). Check after 15 minutes and leave in for longer if necessary to get the pastry really brown and crisp. *Overcooking* is actually better because any greasy layers of undercooked pastry will have to be torn off and discarded after baking.

• *Puff Pastry Starters* •

Traditional vol-au-vents are too fiddly for me, but of course you can, if you like, cut rounds or squares and make a centre which can be filled, as well as a 'hat'. I usually simply cut out fluted rounds from the pastry, bake them well, and then slice across the middle, removing any greasy uncooked layers of pastry. At the last minute I warm the pastry bases and tops through, then fill them with something delicious like creamed haddock (see page 33), scrambled eggs (see page 32), or some of the pâtés (see pages 39–41). Always fill puff pastry at the very last minute otherwise the pastry will become soggy. The sizes can vary from $3\frac{1}{2}$ inches (9 cm) in diameter to 2 inch (5 cm) rounds for canapés. See also the Canapés section for some further ideas on fillings.

These large rounds can also be made into my version of mille-feuilles. Instead of two layers of cooked puff pastry, you use four, and fill each layer with a different pâté – cheese and herb, mushroom and duck, say – for a Miller Howe triple pâté mille-feuilles. Another delicious filling is some mushroom pâté mixed with some Marsala cream (see page 128).

You can, of course, cut puff pastry into any shape you fancy, and a fish shape to accompany a fish dish, for example (see the photograph between pages 112 and 113) is tasty and witty.

Puff pastry is the pastry to use for cornets – the moulds are available in most kitchen shops and department stores – and these can be served as starter or dessert depending on the filling. For a starter, try one of the pâtés again; for a dessert whipped cream and some soft fruit with a good dessert sauce is impressive and unbeatable. The only basic to remember here is that cornets must be baked on a wire cooling tray, not a baking tray, otherwise there will be an uncooked side.

—Grated Courgette and Orange Roll—

This is a very simple dish to do for the family, but it is sometimes cooked at Miller Howe and served in a very thin slice as a vegetable! Personally I prefer it when it is warm, but a precooked one filled when cold with cheese and herb pâté (see page 39), then rolled, is delicious for a cold lunch or picnic.

Serves 6 generously

butter, for greasing
1½ lb (675 g) courgettes, topped, tailed
  and grated
grated rind of 4 oranges
4 oz (100 g) butter

6 eggs, separated
salt
freshly ground black pepper
2 tablespoons finely chopped parsley or
  dill

To serve
2 oz (50 g) Cheddar cheese, grated
1–2 tablespoons natural yoghurt per
  person

Grease a Swiss roll tin well with butter, and preheat the oven to 350°F/180°C/Gas 4.

Mix together the grated courgettes and orange rind. Melt 4 oz (100 g) of butter and add to the courgette/orange rind mixture. Stir in the lightly beaten egg yolks, then season with salt and pepper, and add the herbs. Beat up the egg whites until stiff, and then fold into the mixture, half at a time. Spread lightly into the greased tin and bake in the preheated oven for 20–25 minutes.

Turn out on to greaseproof paper liberally sprinkled with the grated cheese. While still warm, roll into a Swiss roll shape. Serve at once, cut into thick slices slightly on the slant, with yoghurt.

—Potato Baskets—

These deep-fried 'gaufrette' potato baskets are rather professional and you will need to have two basic kitchen gadgets if you decide to make them: a small mandoline for the actual slicing of the potatoes, and a potato basket holder or 'bird's nest maker' for forming and frying. Various kinds of the latter are available: some are hinged, some are two little strainer type baskets that fit into each other. They are obtainable from good kitchen shops and often, surprisingly, in Chinese supermarkets. But the baskets are, believe you me, well worth the faffing about – but must not be attempted on sultry, humid days as they tend to go a little limp. Make them on the morning of the day they are to be eaten and when cold store them in an airtight container.

You will need at least one potato per basket but, of course, it all depends on the size of the potatoes. Peel the potatoes, then wash and dry them.

Set the mandoline to the fine serrated slice, then, holding the potato in the palm of your hand, push it straight down the cutting edge. Discard this first slice. Turn the potato 90 degrees and cut straight down again. This will produce a lacy potato crisp: if it is a mass of strings, or there are no holes, the crisp is either too thin or thick respectively – adjust the blade. Carry on like this, building up your crisps, turning the potato 90 degrees each time.

Open out your basket fryer – of whatever type – and place one potato slice on the base. Place the other slices around the sides, slightly overlapping them all the time, and finish off with another slice on the base to cover the bottom of the side pieces. Form and hold the shape of the basket as appropriate to your gadget.

Heat good frying oil to 365°F/185°C and deep-fry the basket until brown. The first one might break as you try to get it out, but do persevere – the others will be fine. Remove each basket as made to kitchen paper to drain and cool before storing in airtight containers.

When you come to use them, always put a splodge of the filling on the plate first to hold the basket – this should be done as late as possible. Use a piping bag to pipe in a twirl of filling – the duck pâté on page 40 is ideal, and you could use any of the other pâtés in that section. In one Chinese restaurant we know, sizzling garlicky prawns are presented in such baskets . . . and the liver in sweet and sour sauce on page 70 is interesting (cook the liver in strips rather than slices).

Pancakes

This pancake recipe is a very basic one, and the pancakes are ideal stuffed as both starters and puddings. They're superb on Shrove Tuesday simply with fresh orange juice and rind and lots of vanilla sugar.

The recipe can be doubled and half the pancake yield frozen. Place the cooked pancakes on top of each other with interleaving pieces of greaseproof paper, and then wrap in foil and freeze.

And you can serve another kind of pancake as a starter – the new Miller Howe honey wheatmeal pancake on page 189.

Makes about 24 pancakes of 5 inches (12.5 cm) in diameter

4 oz (100 g) plain flour
a pinch of salt
1 egg plus 1 egg yolk

$\frac{1}{2}$ pint (300 ml) cold milk
$\frac{1}{2}$ oz (15 g) butter, melted

Sieve the flour and salt into your electric mixer (or ordinary) bowl. Beat the egg and egg yolk into the cold milk and, using a whisk, slowly beat half this liquid into the flour. Beat in the melted cooled butter, then the rest of the liquid. Beat until very smooth and leave covered in a cool place for at least 30 minutes.

Simply brush a little oil or melted butter over your heated frying pan and add a tablespoon of the batter. Jiggle it around the base and as soon as it is cooked on one side, flip it over and cook the other side, using a large palette knife. Remove to a cut greaseproof paper square and cover with a tea towel. Go on piling up until the batter is finished.

• *Savoury Pancake Fillings* •

Always serve these filled pancakes hot – heat them through in an oven preheated to 350°F/180°C/Gas 4 for about 10 minutes. Cover them first in a dish with some melted butter or a white or cheese sauce. Sprinkle with some grated cheese or breadcrumbs (the savoury ones on page 106 are good), and then grill finally to brown and finish.

The cheese and herb, mushroom or duck liver pâtés on pages 39–41 make good fillings for starter pancakes. You could also mix some mushroom pâté with some Marsala cream (see page 128) for a richer flavour. Coat with a rich cheese sauce if you like.

A thick white or cheese sauce (see page 125) could be pepped up with a variety of other ingredients – some grated raw vegetables, nuts or raisins, leftover cooked minced meat, etc.

Leftover minced meat can be mixed with some other tasty ingredients such as fried onions, or other fried vegetables, spices, herbs, etc.

Some creamed haddock mixture (see page 33) or some calf's liver in sweet and sour sauce (see page 70) would be ideal. Merely top with melted butter.

See also some of the canapé topping suggestions in the Canapés section.

—*Savoury Apple with Tarragon Cream*—

This starter remains one of the most popular on the Miller Howe menu – and this is my excuse for repeating it again. Prepare the cheese and herb pâté, the date mixture and the tarragon cream in advance, but peel the apples at the last minute only, as they will discolour. Many cookery writers say peeled apples come to no harm (colour wise) if soaked in a mixture of cold water and lemon juice – but oh, what a lot of flavour they lose. If you would like to have the apples peeled earlier on, marinate them in either cider or white cooking wine. This way they will not discolour and will also have a little *additional* flavour and the cider or wine can be used in another dish!

Serves 4

2 Granny Smith apples
2 oz (50 g) cheese and herb pâté (see page 39)
1 oz (25 g) each of stoneless dates, bananas and walnuts, minced together

4 tablespoons tarragon cream (see page 130)

Garnish
4 fresh tarragon or parsley sprigs
paprika

Cut the apples in half around their 'equators' and peel them. Remove the cores from each half with a Parisian scoop. Fill these hollowed-out centres with cheese and herb pâté, and use a little pâté to fill out the tiny hollows at top and bottom.

Put some of the minced date mixture on to the flat base of each apple half, to cover the bare flesh and the cheese and herb pâté filling, and carefully invert on to serving plates, rounded sides up.

Pour tarragon cream generously over each apple half to cover, and garnish with herb sprigs and the merest sprinkling of paprika.

—*Poached Pear Stuffed with Cheese and*—*Herb Pâté, Served with Pickled Onion Slices and Curried Mayonnaise*

If your pears are nice and ripe and soft there is no need to poach them, but more often than not bought pears are on the hard side.

You can make a similar dish with peaches or apples, and an alternative topping could be tarragon cream (see page 130).

Serves 6

3 large pears
juice of 1 lemon
1 teaspoon white wine vinegar
1 tablespoon olive oil
6 small pickled onions
6 oz (175 g) cheese and herb pâté (see page 39)

6 tablespoons curried mayonnaise (see page 134)
1 oz (25 g) desiccated coconut, toasted (optional)

Peel the pears, slice in half lengthwise, and remove the core. Mix together 1 pint (600 ml) water, the lemon juice, wine vinegar and oil, and gently poach the pear halves. Make sure you constantly look at them and prod with a sharp pointed knife; you don't want to overcook them. In no way is it possible to give emphatic cooking times as I don't know what state your pears are in. When soft, but still with a resistance to the knife, remove to a tray lined with a double thickness of kitchen paper. Drain well. This can be done about 8 hours in advance.

When you need to use them, place the pear halves flat side up on individual plates. If they wobble, just nick a small slice off to make them more stable. Slice the pickled onions as thinly as possible and fan the slices out around the top of the pear half – or they can be curved around the pear as in the photograph opposite page 64. Into the hollow centre of the pear, pipe some cheese and herb pâté. Top with a generous coating of curried mayonnaise to finish off the dish – but a sprinkling of toasted desiccated coconut on top of it all looks nice and tastes delicious!

Poached Spiced Pear Stuffed with Mushroom Pâté, Served on Spinach Purée and Garlic Croûton with Herbed Hollandaise

A very satisfying starter dish provided you are planning a relatively simple main course such as roast leg of lamb. It can be prepared early on in the day and then assembled just prior to the party.

Serves 6

3 pears, poached as in previous recipe
4 oz (100 g) mushroom pâté (see page 40)
12 tablespoons spinach purée (see page 166), spiced with nutmeg

6 × 2½–3 inch (6–7.5 cm) round garlic croûtons (see page 97)
1 recipe quantity herbed hollandaise (see page 127)

Once the pears are poached, leave to drain. If they wobble, take a slight piece off the bottoms to stabilise them.

When you wish to serve, warm through the mushroom pâté and the spinach purée separately in basins in a bain-marie, and pop the pears and croûtons into a medium oven (350°F/180°C/Gas 4) for 5 minutes.

Spoon a circle of spinach on to the individual serving dishes, and place a croûton in the middle. Put a half pear on top, and stuff it with the mushroom pâté. Coat with the freshly made herbed hollandaise.

If preparing this in summer, a sprig of redcurrants looks super as a garnish – otherwise use a large sprig of fresh herb or parsley.

Deep-Fried Avocado Wedges on Tomato Provençale with Herbed Cream

This beer batter can be used for many deep-fried delicacies, including mushrooms, and pineapple rings as well as the avocado in this unusual starter.

Serves 4

2 slightly under-ripe avocados
oil for deep-frying

Beer batter
½ oz (15 g) fresh yeast
1 teaspoon sugar
salt
freshly ground black pepper

a pinch of dried thyme
½ pint (300 ml) beer of choice
8 oz (225 g) self-raising flour

A poached pear for a starter, stuffed with cheese and herb pâté,
topped with a curry mayonnaise, and served with pickled onion slices
and a savoury salad.

*Pepper circles on hollandaise topped by a croûton spread
with mushroom pâté and two poached quails' eggs. Try my other version
with added onion circles and baked eggs.*

To serve

3 spinach leaves per person, stalks removed, washed and dried

4 tablespoons tomato provençale (see page 132)

4 tablespoons herbed cream (see page 128)

Peel, halve and stone the avocados and cut each half into three or four long wedges. To make the batter, cream the yeast with the sugar, salt, pepper and thyme. Add the beer, and then beat this mixture into the flour, beating well so that there are no lumps.

Heat the oil to 365°F/185°C, and coat the avocado wedges in batter. Deep-fry for 2–3 minutes.

Have ready individual plates with spinach leaves arranged on them. Divide the avocado between the plates and coat with warmed tomato provençale. Top with a spoonful of herbed cream.

—Vegetable Pasta with Roquefort Sauce—

This is a fun dish to prepare and eat – it's tasty and healthy, and whenever I've served it at Miller Howe it's been welcomed with cries of delight!

Serves 6

$\frac{1}{2}$ cucumber

3 large courgettes

3 carrots

2 red peppers (or 1 if large)

3 tablespoons French dressing (see page 136)

2 tablespoons natural yoghurt

1 tablespoon each of olive and hazelnut oil

Sauce

$\frac{1}{2}$ pint (300 ml) double cream

2 oz (50 g) Roquefort cheese

Garnish

a generous tablespoon of freshly chopped herbs

Wipe the cucumber, courgettes and carrots clean and then, using a scorer, score long strips from each until you can score no more. Place these strips in separate containers. Halve the red peppers lengthways, remove their seeds, and then wash them. Cut into similarly thin strips and put into a bowl.

Put some French dressing over the courgette strips, and some over the carrot; mix the natural yoghurt with the cucumber; and the olive and hazelnut oil mixture with the red peppers. Leave for at least 24 hours.

When you wish to serve, preheat the oven to 350°F/180°C/Gas 4. Put the cream for the sauce into a pan and simmer gently until it has reduced by half. Bring all the marinated strips of vegetables together and portion out between six plates. Warm them through slightly in the preheated oven for 5–8 minutes. To complete the sauce, grate the Roquefort into the warm reduced cream, and when it has melted, coat the warmed piles of vegetable pasta with it. Garnish with the freshly chopped herbs.

Savoury Mushroom Pyramids on Peanut Croûtons

These make a good starter for any dinner party as all the work can be done in the morning. They are served lukewarm garnished with sprigs of fresh herbs or parsley stuck in through the savoury breadcrumbs.

Serves 6

6 × 3 inch (7.5 cm) round croûtons, baked (see page 97)
2 oz (50 g) peanut butter (or mushroom pâté, see page 40)
2 tablespoons olive oil (or garlic oil, see page 138)

2 oz (50 g) butter
36 button mushroom caps
4 oz (100 g) cheese and herb pâté (see page 39)
3 oz (75 g) savoury breadcrumbs (see page 106)

Prepare the croûton rounds first. When they are cold, coat one side liberally with peanut butter (or mushroom pâté).

Melt the olive oil (garlic oil is even better) and butter together in a large frying pan, and sauté the mushroom caps for about 5 minutes. Remove from the pan and leave to drain, dry out and cool on a double thickness of kitchen paper.

Fill a piping bag with the cheese and herb pâté and pipe a blob into each mushroom cap. Place the croûtons, peanut side up, on a flat baking tray, and then build up six filled mushrooms on each to form a pyramid. Use the cheese and herb pâté as a 'glue' to help the pyramid keep its shape. Coat each pyramid liberally with savoury breadcrumbs.

Cover the tray with cling film and put in the fridge to chill thoroughly until you need to warm the pyramids through. They only need 10 minutes in an oven preheated to 350°F/180°C/Gas 4.

Mushrooms à la Grecque

Serve these deliciously flavoured mushrooms with a choice of different mayonnaises and slices of well buttered wholemeal bread.

Other vegetables can be treated in much the same way – try red or green peppers and button mushrooms.

Serves 6–8

2 lb (900 g) mushroom caps (use the stalks for pâté or soup)

Marinade
1 pint (600 ml) white wine
$\frac{1}{4}$ pint (150 ml) good olive oil
2 tablespoons white wine vinegar
$\frac{1}{4}$ pint (150 ml) fresh lemon juice with the finely grated rind (about $4\frac{1}{2}$ small lemons)

1 level teaspoon salt
4 tablespoons spring onions, finely chopped
12 parsley sprigs
2 garlic cloves, peeled and crushed
2 celery sticks, finely chopped
1 level teaspoon each of fennel and mustard seeds
24 peppercorns
12 coriander seeds

Bring all the marinade ingredients to the boil and then simmer over a low heat for 20 minutes. Strain and pour over the mushroom caps in a heatproof dish. Leave for at least 24 hours before serving.

——————Quick Marinated Mushrooms——————

I prefer the recipe above as it has such a fine Continental flavour – full of subtleties – but this can be done and served in just a few hours. Serve on a bed of shredded lettuce with aïoli (see page 136).

Serves 4–6

1 lb (450 g) mushroom caps (use stalks as
    above)
1 tablespoon each of freshly chopped
    chives and mint

Marinade
2 tablespoons white wine vinegar
4 tablespoons olive oil
2 teaspoons Dijon mustard
lashings of freshly ground black pepper

Put the mushrooms into a container and coat them with the chopped herbs. Put all the other ingredients into your liquidiser, process well, and then pour over the mushrooms. Put them in the fridge to chill, for at least 4 hours, before serving.

——————Marinated Baby Mealies——————

Mealie is the African name for corn, and these baby corn-on-the-cobs have recently become widely available in better supermarkets and greengrocers (the Chinese have canned and stir-fried them for years). They are delicious and require very little cooking – if any, as here.

Serves 6

36 baby mealies, wiped

Marinade
$\frac{1}{4}$ pint (150 ml) olive oil
$\frac{1}{4}$ pint (150 ml) white wine vinegar
2 garlic cloves, peeled
2 tablespoons finely chopped parsley

12 coriander seeds
4 peppercorns
1 tablespoon honey
a pinch of salt

Combine all the marinade ingredients in a liquidiser and then turn into a saucepan and bring to the boil. Arrange the mealies in a flat heatproof glass or china dish, and pour the boiling marinade over them. Leave to cool, then chill for 12 hours.

    Serve on a bed of assorted greens with watercress sprigs and mustard mayonnaise (see page 135).

Quails' Eggs on a Trio of Sauces, Topped with Herbed Hollandaise

This dish immediately brings out oohs and aahs from guests. It looks magnificent and, although it may sound fiddly, most of its elements can have been prepared earlier on in the day.

The dishes I prefer to serve this in are those rather nice white Apilco dishes, round, about 1 inch (2.5 cm) deep, and with two slightly curved 'handle' edges. They are available in good kitchen and china shops – but whatever you use, the dishes must be ovenproof.

Per person

1 dessertspoon each of spinach purée (spiced with some nutmeg), mushroom pâté and tomato provençale (see pages 166, 40 and 132)

1 tablespoon hollandaise (see page 126)
3 quails' eggs

Arrange the dessertspoons of spinach purée, mushroom pâté and tomato provençale carefully around each individual dish, leaving a ring in the middle about the size of a 10 pence piece. This can be done in the morning and the dishes may then be covered with cling film and left in a cool place.

When you are about to serve, pop them into a preheated oven at 375°F/190°C/Gas 5 to heat through for 8–10 minutes. As your guests are about to be called into the dining room, make a hollandaise (see page 126). As they are sitting down, break the three quails' eggs into the centre of each dish, and the eggs will be cooked nice and soft in 2 minutes at the most. If they are a trifle runny it doesn't matter as you still have to coat the eggs on each dish with the dessertspoon of hollandaise. If you happen to grow borage in your garden, a blue borage flower will set the colour of the dish off.

Pepper and Onion Circles on Mushroom Croûton with Baked Quails' Eggs and Hollandaise

This dish, I must admit, sounds quite a mouthful of verbal garbage, but as most of the work can (at home when entertaining) be done in the morning, it's practical – and oh, how spectacular it looks! It's another starter to set the tongues wagging and the saliva glands working!

Alternatively, as in the photograph opposite page 65, you can use the pepper circles only (baked or unbaked as you like) on hollandaise, then topped with the mushroomed croûton and some poached quails' eggs. It looks more spectacular, but is harder work!

Per person

2 rings green pepper
2 rings red pepper
2 rings yellow pepper
2 rings Spanish onion
1 fluted croûton of 3 inches (7.5 cm) in
  diameter (see page 97)

1 oz (25 g) mushroom pâté (see page 40)
2–3 quails' eggs
1 tablespoon hollandaise (see page 126)

Before you cut your red, yellow and green peppers into rings, wipe each well with a damp cloth. Slice off the stalk end and, using a small sharp-pointed knife, remove the thin strips of white flesh that run along the inside. Make absolutely sure you remove all the wretched seeds (best done under cold running water), then slice the peppers very thinly, making even-sized circles. Top and tail the large onions, remove peel and make onion circles of the same thickness and diameter.

Grease some baking trays well and preheat the oven to 400°F/200°C/Gas 6. Arrange on the trays circles of alternate peppers and onions: have three pepper circles together, separated by an onion ring, times two. This will give you an odd Olympic insignia per person. These circles should be of an internal diameter to sit comfortably on the croûton; the external diameter will overhang the edges (see illustration). Make as many of these circles as you need, and bake them in the preheated oven for 10 minutes until just *partly cooked*. Leave to one side.

Meanwhile, make your fluted round croûtons, and coat them with mushroom pâté. Place on another baking tray, allowing space between them.

When the pepper/onion circles are cool, transfer to the mushroom croûtons using a fish slice.

When you are ready to cook them, finally preheat oven to 400°F/200°C/Gas 6 and warm through for 5–8 minutes. Break the chosen number of quails' eggs on to them, towards the outside of each croûton round, and return to the oven for 2 minutes only. Serve at once with a spoonful of hollandaise.

Marbled Egg Mayonnaise

When I was a kid, Easter was never complete without the traditional hard-boiled eggs cooked in onion skins to give them that stippled coloured effect. Whilst not as enjoyable to eat as their chocolate counterparts, they looked extremely homely with cardboard circle hats and painted faces. If you are a lover of that simple dish, Egg Mayonnaise, try this for a visual effect not dissimilar to those Easter eggs.

Serves 6

6 hard-boiled eggs
1 pint (600 ml) good strong stale Indian tea (stored from returned breakfast teapots)
2 tablespoons dark soy sauce

To serve

6 tablespoons curried mayonnaise (see page 134)
6 lettuce leaves, shredded
6 oz (175 g) shrimps
heads of mustard and cress

Roll the hard-boiled eggs coarsely on a firm surface in order to crack them all over and then place them in the bottom of a saucepan. Pour over the tea mixed with the soy sauce to cover them completely. Simmer for 45 minutes, adding more tea if necessary.

Allow to cool and then shell completely. Cut the eggs in two lengthways, and lay on a base of curried mayonnaise. Garnish with chopped lettuce, shrimps and mustard and cress. The marbled effect is quite stunning.

Calf's Liver *with Sweet and Sour Sauce*

This dish has to be finished off at the last moment, I must admit, but as it literally takes only moments to prepare, it is relatively easy and convenient. It can be served simply by itself with the sauce and a garnish of chopped parsley, but I often tart it up a little more. Using a slightly lipped dish, I lightly paint it with walnut oil, then rub it with a peeled garlic clove. I then line it with various salad leaves – spinach, lamb's lettuce, lettuce and radiccio etc – then serve the hot liver and sauce in the middle. It can also be served in potato baskets (see page 60).

If you find the sweet and sour flavour too strong for the delicate calf's liver, you could simply reduce $\frac{1}{4}$ pint (150 ml) dessert wine by half and then fold in the plumped-up sultanas.

Serves 4

4 very thin slices calf's liver
2 oz (50 g) good lean bacon, rinded and
    diced
4 spring onions, finely chopped
2 tablespoons redcurrant jelly
1 tablespoon red wine vinegar
2 oz (50 g) butter

freshly ground black pepper
2 tablespoons sultanas, marinated
    overnight in 1 tablespoon cooking
    brandy

Garnish
Sprig of watercress or chopped parsley

Trim the liver well. Fry the bacon in a small saucepan until lightly browned. Add the chopped spring onions and cook until golden, and then pour in the redcurrant jelly and red wine vinegar. Bring to the boil and simmer for 2–3 minutes. Leave to cool – this can be prepared well ahead of time.

Just as you are about to call your guests to the table, melt the butter in a frying pan and liberally sprinkle the slices of liver with pepper. Put the sauce on to warm through, having added the few drops of brandy from the plumped-up sultanas. Quickly fry off the liver (about a minute each side if nice and thin), and put on to individual plates (or on to salad on plates). Add the sultanas to the sauce, heat through momentarily, and pour over the liver. Garnish with a sprig of watercress or chopped parsley.

Baked Duck Livers with Smoked Bacon

Try to get fresh duck livers as they taste and cook so much better than the frozen ones.

Per person

2 duck livers, trimmed
milk
1 rasher smoked bacon, rinded and
    chopped
chopped fresh marjoram

To serve
watercress
warmed French dressing (see page 136),
    made with some walnut oil
a scattering of toasted pine kernels

Soak the livers in the milk for 24 hours, then drain them well. Preheat the oven to 375°F/190°C/Gas 5.

Fry the bacon pieces until crisp, and bake the livers, sprinkled with marjoram, in the preheated oven for 8–10 minutes. Serve livers and bacon immediately on individual plates on top of the dressed watercress. Sprinkle the pine kernels on top.

· Miller Howe · Canapés

We don't actually serve canapés or pre-dinner nibbles at Miller Howe – they're more part of my life at Brantlea or the Farm – but it's certainly something I've often thought about and may do in the near future. I will be the very first to confess that they are very time-consuming, but are an excellent 'party warmer', particularly if the guests are offered an identical plate each shortly after being served their first drink. This can often be counted as the first course of the dinner party if you've been imaginative and generous enough. (And you can be putting the finishing touches to other courses while they're eating.)

I wouldn't ever dream of offering run-of-the-mill things like potato crisps (unless home-made), olives or any of the endless savoury nibbles now straining the shelves of the supermarkets – although my toasted curried nuts are quite different and delicious (see page 77). What I would want to offer are goodies that look stunning, taste very interesting, and immediately make your guests realise that you have given them the most precious thing around these days – your *time*.

Canapés can be hot or cold, and as simple or as elaborate as you like. I think you'll get quite a few ideas in the following pages – and from the photograph opposite page 80.

———— CANAPÉ BASES ————

And never do I serve my exotic toppings simply piped or spread on to bought cream crackers and the like: I use instead home-made toast croûtons, puff pastry slices, pastry containers of all sorts – and even occasionally wrap my goodies in pancakes. I also give you a couple of delicious biscuit recipes, good as bases.

· Croûtons ·

There are two ways of making croûtons to use as canapé bases: one utilises plenty of cholesterol-rich butter; the other is slightly kinder to your guests' health and waistlines. Both types of croûton are vital, not only as canapé bases, but in many aspects of Miller Howe general cooking and presentation.

In either case, bought sliced white or brown bread is ideal. Use round fluted pastry cutters, whichever size you fancy (but small for canapés, larger for other uses), and simply cut out as many circles as possible from each slice of bread. (Use the leftover shapes for breadcrumbs.) Cut out the rounds the day before you want to use them; this way they go a little hard, and they won't soak up so much butter if you choose the fattening croûton option.

Preheat the oven to 350°F/180°C/Gas 4. If you're going for the fattening ones, break an 8 oz (225 g) block of butter into pieces and melt in a large saucepan. This may seem a lot, but you'll find a use for any butter left over. (You may, of course, need *more* if you're preparing croûtons for an army.) Dip each croûton round into this melted butter with a pair of tongs and place down flat on a lipped baking tray.

Put the full tray into the preheated oven and after 10 minutes, remove, strain the surplus butter back into the saucepan, and turn each round over. Return to the oven. Depending on how many you put in at once, the circles should be cooked in about 15 minutes. Transfer them to a tray lined with a double thickness of kitchen paper so that surplus butter can drain off.

If avoiding the lovely fattening butter, all you have to do is place the unbuttered circles of bread on to your baking tray and bake in the oven as before.

You want, in both instances, to have something quite brittle that will not go soggy when you pipe on your toppings.

• *Puff Pastry* •

Another relatively easy way of making firmish bases is to roll out sheets of puff pastry (see page 57), as thinly as possible to fit your lipped baking trays. Put in the fridge to chill and then preheat the oven to 450°F/230°C/Gas 8. Place a sheet of greaseproof paper over the chilled puff pastry and cover with another baking tray topped with a couple of pound weights. Bake like this for 15–20 minutes. The object of the exercise is to make the thinnest possible biscuit-textured pastry. Cut immediately while still hot into strips lengthwise, and leave to cool.

• *Savoury Pastry* •

Using the savoury pastry on page 50, make individual canapé pastry cases in the special tins – there are twelve depressions of about 1 inch (2.5 cm) in diameter – available from kitchen shops. Use a fluted cutter to make the circles and drop them into the little depressions. Chill well and preheat the oven to 325°F/160°C/Gas 3. When ready to cook, fill paper fondant or petits-fours cases with rice, dried peas or, better still, the ceramic bake bits (they're smaller than baking beans, and supplied by Lakeland Plastics in Windermere). Place these cases inside the pastry cases. Bake for about 15–20 minutes until nice and firm.

You could also make boat shapes from savoury pastry, using the moulds readily available in good kitchen shops. Drape the pastry over the moulds, and press in gently. Fill – there's no alternative – with foil and baking beans or bits of rice etc, and bake blind as above.

• *Choux Pastry* •

Make tiny choux pastry puffs (see page 55), and pipe any of the soft purée fillings into them.

• *Bread Bases* •

Of course you can use wholemeal or wheatmeal bread sliced in the normal way, but if you have an obliging baker, ask him to bake his bread in longer, slightly smaller tins. Better still, use the wholemeal bread recipe on page 36, and bake it in Le Creuset terrine dishes. This way you can cut the bread *lengthways*, which makes for easier canapé preparation (see later).

If your bread proves to be soft and tricky to slice at any time, simply chill it in the freezer until it firms up.

——— TOPPINGS AND FILLINGS———

No matter what filling I am going to use, I always, but always, butter a bread base first: use very soft butter, or melted butter and a paintbrush. To give added oomph some hollandaise (see page 126) is easy to paint on as well. Depending on what fillings you are to use, this 'base spread' can be flavoured with fresh herbs, tomato purée or your particular favourite mustard. Remember you are wanting people to raise their eyebrows and question what is on and in the selection of titbits.

Then you spread or pipe on your topping. Most of my toppings and fillings are ones that can be piped, but many bases can carry a rougher texture that can simply be spread on. And don't forget about those old faithfuls, all the piping pâtés in the Starter section (see pages 39–41).

The following are a few combinations for which you need to use a liquidiser or food processor. Add, if you feel economical, a little cream cheese as well.

smoked salmon and avocado with a touch of lemon
smoked trout with horseradish and green fennel tops
smoked haddock simmered in milk then processed with spinach and a touch
  of nutmeg
mushroom pâté with ground hazelnuts
mushroom pâté with cooked ham
cooked ham with mustard and soft pear
cooked ham with curry paste (or tomato purée) and parsley
cooked ham with sweetcorn and mustard
tongue with redcurrant jelly and mustard
tongue with fresh cherries and a little thyme
lamb with garlic and rosemary
lamb with apple and mint
chicken with sage and onion
chicken with apple sauce and chives

chicken with peanut butter and garlic
pork with onion and apple sauce
pork with peach or pineapple
pork with mustard and mint
pork with mango, lime and ginger
leftover chicken or duck liver pâté with orange rind and ground hazelnuts
sausage with bacon fat and walnuts
minced smoked salmon offcuts mixed with a squeeze of lemon juice and a hint
   of vodka
tuna fish, cucumber and radish
tuna fish, pine kernels and fennel
tuna fish and avocado pear

And when you're using cooked meats, there is no reason at all why you shouldn't include in the food processor mixing a little of the leftover sauce or gravy you have originally used – in particular the rich jelly-like juices from roast birds. You can also incorporate any leftover cooked vegetables to give a hint of taste and a touch of colour (carrots and sprouts in particular).

And if you want to go overboard, there is no reason why on the baked croûtons (buttery or dry) you should not pipe an outer circle wall of firm meaty filling, and break into the centres of these a quail egg. Warm these through in a preheated oven at 400°F/200°C/Gas 6 until the egg poaches but still has a runny yolk – about 2–3 minutes.

Any of the above spreads can be rougher in texture, and you could also add some finely chopped something to give taste and additional texture. Scrambled eggs with diced smoked salmon or trout mixed in, for instance, makes an ideal spread for the puff pastry strips or bread rectangles. Add some crunchiness by simply mixing in some finely chopped raw apple, fennel, red peppers, mushroom, celery or nuts (preferably roughly chopped).

DECORATING CANAPÉS

If you are piping the topping on – the croûtons or tartlets are best for this – try to use a selection of nozzles so that you can have a variety of contours and shapes. The basic rosette twirl works as well as any.

When preparing the flat puff pastry strips or bread rectangles, spread the mixture over fairly generously with a palette knife. Then, using an alternate mix and a piping bag, pipe either edge borders or pyramid centres (see illustrations). Cut widthwise with a serrated knife into long strips and then either at an angle, quickly and easily making attractive diamonds, or straight across.

Now the fiddly part of the decorating commences, and this undoubtedly needs time and patience (and – for me – a drink of something close to hand). Draw a stool up to your work surface and concentrate on the job in hand. Organise any kind of nuts, in slivers or halves; prepare very small pieces of parsley or other herbs; cut stars and other shapes out of red, green and yellow peppers; use small diamonds of smoked salmon; mustard-spoon portions of black or red caviar roe; thin circles of radishes or pickled gherkins; quarter circles of pickled walnuts; little touches of chutney; a pea, caper or cocktail onion.

Place these on the soft topping of your canapés, then arrange them all on serving dishes in an attractive and decorative pattern. Have a nice time!

——HOT SKEWERED CANAPÉS——

These are perhaps a little more substantial, but I can never resist them, and they're ideal for serving as a first course at an informal party.

The older I get I seem to spend all my hard-earned brass on a few spread-out breaks each year which, apart from recharging my batteries, restore my sanity in this pressurised world of business. The packing (always cause for a row in this household as I travel heavy!) is the only nightmare, but how the adrenalin flows when departure time for the airport slowly draws near – I usually have to resort to a Librium. Check In, the formalities, Duty Free, anxious moments hoping no flight delay will be announced, sauntering to the gate (we play a game that we will always be the last two to board), settling down in the seats, avidly reading the menus, the magical take-off . . . and then the hot canapés. I do not hold back: I simply say, 'A double selection of all the hot ones, please, as I'm starving!'

I have had such ingenious hot canapés on various pampered first-class flights (yes, as I said, *all* my spare money is spent on holidays), that I now like to serve my own variations with the wine before dinner. I grill them on wooden satay skewers or cocktail sticks and then serve each guest with a small individual plate. To prevent the skewers or sticks burning under the grill, they should be soaked in water with a teaspoon of vinegar added (to give additional flavour), for a few hours beforehand.

Very small cubes of various meats – lamb, chicken, beef or pork – must be marinated well before grilling (see pages 181–2 for some marinades), and you could serve prawns or quartered scallops. The following can also be skewered easily along with the meat:

> red and green pepper diamonds marinated in honey and lemon juice
> mushrooms marinated in soy sauce
> halved pickled onions
> pineapple pieces in yoghurt
> water chestnuts in sherry
> baby courgette slices in Marsala
> liver pieces in milk
> olives washed of their brine (make sure they are stoneless!)
> stoned dates and prunes
> fresh fig quarters
> smoked canned oysters

You decide what you have got and what goes with what and then skewer them on the sticks. Grill for several minutes then remove them with a pair of pliers. Serve immediately on plates and hand out thick paper napkins.

Toasted Curried Nuts

These, although very more-ish, can be served as an accompaniment to pre-dinner drinks, without spoiling your guests' appetites too much. They're also wonderful with a mid-morning Bloody Mary after the night before!

2 egg whites
1 tablespoon caster sugar
1 heaped teaspoon curry powder
4 oz (100 g) each of whole almonds,
   cashews, macadamia nuts and pecan
   nuts, making 1 lb (450 g) in total

1 tablespoon each of sesame seeds and
   black poppy seeds

Beat the egg whites until they reach the soft peak stage, and then beat in the sugar followed by the curry powder. Fold in all the nuts and seeds and then spread out on a baking tray. Bake in a preheated oven at 325°F/160°C/Gas 3 for 40 minutes, shaking the tray and turning the nuts every 10 minutes. When completely cold, store in an airtight container.

Cold Pancake Fans

These can be served as canapés or pre-dinner snacks, but they are substantial enough to be counted as a first course, an integral part of the menu.

Using the basic pancake mixture on page 61, make the appropriate number of pancakes, about 5 inches (12.5 cm) in diameter. When they are cold, lay the pancakes out on the work surface. On the top left-hand quarter of the circle put a generous teaspoon of the first filling (see below), and then fold the pancake in half away from you giving you the top of an arch. On the right-hand half of this semi-circle, put your other filling and then fold the left-hand side over the right on top to make a fan-shaped pancake which is easily consumed.

Left-hand top corner
smoked salmon bits
flaked potted shrimps
flaked white fish
small ham pieces
poached spinach leaves
minced pork or veal ends
flaked tuna with apple bits
chopped tomato and avocado
American red salmon caviar roe

Right-hand top corner
cream cheese and caviar
curried mayonnaise (see page 134)
cool herbed hollandaise (see page 127)
home-made chutney
cheese and herb pâté (see page 39)
orange rind cream cheese
mayonnaise (see page 134)
piped soured cream
piped horseradish cream

Cheddar Cheese Wedges

Serve with cheese after dinner, or use as a base for piped duck liver pâté.

5 oz (150 g) plain flour
4 oz (100 g) soft butter

4 oz (100 g) Cheddar cheese, finely
   grated
a pinch of paprika

Preheat the oven to 300°F/150°C/Gas 2.

Put the flour, butter and cheese into a chilled bowl and bring together with your fingers to form a dough. Spread evenly into a loose-bottomed 8 inch (20 cm) flan tin, and sprinkle with a little paprika. Chill for at least 1 hour.

Bake in the preheated oven for 1¼ hours. Remove from the oven and leave to cool. As cooling, portion into wedges.

Lightly Curried Herb Biscuits

These are ideal used as the base of pre-dinner canapés with twirls of pâtés on top, or for serving with cheese at the end of a meal.

Makes 16 (without re-rolling, see below)

8 oz (225 g) plain flour
½ teaspoon curry powder
3 teaspoons baking powder
3 oz (75 g) soft butter

1 teaspoon caster sugar
2 tablespoons chopped fresh herbs of
   choice
1 tablespoon natural yoghurt

Preheat the oven to 350°F/180°C/Gas 4, and line a couple of baking trays with greaseproof paper.

Bring the flour, curry powder, baking powder, butter, sugar and herbs together in the Kenwood bowl, using the K beater. Mix in the yoghurt to make a paste-like dough.

Turn this out on to a floured work surface and roll to a thickness of about ¼ inch (6 mm). Cut out the biscuits using a fluted round 2 inch (5 cm) cutter, and transfer to the lined trays. Bake for 15–20 minutes. Leave on the trays for a few minutes to crisp up then leave to cool. When quite cold, store in airtight containers.

I would not re-roll the dough left to make further biscuits. When I did so, the biscuits were much tougher – and the waste is so minimal.

The Second Course
· *SOUPS* ·

Creamy vegetable soups form the second course of a dinner at Miller Howe. They are colourful and tasty, are always garnished attractively, and served on doyleyed and occasionally beflowered plates. But they don't, however, need to be part of a five-course dinner: the proportions I give below, for both hot and cold soups, make enough soup for *twelve small* dinner portions, but will also serve six generously as part of a three-course meal or a simple lunch.

There is nothing in a can or packet (however expensive) to beat the taste, texture and smell of a good home-made soup; and there is never a time of year when there isn't a relatively inexpensive vegetable on the market that will produce a pleasant pot of potage for your family and friends. I can't think of *any* vegetable that won't make a soup (not always creamed, either) to warm on a chill autumn or winter night – and you can even serve some soups chilled for a summer lunch or dinner party.

Follow my basic recipe for creamed vegetable soup and you will find how easy it is to gain confidence to experiment and ring the changes. Use seasonal vegetables as much as possible, trying some of the more exotic combinations in the recipes below – some using ingredients other than vegetables – for a dish that is easy to prepare and cook, simplicity itself to serve, and one which is healthy and economical, as well as satisfying for both appetite and taste buds.

HOME-MADE STOCKS

The basic secret of a good home-made soup, though, is a good home-made stock. Elizabeth David took me to task recently (in the nicest possible way, in the *Tatler*) about using only a chicken-based stock for my soups – and of course she was right. So here I introduce some variations used at Miller Howe constantly, and they should help bring different flavours to soup recipes, new or familiar.

It horrifies me that there are still many cookery writers who give recipes for soups (some of them ingenious and clever), but say you can use stock cubes. I put my head on the block here and now and definitely, most positively, say you *can't*. If you are taking the time and trouble to produce a soup using everything that is fresh and in season (most of the time), why, oh why, completely ruin the effort by using stock cubes or crystals full of that ruddy monosodium glutamate (as well as various other nasties).

There is surely no household which cannot, at least once a week, make its own home-made stock. Anybody loving food and respecting their bellies (well, maybe we're all a little unkind at times!) will always be capable of making some sort of stock, whether from leftovers, or from specially selected and bought bones and vegetables.

Do be meticulous, though, about cooking and storing stock. It can 'turn' if left for too long on top of the stove after or in between simmerings. If it 'bubbles' on top – and the heat isn't on underneath it – it could have started fermenting, a disaster to which chicken stock is particularly prone. Always cook a stock slowly, cool it as quickly as possible, and chill or freeze.

FREEZING SOUPS AND STOCKS

I find it easiest and best to freeze any leftover cold stocks and cream soups by pouring them into ice-cube trays. When frozen, the cubes are turned out into polythene bags, which are secured and returned to the freezer. This method is far more satisfactory than one whole clump of ice which takes ages to melt and which will never fit your saucepan – and usually over-hangs it and melts on to the cooker top.

Stocks should be reduced by at least half by simmering before being frozen. They take up less space this way, of course, and are a bit like having your own 'stock cubes' to hand. When you want to use the cubes, reconstitute the lot with a little boiling water for soup stock – or use just one or two to add that extra something to a sauce.

When you wish to serve a soup that has been frozen, put the cubes into a double saucepan and heat gently until melted and hot. If you don't possess a double saucepan – no sin – plonk the cubes into a Christmas pudding type bowl and place this over a saucepan of simmering water. It will take about 10 minutes from freezer to soup bowl. Of course if you have a microwave oven these timings are irrelevant.

A selection of colourful and delicious canapés,
● *using croûton and pastry bases, and a multitude of toppings.* ●
*A few of these could be arranged on individual plates and served
as an informal starter.*

A trio of cold soups and their garnishes.
● From the top, clockwise, *cucumber and mint, rhubarb,* ●
ginger and elderflower, and a magnificent
Miller Howe gazpacho.

A cold fish terrine which rather resembles a Battenburg cake!
Long thin strips of salmon and halibut are wrapped around purées
of pea and asparagus, and the whole is wrapped in pancakes.

Lettuce–steamed scallops taste as magnificent
as they look, especially when accompanied, warm,
by a little hollandaise.

It is always a wise person who has bags of soup cubes in their freezer. Apart from being far superior to any canned or packeted soups, they are relatively inexpensive, and are always there ready for a quick snack or for unexpected guests. In fact it's usually worthwhile to make *more* soup than you need specifically so that it can be frozen.

Poultry Stock

You can use the carcass of a bird you've already roasted, or the bones left over from boning breasts or legs or whatever. Raw bones with some fragments of meat left on them, plus the skin, will make a stronger, clearer stock. After Christmas (or Easter, as turkeys are becoming popular then too), you could make gallons of good turkey stock from the carcass; do it in batches, and freeze for use in soups at a later date.

The vegetable and flavouring part of the stock can be almost anything and everything (except potato). Gather together and keep things like onion and garlic skins, outside lettuce and cauliflower leaves, celery tops, leek and carrot tops etc in a plastic bag in the fridge; this way you'll have the basics of a stock for the next time you cook a bird.

poultry bones, skin and trimmings
vegetable flavourings (as above, but try always to include some onion, carrot and celery)

parsley stalks
a few black peppercorns
2 bay leaves

Put all the bones, chosen generous vegetable and other flavourings into a large spotlessly clean saucepan and cover with cold water – at least 5 pints (3 litres). Bring slowly to the boil, skimming clear of any scum that might come to the surface, then turn the heat down immediately. Cover and continue to simmer. Never *ever* continue boiling.

Leave for at least 4 hours simmering away, adding more water from time to time if necessary. Strain and cool, then refrigerate. Any fat will set in a layer on the top overnight, and can easily be removed. Freeze if you like.

However, you can keep a stock going. Either add more vegetable flavourings – some grilled tomatoes left over from breakfast, or a mushroom stalk or two, for instance – and more water, and carry on simmering; or you can strain the stock and start *again* with fresh flavourings for a much more richly and intensely flavoured stock. This can continue for about 3–4 days, after which you will be left with about 3 pints (1.8 litres) of rich stock.

Fish Stock

This basic stock can be used as the basis of any fish soup or as a court-bouillon in which to poach a whole fish such as a salmon, or steaks or cutlets (up to twelve). But well reduced, it makes a wonderful flavouring addition to a cream reduction sauce to accompany fish – it gives an undeniable edge to fish cooking.

head, tails, gills, bones and skin of fish
1–2 teaspoons olive oil
2–3 black peppercorns
a couple of parsley stalks

2 thin lemon slices
1 pint (600 ml) white wine
1 pint (600 ml) cold water

Cut the fish trimmings into evenly shaped pieces and put into a large shallow saucepan with all the remaining ingredients. Bring to the boil. Turn down the heat and simmer for 10 minutes, no more.

Strain into a clean saucepan and simmer to reduce slightly. Reduce much more slowly if you want to use it as a flavouring for sauces.

Vegetable Stock

As there are so many vegetarians about these days, and others who simply do not like meat or chicken stock used with soups (and it isn't always that one has a chicken carcass in the house), a good stock can be made from vegetables alone. Use this stock for any soup to replace the chicken stock.

2 oz (50 g) soft butter
8 oz (225 g) onions, peeled and cut into
    quarters, each studded with 1 clove
2 lb (900 g) vegetables of choice to hand
    (carrots, celery, French beans, leeks,
    parsnips, turnips), all cut into similar
    sized pieces

1 oz (25 g) fresh herbs
5 pints (3 litres) cold water

Melt the butter in a large, thick-bottomed saucepan and add the clove-studded onion quarters. Cook until slightly brown then add the other vegetables. Continue cooking, stirring from time to time, until all are beginning to brown. Add the herbs and cold water and leave to simmer for 3–4 hours. Add a little more water if necessary.

Take a teaspoon of the liquid out at this stage and taste when cool. If the flavour is to your liking, strain the stock, discarding the vegetables. Leave to go cold, and skim the congealed fat off.

Basic Cream Soup

This basic recipe can be applied to each and every soup 'recipe' listed below (which is why they're rather skimpy as far as instructions are concerned). Just remember that you need 2 lb (900 g) of *prepared* vegetables – that is, they've already been trimmed, peeled if necessary, or simply scrubbed before being weighed up. Many vegetables, of course, don't *need* to be skinned or cored or whatever: the soup will be liquidised and then sieved before reheating, and a lot of the vegetable goodness and flavour is contained in or near the skin. Use this quantity of one vegetable alone – any of those in the recipes below, or others such as asparagus, aubergine (yes, it's good), beetroot, celeriac or Jerusalem artichokes, for instance – or use a combination of vegetables, 1 lb (450 g) each of two, for instance. Some of the recipes below are not *just* vegetable – the same rules still apply. I've given combination recipes only in the main – recipes that have been tried, tested and appreciated – as I think you can prepare your own single-vegetable soups without any further aid from me – provided, of course, you follow the basic recipe . . .

Serves 6–12 (see above)

2 lb (900 g) prepared vegetables
4 oz (100 g) butter
8 oz (225 g) onions, peeled and finely chopped
¼ pint (150 ml) cooking sherry

2 pints (1.2 litres) good home-made stock
salt
freshly ground black pepper

Cut the prepared vegetables into even-sized pieces so that they will all cook evenly. This is *most* important.

Melt the butter in a large saucepan, add the finely chopped onions, and cook until soft and golden. Add the vegetables, stir around in the butter and onions, and pour in the sherry. At this point, many flavourings in individual recipes are added.

Dampen a doubled sheet of greaseproof paper well and press down over the vegetables to cover them and keep the steam in. Cover with a lid and simmer on a very low heat for 40–45 minutes. Have a look occasionally, just to check that the contents aren't burning or drying out. They shouldn't if the heat is low enough, there's usually a lot of moisture.

Add the stock to the soft vegetables in the pan and then liquidise the soup in batches. As each batch is liquidised, pour through a sieve into a clean pan: press through with a soup ladle – far quicker than with an ordinary wooden or metal spoon.

Reheat very gently and *only then* taste for seasoning. Add salt and pepper as required, and any other flavourings that may be specified in individual recipes.

The last thing to do is to garnish your soup to enhance both its appearance and its taste. Garnish ideas are attached to many individual soups, and there are a few more ideas at the end of this section.

• Apple •

This soup can be served cold as well. Garnish a cold soup with a generous sprinkling of finely chopped chives and a thin onion slice, or with a pinch of curry powder or powdered cinnamon. Use 1 pint (600 ml) each of chicken stock and dry cider instead of all stock.

2 lb (900 g) Granny Smith apples

Garnish
natural yoghurt
horseradish sauce
grated Lancashire or Cheddar cheese

Add the chopped apples, cores and all, to the onions and cook as in the basic recipe. Add the stock and cider, liquidise and sieve. Garnish each bowl with a tablespoon of yoghurt mixed with 1 teaspoon of horseradish sauce and sprinkle the cheese on top. You could also add some chopped chives if you like.

• Apricot and Marrow •

1 lb (450 g) dried apricots, soaked overnight in the cold stock, then strained
1 lb (450 g) marrow flesh
½ teaspoon ground ginger
1 tablespoon caster sugar

Garnish
fresh mint sprigs

Add the strained apricots, marrow flesh, ginger and sugar to the onions and cook as in the basic recipe. Add the stock, liquidise and sieve. Garnish with the mint.

• Broad Bean and Hazelnut •

2 lb (900 g) broad beans
1 tablespoon caster sugar
4 oz (100 g) ground hazelnuts

Garnish
a few extra broad beans, cooked separately and slowly, tough outer skins removed
lemon juice

Add the broad beans and sugar to the onions and cook as in the basic recipe. Add the stock and ground hazelnuts, then liquidise and sieve. Garnish with the extra broad beans which have been marinated in the lemon juice.

• Broad Bean and Lemon •

2 lb (900 g) broad beans
juice and grated rind of 2 lemons

Garnish
lemon slices
whipped double cream
parsley sprigs

Add the broad beans and lemon juice and rind to the onions and cook as in the basic recipe. Add stock, liquidise and sieve. Garnish each bowl with a lemon slice topped with a twirl of cream and a sprig of parsley.

• Broccoli and Apple •

1 lb (450 g) broccoli
1 lb (450 g) apples

Garnish
apple rings fried in a little butter
tiny broccoli florets

Add the broccoli and the apples, cores and all, to the onions and cook as in the basic recipe. Add stock, liquidise and sieve. Garnish with the apple rings and broccoli florets.

Broccoli with Calvados Apple Purée

2 lb (900 g) broccoli

Garnish
Calvados apple purée (see page 133)

Add the broccoli to the onions and cook as in the basic recipe. Add stock, liquidise and sieve. As the soup is being dished out into the serving bowls, add 1–2 tablespoons of the apple purée to each bowl.

You could also sprinkle a tablespoon of finely grated Cheddar cheese on top – all the flavours blend well together.

Brussels Sprout, Chestnut and Water Chestnut

2 lb (900 g) Brussels sprouts
6 oz (175 g) natural chestnut purée
$\frac{1}{4}$ teaspoon ground nutmeg
$\frac{1}{2}$ tablespoon caster sugar

Garnish
crispy baked bacon bits (see page 99)
1 canned water chestnut per portion, chopped

Add the sprouts, chestnut purée, nutmeg and sugar to the onions, and cook as in the basic recipe. Add stock, liquidise and sieve. Garnish with the bacon bits and the chopped water chestnuts.

Brussels Sprout and Hazelnut

2 lb (900 g) Brussels sprouts
4 oz (100 g) ground hazelnuts

Garnish
orange slices
whipped double cream
chopped hazelnuts

Add the Brussels sprouts to the onions and cook as in the basic recipe. Add the stock and ground hazelnuts, liquidise and sieve. Garnish each bowl with an orange slice topped with a twirl of cream spotted with chopped hazelnuts.

Brussels Sprout and Mustard

2 lb (900 g) Brussels sprouts
2 tablespoons dry English mustard powder

Garnish
crispy baked bacon bits (see page 99) or heads of mustard and cress

Add the Brussels sprouts to the onions and cook as in the basic recipe. Beat the mustard powder well into the stock, then add to the vegetables, liquidise and sieve. Garnish with the bacon bits or mustard and cress.

Carrot and Apple

$1\frac{1}{2}$ lb (675 g) carrots
8 oz (225 g) sharp apples

Garnish
grated carrot
lemon juice

Add the carrots and quartered apples, cores and all, to the onions and cook as in the basic recipe. Add stock, liquidise and sieve. Garnish with the cold grated carrot which has been marinated in the lemon juice.

Carrot and Coriander

2 lb (900 g) carrots
2 tablespoons whole coriander seeds
1 tablespoon caster sugar

Garnish
croûtons (see page 97)
whipped double cream
deep-fried parsley sprigs (see page 98)

Add the carrots, coriander seeds and sugar to the onions and cook as in the basic recipe. Add stock, liquidise and sieve. Garnish each bowl with a few croûtons, a twirl of cream on top and the sprig of parsley (or a sprig of fresh coriander).

• Carrot and Ginger •

2 lb (900 g) carrots
4 whole pieces ginger in syrup, drained

Garnish
finely chopped preserved ginger

Add carrots and ginger to the onions and cook as in the basic recipe. Add stock, liquidise and sieve. Garnish with the ginger.

• Carrot, Leek and Mustard •

1 lb (450 g) carrots
1 lb (450 g) diced leeks
1 tablespoon caster sugar
2 tablespoons dry English mustard powder

Garnish
toasted almonds

Add carrots, leeks and sugar to the onions and cook as in the basic recipe. Add the mustard powder to the stock and beat in well before adding to the vegetables. Liquidise and sieve. Garnish each bowl with some toasted almonds.

• Carrot and Orange •

2 lb (900 g) carrots
1 tablespoon caster sugar
juice and grated rind of 4 oranges

Garnish
1 orange slice, skinned, per portion
whipped double cream
finely grated raw carrot

Add carrots and sugar to the onions and cook as in the basic recipe. Mix the orange rind and juice into the stock, add to the vegetables, then liquidise and sieve. Garnish each bowl with an orange slice, topped with a whirl of cream and sprinkled with grated carrot.

• Carrot and Spinach •

2 lb (900 g) carrots

Garnish
spinach purée (see page 166)

Add the carrots to the onions and cook as in the basic recipe. Add the stock, liquidise and sieve. Garnish each portion with a tablespoon of warmed spinach purée.

• Cauliflower Cheese •

2 lb (900 g) cauliflower florets
$\frac{1}{2}$ teaspoon grated nutmeg
$\frac{3}{4}$ teaspoon dry English mustard powder
$\frac{1}{2}$ tablespoon caster sugar
4 oz (100 g) Cheddar cheese, grated

Garnish
small cauliflower florets, lightly fried in oil and drained
very finely grated Cheddar cheese
sprigs of deep-fried parsley (optional, see page 98)

Add the cauliflower, nutmeg, mustard powder and sugar to the onions and cook as in the basic recipe. Add stock, liquidise and sieve. Add the cheese when reheating. Garnish with the tiny sprigs of cauliflower, and sprinkle each bowl with some cheese as it's being served. A sprig of deep-fried parsley looks good and colourful – and tastes delicious!

• Cauliflower and Fennel •

1 lb (450 g) cauliflower florets
1 lb (450 g) fennel bulb

Garnish
toasted almonds or a generous spoonful of warmed mushroom pâté (see page 40) per portion
a few fennel fronds

Add the cauliflower and fennel to the onions and cook as in the basic recipe.

Add stock, liquidise and sieve. Garnish with the almonds and fennel fronds, or spoon some mushroom pâté into each bowl as it's being served, and top with some fennel fronds.

• Celery and Dill •

2 lb (900 g) celery
2 tablespoons dried dill seeds

Garnish
chopped walnuts

Add the celery and dill to the onions and cook as in the basic recipe. Add stock, liquidise and sieve. Garnish with the walnuts.

• Celery and Fennel •

1 lb (450 g) celery
1 lb (450 g) fennel

Garnish
green fronds of fennel or finely chopped fennel bulb hearts

Add the celery and fennel to the onions and cook as in the basic recipe. Add stock, liquidise and sieve. Garnish with the herb or diced fennel.

• Courgette and Fennel •

1 lb (450 g) courgettes
1 lb (450 g) fennel bulb
½ tablespoon caster sugar

Garnish
thin slices of courgette, dipped in beaten egg and flour, deep-fried and drained (see page 167)

Add the courgettes, fennel and sugar to the onions and cook as in the basic recipe. Add stock, liquidise and sieve. Garnish with the courgette 'fritters'.

• Courgette, Fennel and Orange •

1 lb (450 g) fennel bulb
1 lb (450 g) courgettes
juice and grated rind of 2 oranges

Garnish
fresh orange segments (see page 101)

Add the fennel and courgettes to the onions and cook as in the basic recipe. Add the orange juice and rind and stock, liquidise and sieve. Garnish each bowl with two fresh orange segments.

• Courgette and Rosemary •

2 lb (900 g) courgettes
1–2 tablespoons fresh rosemary

Garnish
chopped fresh parsley and mint

Add the courgettes and rosemary to the onions and cook as in the basic recipe. Add the stock, liquidise and sieve. Garnish with the chopped herbs.

• Curried Apple •

2 lb (900 g) unpeeled cooking apples, roughly chopped
4 tablespoons caster sugar

Curry flavouring
1 tablespoon oil
1 oz (25 g) butter
4 oz (100 g) onions, peeled and finely chopped
1 teaspoon each of cumin, celery and coriander seeds
1 teaspoon ground coriander
a pinch each of ground cinnamon and chilli powder

Garnish
finely diced apple
fresh lime juice
toasted desiccated coconut

If you use dessert apples you don't need to add the sugar. Cook the chopped apples and sugar gently with the onions as in the basic recipe.

Put the stock in the liquidiser goblet. Heat the oil and butter together in a pan, and fry the onions until golden. Add all the remaining ingredients for the curry flavouring and sauté gently until brown. Add this mixture gradually to the stock in the goblet, blending as you go and tasting, until you are satisfied that you have got it right to suit your palate. Do bear in mind that it has to be slightly stronger than you might actually prefer as it still has to be blended with the apples.

Add the liquidised stock and curry mixture to the apples, then return to the liquidiser in batches in the usual way. Sieve. Garnish with the diced apple which has been marinated in the lime juice, and top with a sprinkling of coconut.

• Curried Marrow •

Follow the recipe for Curried Apple, and garnish with toasted desiccated coconut.

• Curried Pumpkin •

Follow the recipe for Curried Apple, and garnish with banana circles fried in a little butter.

• Fennel and Almond •

2 lb (900 g) fennel bulb
4 oz (100 g) ground almonds

Garnish
finely diced fennel bulb hearts
Pernod

Add the fennel to the onions and cook as in the basic recipe. Add stock, liquidise and sieve, and stir in the ground almonds. Garnish with the fennel dice which have been marinated in a little Pernod.

• Fennel and Red Pepper •

1½ lb (675 g) fennel bulb
1 large red pepper

Garnish
finely diced red pepper

Add the chopped fennel and diced red pepper to the onions and cook as in the basic recipe. Add stock, liquidise and sieve. Garnish with the pepper dice.

• Leek, Lemon and Lime •

This soup can be served hot or cold. Use milk instead of stock.

2 lb (900 g) leeks, roughly chopped
2 tablespoons caster sugar
1 lemon, chopped
½ fresh lime, chopped

Garnish
toasted flaked almonds
whipped double cream
finely chopped parsley
1 small wedge of lime per portion

Add the leeks, sugar, lemon and lime to the onions and cook as in the basic recipe. Add the milk, liquidise and sieve very well. Serve, hot or cold, sprinkled with almonds and topped with a swirl of whipped cream and some parsley. Wedge the lime pieces on the top rim of the soup bowl.

• Leek and Mustard •

2 lb (900 g) leeks
½ tablespoon caster sugar
4 tablespoons dry English mustard
  powder

Garnish
heads of mustard and cress

Add the leeks and sugar to the onions and cook as in the basic recipe. Beat the mustard powder into the stock, add to the vegetables, then liquidise and sieve. Garnish with the mustard and cress.

• Leek and Potato •

1 lb (450 g) leeks
1 lb (450 g) potatoes

Garnish
1 slice chilled walnut butter (see page 109) per portion
finely chopped fresh chives

Add the leeks and potatoes to the onions, and cook as in the basic recipe. Add stock, liquidise and sieve. Garnish at the very last moment with the thin slice of walnut butter and a sprinkling of chives.

Mango and Green Pea • with Lime •

1½ lb (675 g) mango flesh
8 oz (225 g) frozen peas
juice and grated rind of 1 fresh lime

Garnish
extra warmed whole peas

Add the mango flesh, peas, and rind and juice of the lime to the onions, and cook as in the basic recipe. Add stock, liquidise and sieve. Garnish with a few warmed whole peas in each bowl.

• Mushroom and Apple •

1 lb (450 g) fresh mushrooms, stalks included
1 lb (450 g) apples

Garnish
apple rings
sherry

Add the mushrooms, stalks and all, and apples to the onions and cook as in the basic recipe. Add stock, liquidise and sieve. Garnish each bowl with an apple ring which has been marinated in sherry.

• Mushroom and Cumin •

2 lb (900 g) fresh mushrooms, stalks included
¼ teaspoon cumin powder

Garnish
2 turned mushroom caps per portion (see page 105), fried in butter and drained
sprig of fresh parsley

Use Marsala instead of the sherry in the basic mixture if you like. Add the mushrooms and cumin to the onions, and cook as in the basic recipe. Add stock, liquidise and sieve. Garnish with two mushroom caps and a large sprig of fresh parsley per bowl.

• Mushroom and Mustard •

2 lb (900 g) fresh mushrooms, stalks included
4 dessertspoons Moutarde de Meaux

Garnish
sprigs of watercress

Add the mushrooms and mustard to the onions and cook as in the basic recipe. Add stock, liquidise and sieve. Garnish with sprigs of watercress.

• Nip and Nip •

It is most important that these vegetables are cut into the same sized pieces so that they both become soft together. Otherwise a lot of their goodness will escape.

1 lb (450 g) parsnips
1 lb (450 g) turnips

Garnish
lightly curried leek rings (see page 167)

Add the parsnips and turnips to the onions and cook as in the basic recipe. Add stock, liquidise and sieve. Garnish with the leek rings.

• Onion •

For this creamy soup, the method is slightly different, and milk is used instead of stock.

2 lb (900 g) onions, peeled and roughly
   chopped

Garnish
small circular croûtons topped with
   grated Cheddar cheese and grilled (see
   page 97)

Cook the onions as in the basic recipe, but then add the sherry, *additional* soup onions and milk all at the same time. Cook gently, with a lid on, as usual, until the onions are mushy. Liquidise and sieve. Garnish with the cheese-topped croûtons.

• Pea, Caraway and Mint •

2 lb (900 g) peas
2 tablespoons caraway seeds
1 large bunch fresh mint

Garnish
a few extra sprigs of fresh mint

Add the peas, caraway seeds and bunch of mint to the onions and cook as in the basic recipe. Add stock, liquidise and sieve. Garnish with the sprigs of mint.

• Pea, Lemon and Mint •

2 lb (900 g) frozen peas
1 lemon, cut into 6 wedges
6 large sprigs fresh mint, or 2
   tablespoons dried mint
2 tablespoons caster sugar

Garnish
extra cooked peas
juice of $\frac{1}{2}$ lemon

Add the peas, lemon wedges, mint and sugar to the onions and cook as in the basic recipe. Add stock, liquidise and sieve. Garnish with the lemon-marinated peas.

• Pea, Lemon and Sweetcorn •

1 lb (450 g) frozen peas
1 lb (450 g) sweetcorn kernels
1 lemon, quartered

Garnish
sweetcorn kernels cooked in butter and
   drained

Add the peas, sweetcorn and lemon quarters to the onions and cook as in the basic recipe. Add stock, liquidise and sieve. Garnish with the sweetcorn kernels.

• Pea, Pear and Watercress •

1 lb (450 g) frozen peas
1 lb (450 g) peeled and cored pears
$\frac{1}{4}$ teaspoon ground mace
2 bunches watercress

Garnish
croûtons (see page 97)
thin slices of fresh pear fried in a little
   butter
double cream
sprigs of fresh watercress

Add the peas, pears and mace to the onions and cook as in the basic recipe for 35 minutes. Add the watercress and continue cooking for a further 15 minutes. Add stock, liquidise and sieve. Garnish with croûtons, slices of fried pear, cream and sprigs of fresh watercress.

• Pumpkin and Apple •

For this soup, use 1 pint (600 ml) dry cider and 1 pint (600 ml) stock.

1 lb (450 g) pumpkin flesh
1 lb (450 g) apples

Garnish
parsley sprigs

Add the pumpkin and quartered apples, cores and all, to the onions, and cook as in the basic recipe. Add the cider and stock, liquidise and sieve. Garnish with the parsley.

• Pumpkin and Saffron •

$\frac{1}{4}$ pint (150 ml) hot milk
4 good pinches fresh saffron
2 lb (900 g) pumpkin flesh

Garnish
freshly chopped parsley

Pour the hot milk on to the fresh saffron and leave to infuse for 20 minutes.

Add the pumpkin to the onions and cook as in the basic recipe, along with the infused saffron and milk. Add the stock, liquidise and sieve. Garnish with parsley.

• Red Pepper and Cauliflower •

$1\frac{1}{2}$ lb (675 g) cauliflower florets
8 oz (225 g) red peppers

Garnish
small cauliflower florets, fried in butter
   and drained
diced red pepper

Add the cauliflower and red peppers to the onions and cook as in the basic recipe. Add stock, liquidise and sieve. Garnish with the cauliflower florets and pepper dice.

• Sage and Onion •

As with the onion soup, use milk instead of stock.

2 lb (900 g) onions
12 fresh sage leaves

Garnish
apple slices, fried in a little butter
tomato provençale (see page 132)
freshly chopped chives or parsley

Add the onions and sage leaves, along with the milk, to the onions of the basic recipe, and cook as usual. Liquidise and sieve. Garnish each bowl with a slice of apple, topped with a tablespoon of tomato provençale and a sprinkling of chopped herb.

• Smoked Haddock •

Use milk instead of the stock for this richly flavoured soup. You could garnish it with spoonfuls of spinach and apple purées instead of the croûtons, cream and roe.

2 lb (900 g) smoked haddock

Garnish
croûtons (see page 97)
whipped double cream
red lumpfish roe

Add the haddock to the onions and cook as in the basic recipe. Add the milk, liquidise and sieve. Garnish each bowl with a few small croûtons, a swirl of cream and a pinch of lumpfish roe.

• Smoked Haddock and Sweetcorn •

Make a fish stock (see page 82), from the skin and bones of the fish.

1½ lb (675 g) smoked haddock
8 oz (225 g) frozen sweetcorn kernels

Garnish
8 oz (225 g) sweetcorn kernels lightly
   tossed in butter

Add the smoked haddock and sweetcorn kernels to the onions and cook as in the basic recipe. Add the strained fish stock, liquidise and sieve. Garnish with the sweetcorn kernels.

• Spinach and Apple •

An alternative to this recipe would be to use 2 lb (900 g) spinach for the soup, and use a purée of apples, a tablespoonful for each bowl, as a garnish.

1½ lb (675 g) leaf spinach
8 oz (225 g) apples, quartered
¼ teaspoon grated nutmeg
1 tablespoon caster sugar

Garnish
lemon slices
apple dice

Add the spinach and apples, along with the nutmeg and sugar, to the onions and cook as in the basic recipe. Add stock, liquidise and sieve. Garnish with a lemon slice per bowl and a scattering of apple dice.

• Spinach and Whiting •

Make a fish stock (see page 82) from the bones and skin of the fish.

1½ lb (675 g) leaf spinach
12 oz (350 g) fresh whiting
½ nutmeg, finely grated
1 tablespoon caster sugar
1 teaspoon anchovy essence

Garnish
a few warmed prawns
toasted almonds

Add the spinach, whiting, nutmeg, sugar and anchovy essence to the onions and cook as in the basic recipe. Add the strained fish stock, liquidise and sieve. Garnish with the prawns and toasted almonds.

• Sweetcorn and Crab •

Use fish stock (see page 82) or milk instead of the chicken stock.

1 lb (450 g) sweetcorn kernels
1 lb (450 g) crab meat

Garnish
a few extra sweetcorn kernels
a few shrimps

Add the sweetcorn and crab meat to the onions and cook as in the basic recipe.

Add fish stock or milk, liquidise and sieve. Garnish with the sweetcorn kernels and the shrimps.

• Sweetcorn and Curry •

2 lb (900 g) sweetcorn kernels
2 teaspoons medium-hot curry powder paste

Garnish
sprigs of fresh parsley
finely diced fresh pineapple

Add the sweetcorn and curry powder paste to the onions and cook as in the basic recipe. Add stock, liquidise and sieve. Garnish with the sprigs of parsley and pineapple dice.

You could also use the curry mixture and method as described in the curried apple soup recipe.

• Sweetcorn and Peanut •

1½ lb (675 g) sweetcorn kernels
8 oz (225 g) salted peanuts
¼ teaspoon ground ginger
½ tablespoon caster sugar

Garnish
small croûtons or toast rounds spread thickly with peanut butter

Add the sweetcorn, peanuts, ginger and sugar to the onions, and cook as in the basic recipe. Add stock, liquidise and sieve. Serve the little peanut-butter coated rounds as an accompaniment, not as a garnish.

• Tomato and Apple •

1 lb (450 g) apples
1 lb (450 g) tomatoes

Garnish
finely grated Cheddar cheese
finely diced sweet gherkins

Add the apples and tomatoes to the onions and cook as in the basic recipe. Add stock, liquidise and sieve. Garnish at the last moment.

• Tomato, Apple and Celery •

a good 10 oz (275 g) each of tomatoes, apple and celery
¼ teaspoon grated nutmeg
a pinch of ground ginger

Garnish
thin apple slices
finely chopped fresh chives

Add the tomatoes, apple, celery and spices to the onions and cook as in the basic recipe. Add the stock, liquidise and sieve. Garnish each bowl with a floating raw apple slice topped with a sprinkling of chopped chives.

• Tomato and Tarragon •

2 lb (900 g) ripe tomatoes
2 tablespoons dried tarragon, or 4 tablespoons fresh
1 tablespoon caster sugar

Garnish
sprigs of fresh tarragon

Add the tomatoes, tarragon and sugar to the onions and cook as in the basic recipe. Add stock, liquidise and sieve. Garnish with the fresh tarragon sprigs.

• Turnip and Dill •

2 lb (900 g) turnips
1 tablespoon dried dill
¼ teaspoon caster sugar

Garnish
croûtons (see page 97)
whipped double cream
freshly chopped parsley or strands of fresh dill

Add the turnip, dill and sugar to the onions and cook as in the basic recipe. Add stock, liquidise and sieve. Garnish each bowl with a few croûtons, a swirl of whipped cream and the parsley or dill.

CHILLED SOUPS

Most of the following soups are made in approximately the same way as the basic cream soups. As they use less liquid – 1½ pints (900 ml) instead of 2 pints (1.2 litres), to intensify the flavour – and occasionally slightly different quantities of butter, onions etc, I have spelled them out. As they can all be made quite considerably in advance, they are a wonderful and easy way in which to start a summer dinner party.

As with the cream soups, these too serve twelve if poured into small bowls (well chilled), or less if you are a little more generous in your portioning.

Cucumber and Mint

For additional garnish you could make up a ring of cucumber slices on a lemon slice topped with a twirl of cream, and decorated with a borage flower and strawberry slice.

1 English garden cucumber, wiped, topped and tailed
2 garlic cloves, crushed with 1 teaspoon salt
1 tablespoon tarragon vinegar
3 tablespoons finely chopped fresh seasonal herbs (dill, mint, parsley, tarragon)
¾ pint (450 ml) cream (double or single)

¾ pint (450 ml) natural yoghurt
2 hard-boiled eggs, finely chopped
4 tablespoons finely chopped fennel bulb

Garnish
2 tablespoons sultanas, marinated overnight in 2 tablespoons brandy

Grate the cucumber on a hand grater into a large mixing bowl. Add all the other ingredients, and mix together. Cover and leave to chill in the fridge.

When serving, double check the seasoning and garnish with the now plumped-up sultanas divided evenly over the tops of the soup bowls.

Fennel and Watercress

This soup could also be served hot, when you should use the usual 2 pints (1.2 litres) stock and omit the Pernod.

8 oz (225 g) onions, peeled and finely chopped
4 oz (100 g) butter
2 lb (900 g) fennel bulb, evenly chopped
¼ pint (150 ml) sherry
4 tablespoons Pernod
1½ pints (900 ml) chicken stock

1 bunch fresh watercress

Garnish
heads of fresh watercress
toasted almonds
whipped double cream

Prepare the soup in the normal way. Simmer the onions in the butter and then add the fennel, sherry and Pernod. Cover with dampened greaseproof paper and cook gently for 40–45 minutes. Add the stock and watercress, then liquidise and sieve. Leave to chill in the fridge, then serve garnished with the watercress, lots of toasted almonds and a blob of cream.

Rhubarb, Ginger and Elderflower

The combination of these three ingredients works well, producing a slightly heady, winey flavour which starts off any meal in a grand fashion! Alternatively, you could garnish the soup with a swirl of cream and some chopped chives.

6 oz (175 g) onions, peeled and finely chopped
4 oz (100 g) butter
2 lb (900 g) rhubarb, cleaned and evenly chopped
2 tablespoons dried elderflowers
¼ pint (150 ml) white wine

1½ pints (900 ml) milk
2 walnut-sized pieces preserved ginger, chopped

Garnish
mint leaves
borage flowers

Prepare the soup in the normal way. Simmer the onions in the butter, then add the rhubarb, elderflowers, and wine. Cover with dampened greaseproof and cook gently for 40–45 minutes. Add the milk and the ginger then liquidise and sieve. Chill well, adjust the seasoning, then serve garnished with the mint leaves and borage flowers.

Smoked Trout and Avocado with Caviar

Earlier last year, quite out of the blue, I realised I had boobed over inviting some people to lunch. As the hotel was closed and my emergency supplies were *low*, I concocted this soup – which has since been served at the hotel!

3 oz (75 g) butter
6 oz (175 g) onions, peeled and finely diced
1½ pints (900 ml) milk
12 oz (350 g) smoked trout, boned, skinned and flaked
3 very ripe avocados, peeled, stoned and mashed

grated rind of 1 lemon

Garnish
1 small can American red salmon caviar roe

Melt the butter in a saucepan and lightly fry the onions. Remove from the heat and add the milk, smoked trout flakes, mashed avocado and lemon rind. Liquidise, pass through a sieve then chill.

Serve chilled in cold soup bowls and sprinkle on the top of each a generous teaspoon of the caviar roe. Accompany with thin slices of buttered wholemeal bread.

Smoked Salmon and Avocado

Substitute smoked salmon for the smoked trout in the above recipe. It is even nicer if garnished with very small cubes of fresh fennel bulb and chopped dill.

Sweetcorn and Smoked Chicken

8 oz (225 g) onions, peeled and chopped
4 oz (100 g) butter
1½ lb (675 g) sweetcorn kernels
¼ pint (150 ml) sherry
1½ pints (900 ml) chicken stock
12 oz (350 g) smoked chicken, finely
  diced

Garnish
chopped herbs
toasted macadamia nuts, chopped

Prepare the soup in the normal way. Simmer the onions in the butter then add the sweetcorn kernels and sherry. Cover with dampened greaseproof paper and cook gently for 40–45 minutes. Add the stock, liquidise and sieve. Chill well in the fridge, check seasoning, then fold in the finely diced smoked chicken. Garnish with the chopped herbs and nuts.

Miller Howe Gazpacho

Gazpacho is to Spain what cock-a-leekie is to Scotland, but this variation on the theme is a Miller Howe adaptation which always goes down extremely well in the summer.

At home make it at least the day before. The actual presentation can be built up during the day of your party, and then you can cover it all with cling film. The cold soup itself is poured into the tomato and round the dish at the last moment. Everything must be well chilled.

4 thick slices stale bread
3 large garlic cloves, crushed with a
  little salt
6 tablespoons good olive oil
1 dessertspoon wine vinegar
4 oz (100 g) butter
8 oz (225 g) onions, peeled and finely
  chopped
2 lb (900 g) tomatoes, roughly chopped
4 red peppers, trimmed and chopped

¼ pint (150 ml) cooking sherry
1 pint (600 ml) tomato juice
½ English cucumber, seeded and finely
  chopped
a touch of Tabasco
a touch of Worcestershire sauce
¼ pint (150 ml) vodka (optional)

To finish
1 large tomato per person
garnishings (see opposite)

Blend the bread in the food processor until it becomes crumbs, and then combine with the crushed garlic, oil and vinegar. Leave overnight, stirring first thing in the morning.

Melt the butter in a saucepan and fry the onions until golden. Add the 2 lb (900 g) tomatoes, stalks and all, along with the chopped peppers and sherry. Cover with a double thickness of dampened greaseproof paper and simmer for 45 minutes. Add the fresh tomato juice, cucumber, liquidise and sieve. When cold, fold in the soaked breadcrumbs and, little by little, add Tabasco, Worcestershire sauce and vodka (if using) until you get the flavour *you* like. Chill well.

Meanwhile take one large tomato for each guest and criss-cross the top of each with a sharp knife. Place in a pan of boiling water for about 10 seconds then remove and take the skin off. The time you submerge them in the boiling water will totally depend on the ripeness of the tomatoes, so experiment with the first. Then cut off the tops and remove the insides.

For the garnishings you can choose from: chopped fennel bulb; further skinned wedges of tomato; chopped red and green pepper; chopped cucumber; orange peel strips; chopped avocado; chopped hard-boiled eggs; chopped herbs, whole leaves or sprigs; tiny cooked croûtons.

The skinned tomato case is placed in the middle of the bowl or dish, and the soup is poured carefully *into* the tomato and around the edges. The garnishes are then arranged round the outer rim of the dish and on top of the filled tomato.

SOUP GARNISHES

You can be as basic or elaborate as you like when garnishing soups. A number of the Miller Howe garnishes for soup are very similar in nature to our garnishes on other courses – see the section starting on page 100 – but I thought I'd give a few details here too, of those most suitable for soups.

• Croûtons •

Most soups are the better for having some tiny croûtons dropped into them just as you take the bowls to the table. They can be made the day before from sliced bread. Simply cut off the crusts and then, using a sharp serrated knife, cut into small cubes. Scatter over a baking tray and leave somewhere warm in the kitchen to dry out quite considerably. The staler and dryer the croûton, the less fat it will absorb, and the more it will keep its shape. Put 2 tablespoons oil into a frying pan to heat through gently, before adding 2 oz (50 g) butter. When melted and amalgamated throw in the croûtons and stir-fry using a wooden spoon until they are evenly browned. Turn out on to a double thickness of kitchen paper and when you wish to serve them simply warm through in the oven for a few minutes.

You could also fry some crushed garlic in the oil and butter first for garlic croûtons, and you could sprinkle plain fried croûtons with ground cinnamon to make cinnamon croûtons – delicious with many vegetable soups.

You can make larger croûtons in exactly the same way, but cut into any shape you like – rounds are ideal for soup bowls – and top them with something interesting and appropriate to the soup – mushroom pâté, peanut butter or some grated cheese. I sometimes make a special cheese topping. Beat an egg with 2 teaspoons cooking brandy, salt, pepper and 1 teaspoon Moutarde de Meaux. Grate about 4 oz (100 g) Cheddar cheese into this to make a firm paste. Spread this on to each cooked and drained croûton and heat under the grill at the last minute. I often make larger croûtons still and pipe on to them a tiny blob of cheese and herb pâté (see page 39), and then cover that with the cheese topping. A good combination of tastes and textures.

• *Vegetables* •

Often the best and most visually interesting garnish for a creamed vegetable soup is a little bit of the actual soup vegetable – a broad bean or two, apple dice, tiny cauliflower or broccoli florets etc. You could marinate them first in a citrus juice or alcohol for extra effect. Vegetables can be grated and then marinated if you like – carrots, courgettes, radishes etc – and many small pieces of vegetable can be par-cooked in some way first: lightly fried in oil or butter in slices, wedges or florets, or whole (peas, sweetcorn, baby mushrooms etc).

• *Herbs* •

These are tailor-made for soup garnishes and their bright fresh green enhances most soups. Serve them finely chopped or in sprigs or fronds – and parsley can be deep-fried crisp. Simply wash and dry large sprigs then deep-fry *at the last moment* in deep fat heated to 365°F/185°C. Drain well and serve.

And never forget about herb *flowers*. Borage's bright blue is particularly pretty.

• *Citrus Fruit* •

Thin slices of lime, orange or lemon – skinned or unskinned and scored – can be floated in soups, and can act as a base for something else, like a blob of cream. A citrus fruit twirl (see page 100), looks even better, and for some soups you can wedge a slice on the edge of the soup bowl itself.

• *Purées and Sauces* •

A spoonful of many purées and sauces can often be used as a soup garnish – try apple purée or Calvados apple purée (see page 133), tomato provençale (see page 132), mushroom pâté (see page 40), and spinach purée (see page 166). Or you can try this recipe for red pepper purée, made in much the same way as a basic soup. It's not only a wonderful contrast of colour, but the taste is delightful too. It goes well, warmed gently (as should be all purées and sauces), with soups such as apple, spinach, sweetcorn, pea, turnip and carrot.

Serves 12 portions

4 oz (100 g) butter
4 oz (100 g) onions, peeled and finely diced
12 oz (350 g) red peppers, roughly chopped

1 tablespoon cooking sherry
¾ pint (450 ml) double cream, reduced by half

Melt the butter and fry the onions gently until golden. Add the peppers and the sherry, cover with dampened greaseproof paper, and cook for 30 minutes. Liquidise, and pass through a sieve into the reduced cream. Warm through gently and serve in spoonfuls.

• *Bacon* •

Crispy baked bacon bits provide an interesting texture to creamed soups. Simply cut rinded bacon rashers – use scissors – up into tiny bits and fry until crisp. Two rashers will do about four portions. Or, easier, bake the whole rashers until crisp and then crumble in your hands or with a rolling pin. Drain well always on kitchen paper.

• *Cream* •

A swirl of runny double or single cream in a soup can look magnificent, but in a hot soup the cream often splits and looks messy (it's fine on cold soups). What looks even better is a piped twirl of whipped double cream on a base – a handful of tiny croûtons, a larger croûton or citrus or apple slice etc.

• *Other Garnishes* •

Use your imagination, and always match to the soup! Finely grated Cheddar cheese, some toasted seeds, nuts or desiccated coconut, a flavoured butter (see page 108), diced gherkins or, for fish soups, some lumpfish roe or a couple of prawns or shrimps. And don't forget the speckled effect and superlative flavour of some coarsely ground black pepper or coriander seeds, or some grated nutmeg.

·*Miller Howe*·
Garnishes

The *look* of the food on the plate is almost as important to us at Miller Howe as is the taste – it should be a feast for the eye as well as for the palate. We take immense trouble over details like these – and they're really so easy. The simplest garnish of all – a sprig of parsley – will enhance a plain piece of fish, but an additional butter twirl adds taste as well as visual interest and shows that you've taken time and trouble. Always try to decorate your food: it really does make everything look more appetising, and your guests will appreciate your efforts enormously.

All food garnishes should be edible – and they must complement the food. The taste of a garnish should never be at odds with the principal food it is accompanying, and it should never be so strong that it will overpower the food. The colour must be considered – use your artist's eye to paint a picture – and positioning on the plate is important too. Don't ever overdo it, but don't be frightened to try out new ideas either.

Most garnishes can be prepared well in advance – on the morning of a party, say – and they can be kept in the fridge on plastic trays or plates, covered in cling film. Make sure they are brought out of the fridge well in advance; really cold garnishes are not very welcome!

• *Citrus Fruit* •

One of the most classic garnishes is a slice of lemon but, to make it more interesting, score the wiped sides of the fruit first with a scorer. To make twirls from your slices cut the fruit, before slicing, from top to bottom *half-way* through. As you cut each slice, one side is already cut through, and you can twist it open (see opposite).

Save the 'scorings' from citrus rind: they're good as a garnish too, adding colour and flavour. And if thin strips are required, use the sharpest vegetable peeler you have, which will allow you to remove the peel in $\frac{1}{2}$ inch (1.25 cm) strip sections. Simply stack four or five strips on top of one another, and then cut thinly with a sharp knife. To remove any bitterness, the strips should be plunged into boiling water and brought back to the boil for under 1 minute. Strain immediately and rinse under cold running water. They can be stored in a screw-top jar in ordinary cold water.

Finely grated citrus rind adds taste and colour sprinkled over a variety of foods, but care must be taken when grating as you only want the rind itself. You need a fine stainless steel grater which will simply take the coloured skin off without digging into the bitter white pith. I keep a strong toothbrush in the kitchen which I use to get off all the peel stuck on the grater itself!

Wedges of lemon, lime or orange are occasionally called for. Don't just chuck a wedge on the plate: cut into smaller thinner wedges and arrange three, say, in a fan shape at the side of the food, garnished perhaps with a leaf of continental parsley. Always use your imagination!

Segments of oranges are useful. Peel the orange by cutting away the skin and pith and the outer thin membrane. Then, holding the orange in your non-working hand over a bowl (to catch the juice), cut down into the centre of the orange alongside the membrane enclosing each individual segment. As each segment comes free, drop it into the juice in the bowl.

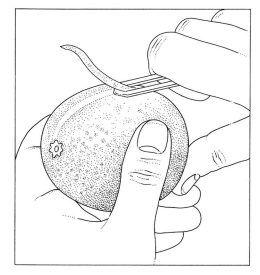

1. Score around the fruit evenly

2. Cut half-way through the fruit

3. Slice the fruit and make your twirls

• *Herbs* •

Whole leaves of herbs, or finely chopped herbs, can be used as one of the simplest garnishes. Deep-fried parsley sprigs are useful too, see page 98. Remember always, though, to choose a herb that will complement your food, many are quite strong in flavour.

• *Cucumber Slices* •

These can be used as a garnish, but score the vegetable lengthwise first before slicing. Courgettes, whether cooked in slices as a vegetable, or sliced raw for a garnish, look good scored as well.

• *Gherkin Fans* •

Place a small sweet pickled gherkin on your cutting board. Slice it lengthways, about five times, keeping it joined at one end. Fan the slices out with your fingers. Strawberries and cooked baby courgettes could be made into similar fans.

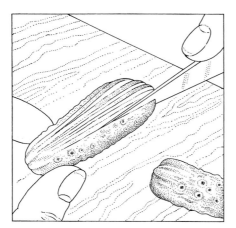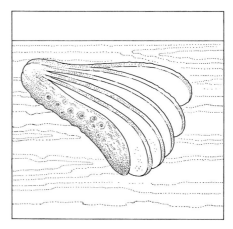

Make several cuts the length of gherkin, and fan out

• *Olives* •

These can be cut into simple slices (stoned of course), but you could also 'vandyke' them, like tomatoes, so that you have two zig-zag halves. You could also be a lot more elaborate and make an olive rabbit. Use large firm olives with stones in. Hold one firmly on the work surface and cut off a small oval slice. This allows the rabbit to sit firmly. Cut a small V shape from one end of the oval slice – the ears – and slot into a nick cut into one end of the olive. Put blobs of mayonnaise for its eyes if you like, and a parsley stalk for its tail (I *know* rabbits have fluffy tails), and sit on a slice of hard-boiled egg (see photograph between pages 48 and 49).

Olives can be served whole as a garnish, of course, but why not try wrapping them in something – an anchovy for a veal escalope, say.

• *Peppers* •

Simple blanched thin strips of contrasting colours – peppers now come in red, green and yellow – make an effective and colourful garnish (good on the vegetable pasta on page 65). Cleaned circles of pepper are good too, and you could cut these circles in half to make 'handles' for a tomato 'basket' filled with something like cheese and herb pâté. Very finely diced peppers are interesting as a colour contrast to many foods.

• *Spring Onion Twirls* •

Top and tail spring onions, remove the outer skin, and then make as many little cuts as you can down the stalk or green part of the onion, leaving the white bulb intact. Leave them to soak in cold water with lots of ice cubes, and the cut tops will fan out extravagantly.

• *Radish Flowers* •

Wash, top and tail your radishes. Place them on their stalk ends, cutting off a thin slice if they don't stand properly. Make tiny curving cuts or slices into the radish, to go about two-thirds of the way down to the base. About eight should be enough. You will see the leafy effect as you finish, but after soaking in iced water, the flowers will open up even further.

R adish slices are pretty too, just by themselves, the red and white looking fresh and colourful.

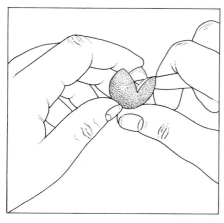

1. Slice two-thirds down each radish as shown

2. Before and after iced-water immersion

• *Celery Twirls* •

Wash and wipe celery sticks, and cut into strips of 2 inches (5 cm) in length. Using a very sharp small knife, cut down into the lengthwise grain of each strip as many times as you can – as if you were fringing the end – but only about one-third towards the middle. Repeat this at the other end of the strip, again making as many tiny cuts as possible, in about one-third. The middle third remains uncut, and holds the two fringed ends together. Now is the difficult bit. Holding the knife at a 90 degree angle to its previous position, cut widthwise *through* those tiny cuts, down towards the middle again, so that you double the amount of fringing. Do this at both ends, then leave each strip of cut celery in iced water. The fringing curls out beautifully.

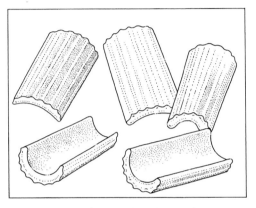

1. Cut celery into 2 in (5 cm) strips

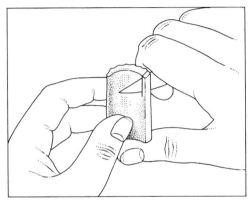

2. Cut in one-third of the way towards the middle

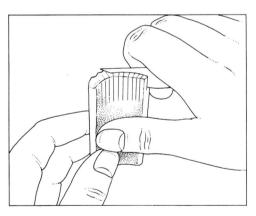

3. Slice *through* these tiny cuts

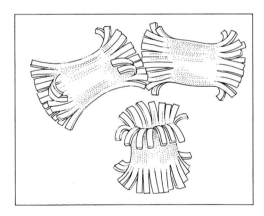

4. Your finished twirls

• *Tomato Roses* •

I don't often do these at Miller Howe, but I'm always being asked how to do them – so here goes. Use extremely firm tomatoes and a very sharp small knife that you're used to handling. Put the tomato stalk side down on your work surface and cut off a slice through the base two-thirds. Then, holding the remaining tomato in your non-working hand, cut a strip of skin off about $\frac{1}{2}$ inch (1.25 cm) wide, running your knife slowly up and down in a sort of sawing motion until half the skin of the tomato is removed in one continuous strip. Cut off, place on work surface, and then remove the balance of the tomato skin to the same thickness. Place the base slice, skin side down, on the work surface, and curl up the first piece of skin, leaving a gap in the middle. Into this you put the second piece of tomato skin rolled up tightly. All this will resemble the petals of a rose. If you want to go the whole hog, use the green ends of spring onions or strips of leek green for stems, and a herb leaf for rose leaves! (And use the remaining tomatoes in a tomato sauce or soup.)

You could also cut tomatoes into wedges, slices, halves plain or vandyked (zig-zag), and the tiny cherry tomatoes make cheerful garnishes in themselves. A seeded and drained tomato case can be filled with something to act as a complementary garnish.

• Turned Mushrooms •

Choose small white mushroom caps, and, using a scorer or a small, very sharp knife, make little cuts or scores radiating out from the centre to the edges at an angle, taking away a tiny strip of flesh each time. Blanch them briefly in some acidulated water (with lemon juice) to prevent discoloration.

• Hard-Boiled Eggs •

These can be used in a variety of ways. Simple slices are colourful, or they can be used as the base for something like a radish flower. They can be cut into quarter wedges, or lengthwise halves – which can occasionally be stuffed. Try vandyking eggs (lengthwise) and, of course, finely chopped white and sieved yolks are familiar garnishes on a number of dishes. And don't forget about the possibilities of the quails' eggs now more readily available.

• Fruit •

Individual small fruit can be incredibly decorative. Think of the shapes, colours and flavours of cherries, strawberries whole or sliced, raspberries, grapes, kumquats, melon balls, sprigs of currants etc.

• Fruit Wedges •

As well as citrus and tomatoes, apple and avocado wedges can look good – dip them in lemon juice to prevent discoloration. Peaches, pears and tiny melon wedges can also look good – and they could all be arranged, if small enough, as the citrus wedges above.

• *Apple Slices* •

Circles of cored apples can be used raw as a garnish (dipped in lemon juice), but they can also be cooked in a mixture of runny honey and wine vinegar (twice honey to vinegar) until virtually transparent. These are good for garnishing roast pork or ham.

• *Piped Garnishes* •

Use any of the piping pâtés or flavoured butters (see below), and pipe into a small twirl. A whipped double cream or double cream sauce twirl also looks and tastes good. And don't forget about how decorative are simple spoonfuls of a hollandaise or mayonnaise, plain or natural yoghurt.

• *Croûtons* •

See page 72 for instructions on how to make croûtons. A large croûton can be used as the base for a number of foods – particularly things like small steaks. Spread them with mushroom pâté to add zest to the serving of a fillet steak or thick lamb loin round. To make a large croûton more 'upmarket', roll the complete round edges of the croûton in melted redcurrant or blackcurrant jelly (or spread on the top), and then immediately roll the edges on to a saucer of finely chopped parsley or mixed herbs.

Tiny soup croûtons (see page 97) are often a welcome texture addition to a salad. And shapes can be cut out of bread before it is staled and prepared as a croûton – think of the effect of small fish, of half-moons or hearts. Cutters are readily available.

• *Garlic Cloves* •

Large whole peeled cloves can be used as a garnish for a number of meat dishes. Soak them in milk for a few hours (this takes away the majority of the garlic flavour – and always use the garlicky milk afterwards for a sauce), then fry in butter or dripping until brown. They could also be boiled in the milk, or deep-fried.

• *Savoury Breadcrumbs* •

These have a multitude of uses and you should always have a jar of them in the fridge to save any last-minute grating and messing around. They're delicious on simple boiled cauliflower, as a coating for fried or baked fish, a topping for any gratin dishes – or the pyramid of mushrooms on page 66. Simply combine 2 oz (50 g) finely grated Cheddar cheese, 6 oz (175 g) fine breadcrumbs (brown or white), a pinch of dry English mustard powder and 1 tablespoon very finely chopped parsley. Use or store – they will keep for up to 7–10 days in the fridge in an airtight container.

You could add other ingredients, depending on the usage intended. A clove of crushed garlic adds tang, as does about 2 oz (50 g) very finely chopped onion. If you use either of these, the crumbs won't store for quite so long.

• *Pastry Garnishes* •

As with croûtons, small shapes can be cut out of pastries – the rough puff is perhaps best for this. Small canapé-sized tartlets can be made from savoury pastry and look very effective as garnishes: try filling them with the stuffing for roast chicken or pork; with cranberry sauce for turkey; or with horseradish or mustard cream to garnish beef. Small choux pastry puffs, too, can be stuffed with various fillings – try the creams for beef (spectacular with cold slices of beef fillet).

• *Home-Made Potato Crisps* •

The American Bar and guest suites at the Savoy in London all sport very generous bowls of home-made crisps, and I always picture some poor new commis chef spending his first month doing nothing else in order to keep up with the demand.

A mandoline is necessary for making these, but they are so delicious served as a snack or canapé, or used as a garnish. Slice peeled potatoes fairly thinly, either plain or criss-cross (see page 60), and put into water. Preheat your deep fryer to 355°F/182°C, and when ready remove the potatoes from the water and pat dry. Simply place sufficient potato slices in to spread fairly evenly over the bubbling top of the oil (never overload). Using a wooden spoon – but holding the spoon part rather than the handle – keep on breaking up clusters which try to form. When cooked brown, turn out on to a double thickness of kitchen paper and be fairly generous with a sprinkling of salt.

• *American Red Salmon Caviar Roe* •

When this was seldom to be seen in this country, I never left on the evening flight from New York without going into the Russian Tea Room mid afternoon and having their inimitable blinis and soured cream topped with this caviar – helped along, of course, as is my wont, with the odd chilled vodka and half bottle of Pouilly Fumé.

Now, however, American red salmon caviar roe is sold by Whites of London, and several other upmarket grocers as well. It comes in 100 g sealed cans which have lovely attachable plastic storage lids (of little use to me as I always finish a can as soon as it is opened). Treat yourself to a can even if just to garnish your scrambled eggs one Sunday brunch, or to eat with soured cream or yoghurt along with pancakes. You can make very, very small pastry tartlets and pipe into them some cream cheese flavoured with a little lemon juice and then put a teaspoon of the caviar on top with a sprig of dill: any fish dish is immediately transformed.

Red and black lumpfish roes are useful too for garnishes.

• *Butter Garnishes* •

Whenever I go to a local market I seek out the dairy produce stall as a top priority in order to secure real home-made farm butter. I still remember going to the local Co-operative, years ago, and watching the butter being taken out of the wooden casks. It was cut up into portions and slapped on to the lovely marble and brass weighing scales. Then, with two wooden butter shapes, before my very eyes, it was made into a splendid rectangle with wiggly lines all over it. It's *so* boring buying butter nowadays, but whenever I do find farm butter, I buy in quantity and freeze some.

When I want to serve butter on the dinner table, or for a supper party, I always like to make it look good. For a block, large or small, I let it come right round to room temperature and then, using a table fork, leisurely run a fork up and down all round the five revealed sides, making V-shaped lines. It's then returned to the fridge to harden up, and served on a block of wood on lettuce and parsley. You can still find butter shapers in antique shops, so you could shape your block in a more traditional way. And, of course, tiny butter moulds are around too, some antique, some modern reproductions: a small block of butter could be imprinted with a pattern or picture.

You can have butter curls – use the special implement which, drawn across hardish butter, produces those ridged curl slices – but remember to prepare only a short time before serving, and do so along with some ice, so that they retain their shape. At Miller Howe we shape butter into swans – and you can try this if you like. Hotels of course can have one particular member of the kitchen staff devoting time to such a chore – it's a little more difficult in the home situation! It's all done by piping and quick freezing.

Flavoured Butters

In my vegetable book, I discussed flavoured butters – they're such a wonderful addition to vegetables – but they are also useful in a myriad other ways. A plain baked fish is transformed by the addition of a circle or twirl of a flavoured butter – particularly the trout on page 115 – and many grilled meats can be similarly garnished. The butter not only looks good as the dish is brought to the table, but it also adds considerable flavour. Certain flavoured butters – garlic and curry, for instance – could be used for frying croûtons, and others, the garlic in particular, are good for stir-frying vegetables. And don't forget about flavoured butters in sandwiches: horseradish butter is ideal for a beef sandwich, for instance.

I have given each flavoured butter suggestion in a 1 lb (450 g) quantity, which is a lot, but you can halve it – and do remember that butters freeze well (but not for *too* long). The butter must be soft before mixing in the flavouring, particularly if you're going to pipe it into twirls, the most visually effective way of presenting it. Pipe on to baking trays and open-freeze, then scoop off into a freezer bag. You can also roll the butter up like a sausage and freeze wrapped in foil. Cut circles off the sausage as you want them. Or simply freeze in a block – in a container to get the shape – and cut into small squares or rectangles.

For each 1 lb (450 g) of butter

Anchovy
2 tablespoons anchovy essence.

Coconut
4 tablespoons toasted desiccated coconut.

Curry
2 tablespoons reduced curry essence as used for mayonnaise (see page 134).

Fennel
4 tablespoons chopped fennel herb (and tops of fennel bulb) liquidised first with a little of the soft butter.

Garlic
6 garlic cloves, peeled and finely crushed with 1 teaspoon salt.

Hazelnut and Honey
4 tablespoons ground hazelnuts and 2 tablespoons runny honey.

Herb
Be as generous as you fancy with individual or mixed herbs.

Horseradish
2 tablespoons horseradish cream.

Lemon
Juice and rind of 1 lemon.

Lime
Juice and rind of 1 lime.

Mustard and Lime
1 tablespoon dry English mustard powder and juice and rind of $\frac{1}{2}$ lime.

Orange
Juice and rind of 2 oranges.

Raspberry Vinegar
2 tablespoons raspberry vinegar.

Red Pepper
2 tablespoons red pepper purée (see page 99).

Relish
2 tablespoons Worcestershire sauce.

Tomato
4 tablespoons tomato purée (see page 131).

Tomato and Mustard
2 tablespoons tomato purée and 2 tablespoons dry English mustard powder.

Walnut
4 oz (100 g) finely chopped walnuts.

Café de Paris Butter

Many restaurants have their own particular version of this savoury butter, and I must admit I always looked upon it simply as butter mixed with garlic and herbs until I worked with a super chef at the Windsor Hotel in Toronto. The daily task of one of the commis chefs intrigued me: he had to turn out about 14 lb (over 6 kg) of butter daily to be used in the splendid Garden Restaurant (doing up to a thousand covers a day). As it was done with such care and was always taken to the busy head chef for tasting prior to being piped into rosettes, I got the recipe from them.

8 oz (225 g) soft butter
2 egg yolks
2 small anchovy fillets
2 small garlic cloves, peeled, green shoot
  removed, and lightly mashed with 1
  teaspoon English mustard and a
  generous pinch of freshly ground
  black pepper

3 teaspoons fresh lemon juice
1 tablespoon freshly chopped parsley
½ teaspoon Worcestershire sauce

Simply put everything into the blender and whizz round until completely blended. Pipe into rosettes or twirls and chill (or freeze).

Use on jacket potatoes, fish, steak, meats for barbecues and grilled sausages.

• *Savoury Salads* •

These silly little garnishes do so much to make a dinner party an occasion and are, in my opinion, well worth the time and trouble taken to do them. Normally – when entertaining at home – there is a time of day when the kitchen is a shambles: sinks full to the brim, work surface cluttered in confusion, leftover bits and pieces everywhere, not a clean pan in sight, and, worse still, tempers just a trifle frayed! That's the time to have a clean-up blitz operation, open a bottle of wine, and sit down quietly to do the savoury salads and garnishings.

Have ready in front of you a small plastic tray with a side lip on which to arrange the salads. Each is based on a piece of lettuce and radiccio about 3–4 inches (7.5–10 cm) in diameter. An 'anchor' is essential, and I usually pipe a blob of flavoured whipped double cream in the middle. This allows you easily to arrange a variety of things: an orange or lemon twirl with a sprig of parsley; a half walnut; a halved stuffed olive or quarter slice of thin cucumber; fanned gherkins; radish flowers; celery twirls; herb flowers; red pepper or onion circles (don't let your savoury salad clash *too* violently with the actual dish). None of these is expensive but the task is very time-consuming – it will take, say, half an hour for eight guests at first.

When you are satisfied with your artistry, simply cover the tray well with a double thickness of cling film, making sure it is securely wrapped underneath to keep the salads from going limp. Store them in the fridge until needed. Take them out to room temperature a bit before you want to serve them, remove the cling film and, using a palette knife, transfer them with consummate ease to your serving plates!

The Third Course
· *FISH* ·

A small portion of fish forms the third course of a Miller Howe dinner. It could be hot – fried or baked in a savoury coating – or it could be a slice of a cold fish terrine – but, if served as part of a five-course dinner, the operative word is always *small*. Many of the following recipes can, of course, be served as a starter rather than a fish course, or expanded for a main course if you like. Some of the following ideas you will have encountered before, but I have added and expanded, as well as invented lots of new recipes.

There is little art in cooking fish but a great deal of skill in buying it as it simply has to be *fresh*, fresh for me – not caught at sea and blast-chilled then left to come round as happens at our nearest main seaport fish market. Look for eyes as bright as a daisy, mouth clenched shut and a slippery oily feel: it should smell of the *sea* and *salt*, not off and of ammonia. When you find a good reliable fishmonger, hang on to him with your hook and cultivate him, as he is worth his weight in gold. (I once said this to a canny North Country lass who immediately quipped back – 'At his prices, no wonder!')

Try to use any fish you buy within 24 hours and, if stored in the fridge, do so loosely encased in foil, and side by side, *never* stacked on top of one another.

If you buy fillets it's much easier to judge how much to get for each person, but when on the bone with the head allow about 1 lb (450 g) in weight per person. It's best to buy the latter as you then have the basics for a fish stock to flavour your sauce. Normally the fishmonger trims, cleans and scales the fish for you – with a display of artistry involving the sharpest of knives – but if you have to start from scratch, here are a few tips.

111

Clear a vast working space and place a generous thickness of old newspapers around where you will be performing. Wash the fish well under running water. (I have been known to do this underneath the bath taps, and a friend puts the salmon or halibut in the bottom of the bath and uses the portable shower unit – but after seeing her do this, I was convinced the cooked fish tasted of Badedas!) Partly dry the fish and then lay it flat on your board. Holding the tail with a J-cloth, start to scrape the scales away from you with a very firm knife. Yes, they do seem to fly all over the place, no matter how neat you endeavour to be!

— *GUTTING AND FILLETING* — *FISH*

To gut a round fish, use a small sharp knife to cut the length of the belly from head to tail, exposing the guts and entrails. Take these out, a relatively easy operation, and one which my neighbour's cat is partial to – whenever I'm gutting fish, there she is, yowling at the back door. The fish should then be washed again under a running cold tap. If it's going to be cooked whole, the dark vein under the backbone must be removed also.

To gut a flat fish, make two diagonal cuts in from just above and below the head to the fin behind the gills. As the head is removed, most of the intestines etc come away too. Wash well.

To fillet round fish into two fillets – trout etc – place on the board, tail towards you. Make a cut along the backbone from just behind the head down to the tail, cutting deep enough to expose the backbone. Cut the fillet from the head, then, with the knife parallel to the ribs, insert it between fillet and bones. Cut down the length of the fish again, separating fillet from bones in short strokes. Lift the flesh up towards you, and nip it off at the tail end. Turn the fish over and repeat on the other side. If there are any bones left in the fillet, pick them out with tweezers.

Flat fish such as sole and plaice will produce four fillets. Lay the fish down on a board, eyes up and tail towards you, and start by cutting down the middle, following the backbone from head to tail. Cut behind the head on one side, separating fillet from bones, then slide the blade in short strokes along the bones to the tail. This is one fillet, and then you do the other. Turn the fish over and repeat the process.

The actual skinning of fish fillets is easy once mastered, and a very sharp knife is needed. Place the fillet skin side down and make a small cut through the flesh at the tail end, lifting a little flesh up. If *right handed*, take hold of the fish tail skin with a J-cloth-covered left hand. Insert the knife at an angle beneath the flesh to prise it from the skin in short strokes. Gently tug the tail end towards you at the same time.

Strips of salmon, with a little wine and some herbs,
are wrapped in a paper package and baked for less than 10 minutes.
All the goodness, flavour and savour of the fish are captured, and released
only when the diner opens the package at the table. Try other fish varieties,
as well as adding some very finely chopped vegetables.

Rolled poached sole with hollandaise, garnished with
● *a tiny savoury salad and a puff pastry fish filled with American* ●
red salmon caviar roe.

A breast of chicken can be garnished in many ways:
try a coating of hollandaise or béarnaise, and add home-made
potato crisp wings and a colourful decoration of herbs
or vegetable strips.

*A magnificent leg of lamb roasted with coriander
presented in all its complete cooked glory.*

HALIBUT

These deep-sea fish can grow to enormous sizes, but they are best weighing around 3½ lb (1.5 kg). Steaks can be cut from these. Chicken or baby halibut are also available. For a first course, 4 oz (100 g) halibut is more than adequate; 6 oz (175 g) makes a generous main course.

Halibut Steaks Poached in Yoghurt

A splendid way to cook this rather meaty fish but, I must warn you, the yoghurt will split and run off the steaks. The flavour that gets through to the fish flakes, though, and the difference it makes to the texture – for halibut can be dry – is very worthwhile indeed.

Per person

1 halibut steak, about 4 oz (100 g) in
    weight, and measuring about 3 × 2½
    inches (7.5 × 6 cm)
butter
salt
freshly ground black pepper
2 tablespoons natural yoghurt

To serve
1 tablespoon cream sauce or hollandaise
    (see pages 128 and 126)
a parsley sprig

Place the steaks on a buttered seasoned baking tray or dish – allowing a little space around each – and then liberally coat with yoghurt. Leave to marinate for up to 24 hours.

Preheat the oven to 400°F/200°C/Gas 6, and cook the fish for about 10–15 minutes. Serve immediately on hot plates with a sauce of choice, garnished with the parsley.

This basic recipe can be varied. Some finely diced fennel, celery or apple could be scattered on top of each steak before baking; to finish the dish off, sprinkle with some finely grated Cheddar cheese and flash under the grill until browned. The marinating yoghurt could contain some lime rind and juice and a little grated fresh root ginger. A mixture of chopped herbs could be sprinkled on to the top of each steak before baking. To serve the fish, as well as one of the suggested sauces, you could scatter it with some colourful vegetable pasta (see page 65), or you could serve the plain fish on a spinach and apple purée with a spoonful of tomato provençale (see page 132) on top.

113

THE MILLER HOWE COOKBOOK

Halibut Steaks Poached in Wine on Diced Vegetables and Bacon

Serves 6

6 halibut steaks as above
white wine
4 oz (100 g) butter
4 oz (100 g) carrots, scrubbed and finely
    chopped
4 oz (100 g) onions, peeled and finely
    chopped

4 oz (100 g) mushrooms, finely sliced
4 tablespoons finely chopped celery
6 rashers smoked bacon, rinded
6 thin scored lemon slices, pips removed
a little salt
freshly ground black pepper
freshly chopped herbs

Place the steaks flat in a baking dish and coat with white wine. Leave to marinate for up to 6 hours. Then, when ready to cook, preheat the oven to 425°F/220°C/Gas 7.

Use 1 oz (25 g) of the butter to grease a roasting tin that will take the steaks in one layer. Pour in the wine from the marination along with all the chopped vegetables and the bacon. Bring to the boil on top of the stove. Spread the bacon rashers evenly and place a slice of lemon on top of each. Place a steak on top of this in turn. Season with salt and pepper and put ½ oz (15 g) butter on each steak. Cover the tin tightly with foil and bake in the preheated oven for 20 minutes. Serve immediately, with a generous sprinkling of freshly chopped herbs for a simple garnish.

Baked Halibut with Spiced Yoghurt Sauce

Serves 6

6 halibut steaks as above
butter
6 oz (175 g) onion, peeled and finely
    chopped
2 tablespoons finely chopped parsley

Marinade
4 tablespoons tomato purée
¾ pint (450 ml) natural yoghurt
2 garlic cloves, crushed with 2 teaspoons
    salt
juice and finely grated rind of 2 lemons
1 teaspoon ground turmeric
1 tablespoon coriander seeds, crushed

Dry the halibut steaks well and place on a well-buttered, lipped baking tray. Mix together the marinade ingredients with an electric hand-beater or, better still, in a food processor. Coat the fish with the marinade and leave lightly covered for at least 8 hours in a cool place. Preheat the oven to 400°F/200°C/Gas 6.

Coat the halibut steaks with the chopped onion and cook in the preheated oven for 12 minutes. Serve immediately, garnished with the chopped parsley.

TROUT

Trout – usually rainbow, but sometimes brown – are now available all year round from farms. Although it all depends on what they have eaten, their flesh should be deep pink, fresh and moist. They're a very good choice for a dinner party as not only do they taste and look magnificent – especially with some of my garnishings – they're so easy to prepare.

For a main course, serve a whole trout per person. They usually weigh between 6 and 12 oz (175–350 g). Gut the fish through the belly as described on page 112. For a fish course, a fillet – or half fish – is generous. See my filleting instructions on the same page.

Baked Trout

This is so simple that I barely need to give you a recipe. Place the fillets – one per person – on well buttered baking trays, skin side down. Baste them well with melted butter and leave until you want to bake. They take 7–8 minutes to cook in an oven preheated to 375°F/190°C/Gas 5. Serve immediately on warmed plates and garnish as you fancy.

The basic recipe can be varied in a number of ways. You can squeeze lime or lemon juice over the fillets before baking: serve them with a twirl of lime or lemon butter (see page 109). Another idea is to cover both sides of the fillets on the baking tray with ground hazelnuts; serve when cooked with a couple of grapefruit or orange segments. Instead of butter alone, mix some bacon fat and melted butter and coat the fillets, then cover them with fine oatmeal on both sides; serve with bacon rolls wrapped round wedges of banana or pineapple (bake for 8–10 minutes alongside the fish), or with a thin slice of cooked bacon spread along each fillet, topped with four or five thin banana rounds. You can use savoury breadcrumbs (see page 106) as a coating, or lashings of cheese and herb pâté (see page 39).

As well as the garnishes indicated above, try any of the flavoured butters on page 109: anchovy, mustard and lime, hazelnut and honey, and fennel are particularly good with trout. A plain butter twirl could be attractively garnished in its turn with fresh prawns and shrimps; and a delicious garnishing and flavouring twirl is made by blending together mushroom pâté and peanut butter.

Nothing looks more stunning alongside a fillet of baked trout than a sprig of redcurrants and, believe it or not, fresh raspberries; used as a garnish on each plate – three per person – these not only look delightful but do actually blend with the taste and texture of the trout.

Smoked Trout or Mackerel on Warm Salad with Eggs

A delicious supper dish any time of the year, combining fascinating flavours that all blend well together. Eaten with home-made bread, it's also very satisfying.

Serves 4

½ iceberg lettuce, shredded
1 bunch fresh watercress, washed and
  dried
2 tablespoons chopped chives
2 tablespoons chopped dill
8 oz (225 g) smoked trout or mackerel
  (all bones removed), skinned and cut
  into ½ inch (1.25 cm) cubes

3 tablespoons white wine vinegar
1 tablespoon soft brown sugar
2 tablespoons Dijon mustard or
  Moutarde de Meaux
¼ pint (150 ml) good olive oil
2 tablespoons double cream
2 oz (50 g) butter
4 eggs, lightly beaten

Shred the lettuce and use to line individual plates, along with the watercress. Scatter over the chopped chives and dill along with the trout or mackerel cubes. At this stage you can cover the plates with cling film and leave for up to 8 hours.

Pour the wine vinegar, sugar, mustard, oil and double cream into a saucepan and beat until combined. Bring to the boil, pour into a container and keep warm.

Melt the butter in a separate pan and scramble the eggs lightly (see page 32). Pour the warm dressing over the fish and lettuce and top with the scrambled eggs. Serve immediately – with a scattering of finely grated Cheddar cheese if you like.

SALMON

We are particularly fortunate in the UK in that fresh salmon is now available over a much longer period than before due to salmon farming becoming a growth industry in Scotland. I once went on a promotional trip: we were served fresh Scotch salmon twice a day in various forms with different sauces and asked to make notes as to whether we thought the salmon were wild or farmed. The five of us were invariably wrong on every occasion as it was always the farmed version that was served. I defy you to tell the difference!

By all means when entertaining a lot of people poach your whole salmon in the traditional way in the fish kettle; I've described this in previous books, but remember, only poach for *1 minute* per lb (450 g) weight. However, when there are just a few of you, I would buy a whole fish, gut and bone it and then *halve* it as I describe below. In this way, rather than simply getting conventional salmon steaks with bone in the middle, you get smaller neater pieces rather like cutlets, and you can also slice it like smoked salmon for escalopes.

If your salmon is very fresh and slithery, you must first wash it well in cold running water, then you must gut it as described for round fish. Using a much stronger knife – one that is as sharp as possible – cut off its head immediately behind the gills and remove the tail. You will be able to see the main bone at the neck end and it is this you have to find with your sharp – preferably serrated – knife, as you want to saw your way from head to tail very slowly and carefully. The backbone then comes away and you are left with two sides of salmon such as you would buy smoked from your delicatessen. Skin these sides as described on page 112 if you like. This is now much easier to cut into steaks or pieces, or to slice into escalopes.

Poached Salmon Pieces

Put your skinned salmon pieces into a well-buttered roasting tin, and top each with a generous slice of salted butter. Make up a fish stock (see page 82) with the head, tail and bones of the fish, using more olive oil than normal for additional flavour. (The basic stock recipe will poach up to twelve normal steaks or cutlets.) Carefully pass the warm stock through a sieve into the tin over the fish, then cover the whole thing with a double thickness of foil. Bring back to a quick simmer on top of the stove and cook for 3 minutes only. Remove the dish from the heat and allow to go cold *without uncovering*. Serve cold with home-made mayonnaise (see page 134).

Grilled Salmon Pieces

Preheat the grill for a good 40 minutes to get it really *red, red hot*. Put your salmon pieces under the hot grill and cook for 4 minutes only (you don't need to turn them over), and they will be ready to eat, served on very hot plates, with hollandaise (see page 126). They continue to cook as they begin to cool slightly. A teaspoon of American red salmon caviar roe will make this dish even more memorable.

Barbecued Salmon Pieces

My good friends Hilary and David Brown, who run the very successful restaurant La Potinière at Gullane, always stay overnight with me en route for their food fact-finding holiday in France, and they introduced me to this rather special dish. What makes it so stunning is the dark, nigh burned, skin which, when cut into, is superbly oily and rich in contrast to the lovely moist-textured fresh flesh. So, prepare the salmon as described previously, but *leave the skin on*.

You need to have barbecue fish holders – two wire fish-shaped contraptions linked at one side – which hold the fish inside and in shape by means of a moveable ring along the handle. (When you buy one you will see what I mean.)

The barbecue coals must be *white, white hot* and what I do is coat my slotted barbecue cooking tray with three or four thicknesses of foil then actually place the barbecue briquettes on this. The lightly buttered steaks are then lowered directly on to the coals *flesh* side down and cooked for no more than 10 seconds simply to seal. Then the skin side is put down on to the hot coals for 2–3 minutes.

I know each and every barbecue is different – in fact it's different every time you cook – but the art of this dish is to *under*cook rather than murder, to have a wonderfully crisp skin and a loose and smooth flesh.

Baked Escalopes of Salmon

These are cut from boned halves of salmon. Lay the salmon, skin down, on a tea towel or cloth – to help secure the slippery creature – and, using a large serrated knife, begin to saw through *horizontally*, 6–8 inches (15–20 cm) up from the tail end, into thin slices resembling smoked salmon. Initially your slices will probably be thicker than you want – but you will get the hang of it eventually.

Transfer each escalope as it is cut to a well-buttered baking tray and then lightly cover with cling film. Avoid the black oily patches of meat lying close to the skin, and any scraps left over can be kept to one side for a fish stock.

When you wish to cook, turn the oven to its highest temperature (about 475°F/ 240°C/Gas 9 in most cases), and when this is reached – and *only then* – remove the cling film from the escalopes, sprinkle some white or rosé wine over them (as if putting vinegar on your chips at the local fish and chip shop), and put in the oven. They will only take 4 minutes to cook and you should then transfer them to a hot plate and to the table immediately.

Serve with lime or lemon butter twirls, or hollandaise or Noilly Prat and chive cream sauce (see pages 109, 126 and 129). New potatoes and a wonderful seasonal salad are good accompaniments.

Smoked Salmon and Gravadlax with Marinated Melon Balls

A deliciously tempting starter or fish course, and it looks magnificent. Instead of the melon balls, you could arrange slices of avocado on the plates.

Per person

2 thin slices smoked salmon
2 thin slices gravadlax (see opposite)
1 tablespoon savoury mayonnaise (see page 135)
4 melon balls, marinated in French dressing (see page 136)

1 parsley sprig
2 slices well buttered wholemeal bread
½ teaspoon American red salmon caviar roe (optional)

Carefully cut the thin slices from each type of salmon, making them measure about 3 × 2 inches (7.5 × 5 cm). If necessary, leave them on a tray under cling film until needed.

When ready to serve, take a piece of smoked salmon and, holding each end, push it up on a circular plate, to form a letter 'M' on the top left-hand corner. Next to it put a similar piece of gravadlax then smoked salmon and gravadlax to cover the whole top left-hand quarter of the plate. In the middle pipe a blob of the savoury mayonnaise and on to this arrange the marinated melon balls.

Garnish each plate with a sprig of parsley and arrange the slices of buttered bread on the side. A little caviar roe does not go amiss cascading over the melon balls and mayonnaise.

Gravadlax

This is my version of the justly famous Scandinavian pickled salmon. Use as much dill as you can, no less than 4 tablespoons though, for a pure and aromatic flavour.

Serve as a starter, cut into thin slices like smoked salmon, or thicker slices, the way the Norwegians like it. Accompany with brown bread and a sweet-sour mayonnaise (see page 135). Or use it in a luxurious recipe like that opposite.

Serves 6

1 tail piece of salmon, about 1½ lb
  (675 g) in weight
3 tablespoons brandy
4 tablespoons sea salt

3 tablespoons demerara sugar
1 teaspoon black peppercorns, crushed
chopped fresh dill

Bone and halve the salmon piece as described opposite, but do not skin. Place the salmon pieces on a large piece of doubled and oiled foil, and massage on all sides with the brandy. Mix all the other ingredients together and use to coat the fish pieces on all sides.

Bring the pieces of fish together, back into the fish tail shape, and wrap tightly in the foil. Place this packet in a small tray and top with another tray. Weight down and leave in a cool place for 5 days, turning the salmon packet morning and evening.

Smoked Salmon with Caviar Roe and Cucumber

Use the basic pancake recipe on page 61, but make the pancakes slightly smaller than usual. You could use smoked trout instead of salmon.

Per person

1 small thin pancake
2 tablespoons double cream, whipped
1 dessertspoon natural yoghurt
½ teaspoon horseradish cream
1 oz (25 g) sliced smoked salmon (or
  trout), cut into strips

3 thin slices scored cucumber
1 teaspoon American red salmon caviar
  roe
fresh fennel or dill

Prepare the pancakes in advance and leave to cool. When ready to serve, simply lay the pancakes out flat on your work surface. Mix together half the cream, the yoghurt and the horseradish cream, and spread in a ¼ inch (6 mm) layer half-way over the right-hand side of the circle. Place on this the strips of smoked salmon or trout, along with the cucumber slices. Pipe the remaining cream in a blob on top, and garnish with the caviar roe and some finely chopped fennel or dill. Fold the uncreamed section of pancake over and serve with sprigs of fennel or dill sticking out.

SOLE

Sole are wonderful plainly grilled or fried, but for a fish course, divide them into fillets (see page 112). As with halibut, a 4 oz (100 g) fillet makes a good fish course, and 6 oz (175 g) a generous main course.

Sole fillets can be simply baked in the oven like trout fillets. Coat them first with melted butter and breadcrumbs – the savoury breadcrumbs on page 106 are the tastiest – and bake on a buttered tray in a preheated oven at 350°F/180°C/Gas 4 for 20 minutes. You can flirt with this basic recipe – you must know the Miller Howe style by now – and add things like desiccated coconut, ground hazelnuts or almonds, or grated citrus rind to the breadcrumbs. Garnish with baked banana slices (good with coconut), baked red pepper and fennel dice (good with the almonds), or orange segments (hazelnuts), or lemon or lime butter twirls (in fact most of the flavoured butters on page 108). Always garnish as well with wedges of fresh lemon and sprigs of parsley.

However, sole can also be stuffed and rolled, slightly less simple, and then baked in greaseproof paper or the new film sold by Lakeland Plastics, and considered to be safe for cooking.

Rolled Poached Sole

Per person

4 oz (100 g) sole fillet
1 oz (25 g) filling of choice (see below)

To serve

1 generous tablespoon hollandaise (see page 126)

Wash the fillets under a slow-running cold tap, skin them, and dry well on kitchen paper. Put the fillets, skinned side up, on your work surface, and spread with the filling of your choice. Roll the fillets up like a small Swiss roll, encasing the filling, and wrap firmly in food film. Pack the little parcels on to a wire cooling tray placed inside a roasting tin.

When about to cook, preheat the oven to 350°F/180°C/Gas 4, and pour enough boiling water into the roasting tin to come up to the base of the cooling tray. Bake in the oven for 20 minutes. Carefully remove the film, and serve immediately with hollandaise.

• *Rolled Sole Fillings* •

Use any of these, varying the combinations, proportions and flavours as you fancy. Always use your imagination!

It goes without saying that you could use mushroom pâté or cheese and herb pâté, but add some ground hazelnuts to the former and some fresh breadcrumbs to the latter.

A thin slice of smoked salmon wrapped around a wedge of mango – or a firmish piece of avocado. Gravadlax could be used as well. And try a par-cooked asparagus tip occasionally.

Liquidise together some avocado and smoked salmon. Or mince some smoked salmon and mix it with diced cucumber.

Sprinkle a little fresh lime juice on to the fillet and then roll round a wedge of mango coated with desiccated coconut.

Cook some finely diced peppers and onion in a little oil momentarily, and then bind with toasted breadcrumbs.

Chop and cook some bacon, mix with chopped sage and onions, and bind with breadcrumbs.

Fry some finely chopped red pepper and pineapple in a little oil and then bind with toasted desiccated coconut and a little soy sauce.

Wrap the fillet round a chunk of banana dipped in toasted desiccated coconut.

Cook some finely diced onion in oil, add some tomato concasse (see page 132), and then bind with toasted savoury breadcrumbs (see page 106).

Hollow out a small hole, using a Parisian scoop, from a quarter pear wedge. Put a small blob of well-chilled Roquefort cheese (or, dare I say it, cheese and herb pâté!) into it, and use as the filling for the sole.

Coat an apple wedge liberally with toasted sesame seeds.

Liquidise 1 oz (25 g) shrimps or prawns per portion with a little butter.

⋆   ⋆   ⋆

Piquant Prawns

This quantity of prawns and sauce will serve four for supper, six for a starter or fish course. It's very nice indeed!

1 lb (450 g) prawns

Sauce

2½ fl oz (75 ml) white wine vinegar	1 tablespoon honey
2 oz (50 g) soft brown sugar	½ onion, peeled and finely chopped
salt	1 red pepper, trimmed and finely
freshly ground black pepper	chopped
a pinch each of ground ginger and	juice and grated rind of 1 orange
cinnamon	8 green and 8 black grapes, halved and
2 tablespoons sherry	pipped

If the prawns are frozen, do make sure to defrost them thoroughly, draining them of every drop of moisture.

Heat the vinegar, add the sugar and allow it to melt. Add all the other ingredients and stir until well mixed. Add the prawns and cook for about 4 minutes or until thoroughly heated through. Serve with some rice, in a piped mashed potato ring, or in a potato basket (see page 60).

Halibut, Salmon, Asparagus and Pea Terrine

A splendid dish that takes some time to prepare, but it's a stunner at a dinner party – it looks very attractive, rather like a Battenburg cake! – and, provided you use a sharp, serrated knife to slice it, is easy to serve either by itself or with a flavoured and thinned mayonnaise, as in the photograph between pages 80 and 81.

Serves 15–20

6–8 cold pancakes (see page 77)
8 oz (225 g) peas
8 oz (225 g) asparagus, trimmed
4 fl oz (120 ml) double cream

1 oz (25 g) powdered gelatine
1½ lb (675 g) halibut, boned and skinned
1½ lb (675 g) salmon, boned and skinned

Using a 14 × 3 × 3 inch (35 × 7.5 × 7.5 cm) terrine, line it with the pancakes, overlapping them, and allowing some to hang over the edges so that they can cover the top. Preheat the oven to 350°F/180°C/Gas 4.

In two separate saucepans, cook the peas and the asparagus until soft. Liquidise these separately, each with half the cream, then pass each through a sieve. While both purées are still hot, beat half the powdered gelatine into each. Leave to cool.

Each fillet of fish should be the length of the terrine and about 2 inches (5 cm) square in thickness. Lay them down flat on your work surface and, using a sharp knife, score through the middle of the fillet, only three-quarters along the length; do this again on either side so that the fillet will roll easily lengthwise when the fillings are piped in.

When the fillings are cold, pipe the pea mixture on to the halibut fillets, dividing it between them; and then do the same with the asparagus purée and the salmon fillets. Put a halibut and a salmon fillet on the base of the terrine, with the other two alternately on the top to get the Battenburg effect.

Cover the terrine with doubled greaseproof paper and then the lid, and put in a bain-marie. Pour in enough hot water to come half-way up the dish and then bake in the preheated oven for 1¼ hours. Remove from the oven and leave to go cold before turning out.

Fish in Paper Packages

This dish, for from one to a dozen, can be prepared earlier in the day (or the day before, even). It is always commented upon by guests as it comes to the table in its dark, slightly browned paper parcel which, when opened, reveals the most succulent flesh and tempting smells. It's not terribly elegant, though, I must admit!

I give you lots of vegetable flavourings in this recipe, but something like salmon, as in the photograph facing page 112, can simply be cooked with a little wine and some herbs of choice.

Per person

4–6 oz (100–175 g) fish (salmon, halibut, sole, hake or cod), skinned and boned
1 oz (25 g) butter
½ oz (15 g) celery, finely chopped
½ oz (15 g) onion, peeled and finely chopped
1 oz (25 g) carrot, finely chopped
1 oz (25 g) fennel, finely chopped

1 oz (25 g) small mushroom caps, finely sliced
sprigs of fresh herbs – dill, fennel tops and a little tarragon
1 teaspoon fresh lime juice
salt
freshly ground black pepper

Make sure all the bones have been removed from the fish, and then cut the flesh into strips. Preheat the oven well to 400°F/200°C/Gas 6.

Melt the butter in a large pan and gently sauté all the vegetables except for the mushroom slices.

Using the best greaseproof paper available, cut out an 8 inch (20 cm) square for each portion. Divide the cooked vegetables between each square, placing them in the centre, then place the fish strips on top. Put in the mushroom slices, herb sprigs, lime juice, and salt and pepper to taste.

Bring the paper together in two to form a triangular shape, and fold over the edges to seal the bag completely.

Put the packages on a baking tray and place in the preheated oven. Cook for 8 minutes if 4 oz (100 g), 10 minutes if 6 oz (175 g). Serve immediately.

—————— *Lettuce-Steamed Scallops* ——————

Served warm, with a little hollandaise, these are delicious.

Serves 6

12 large scallops, out of their shells
3 tablespoons Kummel
2 fresh sage leaves, chopped
12 fresh mint leaves, chopped
12 fresh tarragon leaves, chopped

12 large lettuce leaves
3 tablespoons tomato provençale (see page 132)
freshly ground black pepper
2 oz (50 g) butter

In the morning, marinate the scallops in the Kummel along with the chopped herbs, turning from time to time.

Bring a large saucepan of lightly salted water to the boil. Put the lettuce leaves individually into a strainer that will comfortably fit into the saucepan. Blanch leaves for a minute, and then immediately put under the running cold water tap. Unfurl the leaves, dry firmly on a tea towel and, if the stems are toughish, cut out with scissors. This too can be done in the morning.

On your work surface, slightly overlap two leaves per portion. Put ½ tablespoon tomato provençale into the middle and on this place the two marinated scallops. Grind black pepper generously on and divide the butter between the six portions. Bring the leaves together around the scallops to form six well wrapped balls and place in a colander – or a proper steamer if you have one.

When you wish to cook, the parcels should be steamed, covered, for 10 minutes over a pan of boiling water. Serve immediately they are cooked.

Savoury Fish Slice

This can be made quite easily the day before you wish to serve, but no longer, and you mustn't freeze it. Make it in a terrine mould of 14 × 3 × 3 inches (35 × 7.5 × 7.5 cm).

Serves 15–20

½ oz (15 g) powdered gelatine
5 tablespoons white wine
12 oz (350 g) good cream cheese
2 egg yolks
1 tablespoon horseradish cream
1 tablespoon finely chopped chervil,
    fennel or dill
1 tablespoon finely chopped parsley
1 tablespoon grated onion
juice and grated rind of 1 lemon
¼ pint (150 ml) home-made mayonnaise
    (see page 134)
¼ pint (150 ml) double cream, lightly
    whipped

1 lb (450 g) defrosted prawns
8 oz (225 g) smoked salmon, minced
½ small jar red lumpfish roe
¼ cucumber, skinned, seeded and finely
    chopped

Garnish
tomato wedges.
lemon wedges
cucumber twirls
sprigs of parsley

Put the gelatine in a small saucepan and add all the wine in one fell swoop (see page 191 for more detailed advice). In a large mixing bowl, beat together the cheese and egg yolks, and then gently beat in the horseradish cream, herbs, onion and lemon juice and rind. Fold in the mayonnaise and cream, followed by the prawns, smoked salmon, roe and cucumber. Stir in the reconstituted gelatine.

Spoon into the greased mould and chill for 4–6 hours, until set. To serve, turn out on to a serving platter and portion. Garnish with wedges of tomato, lemon and cucumber twirls, and nice big sprigs of parsley.

·*Miller Howe*·
Sauces and Dressings

Sauces and dressings are important in Miller Howe cooking and presentation, but most of them are extremely basic: a simple amalgamation of ingredients and flavours, a reduction of cream with a little added something. Many of these sauces have been published before in my other books, but as they're so fundamental to so many aspects of Miller Howe cuisine, I unashamedly reproduce them again here – albeit in a simplified or slightly altered – and occasionally expanded! – form.

Basic White Sauce

This is the 'mother' white sauce, which has many 'daughters', and which can enhance your cooking enormously. It is simple to make, can be prepared in advance (as long as you cover it with a butter paper to prevent a skin forming), and it even freezes well – so is ideal for care-free entertaining. It is a fairly thick sauce, so thin it down if you want by mixing in a little more milk – or some cream.

Makes $\frac{3}{4}$ pint (450 ml)

$1\frac{3}{4}$ oz (45–50 g) butter
$\frac{3}{4}$ pint (450 ml) milk

a pinch of salt
$1\frac{1}{2}$ oz (40 g) plain flour, sieved

Melt the butter in a saucepan – a narrow one is better than a wide one – and warm the milk through with the salt in another pan. When the butter is melted, add the flour in one fell swoop. Stir vigorously with a wooden spoon until the roux mixture is smooth.

Add the warm milk very gradually – I use a small ladle, adding about $\frac{1}{8}$ pint (75 ml) at a time – and stir thoroughly after each addition, so that the milk is well absorbed before adding any more. When all the milk has been added, tip the pan a little so that all the sauce falls down to one side, and beat very thoroughly indeed.

Once the sauce is shiny smooth – without the merest hint of a lump – pass it through a sieve (just to make sure!) and store in the top of a double saucepan, covered with a butter paper. When you want to use it, heat through gently over simmering water.

Add flavourings to this basic recipe, as below, and stir in well. Reheat gently in the double saucepan.

• Cheese Sauce •

Add 4 oz (100 g) finely grated cheese to the basic white sauce. Heat gently to melt the cheese and mix well. I often add a little Kirsch or brandy too!

• Mustard Sauce •

Add 2 tablespoons Moutarde de Meaux to the basic white sauce.

• Cheese and Mustard Sauce •

Add 2 oz (50 g) grated cheese and 2 tablespoons Moutarde de Meaux to the basic white sauce.

• Tomato Sauce •

Add 2 tablespoons tomato purée (see page 131) to the basic white sauce.

• White Wine Sauce •

Put a half bottle of white wine (the best you can afford to use in this way) into a pan and add 4 black peppercorns. Reduce this over a low heat to about 4 tablespoons. Strain into the basic white sauce when cool, and beat well to amalgamate.

• Curry Sauce •

Make the curry mixture described in the curry mayonnaise recipe on page 134 and strain it. Reduce the 'liquid' to 2 tablespoons and add to the basic white sauce.

• Mushroom Sauce •

Add about 4 oz (100 g) mushroom pâté (see page 40) to the basic white sauce.

• Parsley or Herb Sauce •

Add a huge amount of finely chopped parsley or herb of choice to the basic white sauce so that it is really green and flavourful.

• Shrimp Sauce •

Liquidise 8 oz (225 g) shrimps and pass through a sieve into the basic white sauce. Add a touch of anchovy essence if you like.

—— Blender or Liquidiser Hollandaise ——

Although perhaps frowned upon by those on high, hollandaise made in a blender or liquidiser is quick and very reliable. You can halve but not double the recipe when making it at home.

Serves 6

3 tablespoons fresh lemon juice
1 tablespoon white wine vinegar
8 oz (225 g) butter

4 egg yolks
1 teaspoon caster sugar
a pinch of salt

Put the lemon juice and vinegar in a small saucepan and heat to bubbling point. At the same time, melt the butter in another pan – be careful not to burn it.

Put the egg yolks, sugar and salt into the blender and blend for a few seconds, then start to trickle in the boiling lemon juice and vinegar with the machine on at top speed. (Do it from a jug rather than from the pan, it's easier.) When all this has been absorbed by the yolks, start to trickle in the hot melted butter. As soon as this has been absorbed the sauce is ready!

Add flavourings to the basic hollandaise recipe, as below, stirring in well. Always serve warm (except when you use cold hollandaise left over as a canapé or sandwich spread). You could put it into a wide Thermos flask to keep warm, but a lot will cling to the sides.

• Citrus Hollandaise •

Simply mix in more lemon juice – or other citrus juice – to taste.

• Tomato Hollandaise •

About 2 tablespoons of tomato purée (home-made preferably, see page 131) both flavours and colours.

• Watercress Hollandaise •

Liquidise a bunch of watercress with 2 tablespoons white wine. Sieve before amalgamating – often not very smoothly – with the basic hollandaise.

• Calvados Apple Hollandaise •

Mix in some Calvados apple purée (see page 133) – about $\frac{1}{4}$ pint (150 ml). It's delicious with pork.

• Red Pepper Hollandaise •

To accompany chicken, fold 2 tablespoons red pepper purée (see page 99) into the basic hollandaise.

• Avocado Hollandaise •

For a simple baked fish, combine the basic hollandaise with a whole very ripe avocado that you have puréed in the blender.

• Herbed Hollandaise •

Add about 2 tablespoons finely chopped fresh mixed (or single) herbs.

• Horseradish Hollandaise •

A tablespoon of grated horseradish or some horseradish cream makes a tangy hollandaise to accompany beef and trout.

• Walnut Hollandaise •

Fold in 4 tablespoons finely chopped walnuts. Good with chicken drumsticks.

• Curry Hollandaise •

Make the curry mixture given in the curry mayonnaise recipe on page 134, and strain it. Reduce the 'liquid' to 2 tablespoons and mix into the basic hollandaise.

• Spinach Hollandaise •

Mix 1–2 tablespoons spinach purée (see page 166) into the basic hollandaise.

• Cheese Hollandaise •

Make the hollandaise in the normal way, but using 6 oz (175 g) butter instead of 8 oz (225 g), and adding 2 oz (50 g) of grated cheese. Dribble this into the blender along with the butter.

Blender Béarnaise

This is prepared in exactly the same way as hollandaise, but you should replace the white wine vinegar with tarragon wine vinegar, and generously add chopped fresh tarragon.

Basic Double Cream Sauce

Fattening – but quite delicious, and so useful in its many manifestations for both savoury and some sweet dishes.

Serves 6

1 pint (600 ml) double cream $\frac{1}{4}$ teaspoon sea salt

Pour the cream into a large pan and add the salt. Place the pan over a low heat, half on and half off the element or flames, and leave to bubble – about 45 minutes – until it has reduced by at least half. Do have the heat low, as cream tends to bubble over. After reduction it should be a nutty buttery colour and slightly bubbly around the edges.

Keep warm in a double saucepan at the side of the stove. Add flavourings, as below, to this warm reduction.

• Herbed Cream •

Add about 2 tablespoons finely chopped mixed fresh herbs. Good with a number of things, particularly avocado or other fritters.

• Tomato and Mustard Cream •

Combine 1 tablespoon dry English mustard powder with 2 tablespoons good tomato purée (see page 131). Beat until smooth and then gradually beat into the reduced cream.

• Marsala Cream •

Reduce $\frac{1}{4}$ pint (150 ml) Marsala down to a tablespoon in a small saucepan then add to the reduced cream. Good with kidneys, pork, chicken and veal. You could use Madeira instead of Marsala.

• Spinach Cream •

Beat some spinach purée (see page 166) into the reduced cream.

• Watercress Cream •

Liquidise a bunch of watercress with a tablespoon of white wine and sieve into the reduced cream. Good with chicken.

• Horseradish Cream •

Add 1 tablespoon horseradish cream from a jar to the reduced cream. Good with some fish dishes and with beef.

• Pernod Cream •

Add 2 tablespoons Pernod to the reduced cream. Good with hot fish mousses.

A fillet steak stuffed with mushroom pâté and fried garlic,
served on a croûton with fried turned mushrooms, steamed carrot sticks
and mangetouts, and a rich brown sauce.

*Slices of roast lamb served with a (modest) number
of Miller Howe vegetables – turnip and swede dice, Kenyan 'Frenchies'
in a red pepper ring, scored courgettes with toasted almonds,
red cabbage with grated orange rind, and broccoli.*

• Noilly Prat and Chive Cream •

Reduce $\frac{1}{4}$ pint (150 ml) Noilly Prat down to a tablespoon in a small pan then add to the reduced cream with 2 tablespoons of finely chopped chives.

• Brandy Cream •

Reduce $\frac{1}{4}$ pint (150 ml) brandy down to a tablespoon in a small saucepan and then add to the saltless reduced cream. Good with Christmas pudding and mince pies.

• Calvados Apple Cream •

Add about $\frac{1}{4}$ pint (150 ml) Calvados apple purée (see page 133), reduced well, to the reduced cream. Serve with pork or with halibut.

• Orange Cream •

For this dessert sauce, replace the salt with 2 tablespoons cube or preserving sugar. Add the juice and finely grated rind of 2 oranges to the warm reduced cream. Good with steamed puddings and farmhouse pies.

—— Whipped Cream Coating Sauce ——

In *Entertaining with Tovey*, this was called, rather uninspiredly, 'Flavoured Essences and Creams' which gave little real indication of what it was about. It's basically a whipped double cream garnishing and coating sauce, more fluffy and thick than the one above, which is flavoured by a 'pre-cooked' essence. The fact that the essence can have been prepared a couple of days in advance and kept in the fridge, makes it an ideal sauce for entertaining. All you need to do on the night is whip the cream and add the essence. The essence of simplicity!

Serves 12 generously

1 pint (600 ml) double cream

Basic essence
2 eggs
4 oz (100 g) caster sugar

$\frac{1}{4}$ pint (150 ml) chosen flavouring (see overleaf)

Sit a Christmas pudding type bowl over a saucepan of water which should come half-way up the sides of the bowl. The base of the bowl should not touch the base of the pan.

To make the essence, break the eggs into the bowl, add the sugar and beat together lightly. Trickle in the chosen flavouring, beating all the time. Place over a medium heat, beating continually, and when the water begins to bubble, turn the heat down. Stir occasionally, for about 12–15 minutes, with a wooden spoon. The egg yolks should thicken up like a lemon curd. Do not overcook. Remove from the heat and leave to cool. Store in the fridge if you want for up to 4 days.

When you wish to serve your sauce, beat up the double cream – lightly only. Pass the cold essence through a fine sieve into the cream, stirring it in with a large spoon.

• Garlic Cream •

Use garlic vinegar as the flavouring. Good with poached leeks as a starter, with apple or pear starters, and on salads.

• Mint Cream •

Use mint vinegar as the flavouring. Good with a savoury apple starter, with cold peas or potatoes, or on a potato salad.

• Tarragon Cream •

Use tarragon vinegar as the flavouring. Good with savoury apples, pears and peaches and a host of other things.

• Cider Cream •

Use cider vinegar as the flavouring – but only ⅛ pint (75 ml). A spoonful is nice on a seasonal salad.

• Raspberry Cream •

Use raspberry vinegar as the flavouring – but only ⅛ pint (75 ml). Good on baked potatoes.

• Sweet Creams •

Use Drambuie, rum, cherry brandy or Frangelico as the flavouring along with the eggs and sugar. Drambuie is good with warmed-through Christmas pudding, the others are all good with hot sponge puddings or fruit crumbles.

• Strawberry and Pernod Cream •

This is slightly different, and doesn't use the eggs. Liquidise 4 oz (100 g) strawberries with 2 tablespoons Pernod. Beat up the cream with 2 tablespoons soft brown sugar, then fold in the purée. You can do the same with raspberries.

Rich Brown Sauce

When entertaining, I always make a rich gravy or brown sauce well in advance. It's a time-consuming and tricky process making a good sauce, and not really feasible when guests are about to arrive or are already there. This sauce stores well for a few days in the fridge (I usually use screw-top jam or honey jars) or in plastic containers in the freezer. Thus, on the night, it is only a simple matter of a few moments of heating through.

Makes 1½ pints (900 ml)

4 oz (100 g) butter
4 tablespoons plain flour, sieved
about 2 oz (50 g) each of finely diced
    carrot, celery, mushroom stalks and
    onion
skins from 2 onions
2 tablespoons tomato paste

3 pints (1.75 litres) fresh home-made
    stock (see page 81), strained
fresh herbs (parsley, rosemary, marjoram
    etc, nothing *too* overpowering), 1
    tablespoon to begin with
2 tablespoons sherry

You need two separate saucepans – one for the sauce and one for cooking the vegetables – but the end result is worth the extra washing up, believe you me.

In a thick-bottomed saucepan with about 3½ pint (1.5 litre) capacity, melt half the butter over a low heat. Turn up the heat to moderate, mix in the flour and stir vigorously and continuously, bashing the 'roux' up against the side of the pan to eliminate any lumps. (A good wooden spoon is *vital*.) Cook for up to 10 minutes as you want the flour to be evenly cooked to a walnut brown colour.

Meanwhile, melt the remaining butter in the other pan, and simmer the finely diced vegetables and onion skins until crisp and brown.

Beat the tomato paste into the fresh stock, and remove the flour roux from the heat. Add the strained stock – little by little – to the roux and vigorously beat, using an electric hand whisk. Add the cooked vegetables along with the herbs (use just 1 tablespoon of these at first, but you can taste after a while and add more if you like).

Turn the heat up high under the virtually empty vegetable saucepan and 'deglaze' with the sherry. Just boil for a minute or two and stir, until all the buttery goodness merges with the sherry. Add this to the saucepan containing all the sauce ingredients.

Return the pan to a low heat and bring back to simmering point. Put the lid on at an angle (in other words so that the sauce can evaporate), and simmer very gently for up to 3 hours, looking at it every half hour to make sure it isn't disappearing too fast. What you are eventually looking for is a sauce the consistency of one of the cream soups.

When reduced as you want it, liquidise the sauce and pass it into storage container(s) through a sieve. Leave to go cold and then put into the fridge. When chilled, it is easy to remove the fat from the top (use it for frying off your next batch of onions when needed).

Your basic sauce is now complete, but you can still play about with flavourings: use a few drops of wine vinegar, some Worcestershire sauce or mustard paste, some brown sugar, honey, reduced sherry or Madeira, some redcurrant jelly, or some green peppercorns.

Tomato Purée

Easy to make, and so economical when you can buy ripe tomatoes in large quantities cheaply – or you have a load growing in the garden. Simply liquidise any quantity you like – I make purée in 5 lb (2.25 kg) batches – then pass through a sieve into a saucepan. Cook gently until thick. If the pips have made it a little bitter, add some sugar.

Fresh Tomato Sauce

This sauce can be kept in the fridge for up to a week, but can also be frozen most successfully.

Makes 2 pints (1.2 litres)

$\frac{1}{4}$ pint (150 ml) olive oil
2 medium onions, peeled and finely chopped
6 large garlic cloves, peeled and chopped
about 2 tablespoons fresh basil, tarragon and marjoram mixed, or to taste

5 lb (2.25 kg) ripe tomatoes, quartered
salt
freshly ground black pepper

Heat the oil in a large saucepan, add the onions and fry until golden brown. Add the chopped garlic along with the herbs and quartered tomatoes. Bring to the boil, cover and leave to simmer for about an hour. Look at the contents every now and again, and stir gently with a wooden spoon. The juice from the tomatoes should evaporate, leaving a thickish mixture. Pass through a sieve and, if it is still a bit runny for your purposes, return to the heat to reduce further. Season to taste with salt and pepper before cooling and storing.

Tomato Provençale

A tomato sauce which is more piquant than the sauce made in quantity above.

2 oz (50 g) butter
4 large garlic cloves, peeled and crushed with 2 teaspoons salt
4 oz (100 g) onions, peeled and finely chopped

$1\frac{1}{2}$ lb (675 g) tomatoes, peeled, seeded and roughly chopped

Melt the butter in a saucepan and fry the garlic paste and onions until nice and golden. Add the tomatoes and simmer slowly until you have a lovely thick consistency. This will take at least an hour. Cool and store in the fridge for up to a week. It will freeze as well.

Tomato Concasse

This is raw finely chopped tomatoes. You must skin and seed them first though. Make a nick in the skins, and pour boiling water over them in a bowl. Leave for about 10–15 seconds, then drain and slip off the skins. Cut a small slice off the top of each tomato and spoon out all the seeds. Drain the tomato, upside down, to remove all the liquid. Then chop as finely as you can for a wonderful garnishing sauce for hot mousses, cheese and herb pâté and many soups.

Fruit Purée Sauces

More and more, I like serving a small portion of a fruit purée with certain main-course joints. There is nothing new about this. Everybody automatically accepts apple sauce with roast pork or cranberry sauce with roast turkey. But as fresh produce appears in your kitchen (some of you will be lucky enough to actually pick from your own garden), do not be hide-bound by convention, but experiment with some of the following combinations. I haven't given very detailed quantities or proportions, but 1 oz (25 g) butter with 3 oz (75 g) onions and 1 lb (225 g) fruit and other flavourings will make enough purée to do about eight servings. The ones that you particularly like can be made in bulk and stored in your freezer for future occasions.

Melt the butter and fry the finely chopped onions until soft. Add the appropriate fruit and flavourings, simmer slowly until nice and soft, then liquidise and pass through a coarse sieve.

That irreplaceable kitchen item, *your finger*, and a good old lick, will soon provide you with the actual combination *you* like. Sugar, curry powder, vinegar and mustard can also be used in varying quantities to excite the palate further.

Warm through gently and serve a dollop *underneath* plain cooked chicken breasts, roast turkey, pork etc.

gooseberry and elderflower	plum and gin
apple, sage and onion	apple and cranberry
cranberry and orange	apple, chive and Calvados
apple, chive and cheese	gooseberry, sage and onion
pear and Stilton	apple and blackberry
pea, apple, lemon and mint	peach and ground hazelnuts
apricot and orange	

Calvados Apple Purée

This sauce is one of my favourites – as you might have noticed, it crops up all over the place – and it can be stored in the fridge or frozen. It can be added to many of the basic sauces – the white or cream sauces – and can be used instead of a basic apple sauce with pork or duck. (*Without* the Calvados, it is, of course, a basic apple purée or sauce.) A dollop is delicious on some creamed vegetable soups. It can also be used as an apple filling – with meringues, pastries and in pies or pancakes – or a sauce for puddings.

butter	$\frac{1}{2}$ teaspoon ground cinnamon
2 lb (900 g) Granny Smith apples, peeled, cored and thinly sliced	$\frac{1}{2}$ tablespoon soft brown sugar
	Calvados

Lightly butter a heatproof and flameproof casserole dish, and preheat the oven to 375°F/190°C/Gas 5.

Mix the apples with the cinnamon, 1 oz (25 g) butter and the sugar, and place in the casserole. Bake in the preheated oven for about 40 minutes, stirring occasionally with a wooden spoon.

When the apples are soft, bring out of the oven and place the dish over a high heat. Heat some Calvados – be generous – in a soup ladle and then flame over the apples. When it's all cooled, pass through a plastic sieve. Use, warmed or chilled, or freeze.

Mayonnaise

For me there is simply *no* substitute for home-made mayonnaise, no matter what the telly adverts tell you. It is so easy to make and works out – I am sure – much cheaper than the bottled or jarred stuff. My electric hand-beater is ideal for making this and you need a round bottomed bowl (the Christmas pudding type is ideal). Settle it well on a dampened J-cloth or rag to keep the bowl in position while you are beating.

Makes ½ pint (300 ml)

2 egg yolks
a few drops of fresh lemon juice
½ teaspoon each of dry English mustard
    powder, salt and caster sugar

½ pint (300 ml) olive oil
1 tablespoon white wine vinegar

Put the egg yolks, lemon juice, mustard, salt and sugar into the bowl and beat together. Measure the olive oil into a jug (use an oil to suit your pocket and palate). Dipping the finger tips of your free hand into the oil, allow it simply to dribble off into the mixing bowl while your hand-beater is whizzing away on top speed. When you can see that all this initial dribbling of oil has been beaten in it is time to dip your fingers back in the oil and dribble more in. In this way – slow but sure – the basic mixture will never curdle. It will take you only about 3–4 minutes to get two-thirds of your oil into the egg yolk mixture.

It will be fairly stiff. Now you add the wine vinegar which will thin it down considerably, and then you simply pour in the balance of the oil in a very steady trickle, continuing to beat away on high speed.

According to your personal taste you can adjust the flavour by adding more or less mustard and sugar, and by using different vinegars such as garlic, mint or tarragon – but *never* malt. Or you can vary your mayonnaise more substantially, as below. Store in a screw-top jar in the fridge – it keeps as long as eggs.

• Curry Mayonnaise •

Heat 1 tablespoon olive oil gently in a pan and fry 1 oz (25 g) finely chopped onion until transparent. Add 1 dessertspoon curry powder, 1 teaspoon tomato purée, ⅛ pint (75 ml) red wine and 1 tablespoon apricot jam. Simmer slowly for about 30 minutes and then strain and cool. Expand the basic mayonnaise recipe with 4 tablespoons whipped double cream, and then incorporate the strained curry 'liquid'.

• Herbed Mayonnaise •

Simply mix 2 tablespoons finely chopped mixed herbs (or use one only) into the basic mayonnaise.

• Apple Sauce Mayonnaise •

Simmer together 1 lb (450 g) peeled, cored and sliced apples, ¼ pint (150 ml) white wine and a sprig of mint. When the apples are soft, liquidise, pass through a sieve and leave to cool. Mix with the basic mayonnaise.

• Tomato Mayonnaise •

Simply add 1 tablespoon tomato purée (preferably home-made, see page 131), to the basic mayonnaise.

• Savoury Mayonnaise •

Mix together 1 dessertspoon black treacle, 1 tablespoon Dijon mustard and 2 tablespoons chopped dill. Add to the basic mayonnaise.

• Avocado Mayonnaise •

Mash the flesh of a very ripe avocado very well and mix into the basic mayonnaise.

• Sweet and Sour Mayonnaise •

Mix together 1 tablespoon black treacle, 1 tablespoon Moutarde de Meaux and 1 dessertspoonful soft brown sugar. Add to the basic mayonnaise.

• Red Pepper Mayonnaise •

Add 2 tablespoons red pepper purée (see page 99) to the basic mayonnaise.

• Lemon or Orange Mayonnaise •

Add the finely grated rind and juice of 1–2 lemons (or oranges) to the basic mayonnaise.

Mustard Dill Sauce

This goes well with gravadlax (see page 119), cold smoked trout or mackerel, and is nice with cold meats.

¼ pint (150 ml) prepared English mustard
2 egg yolks
a pinch each of salt and white pepper
3 tablespoons soft brown sugar

about 3–4 tablespoons fresh dill
1 tablespoon white wine vinegar
6 tablespoons good olive oil

Place the mustard, egg yolks, salt, pepper, sugar and dill into your blender and whizz around until it is frothy and bubbly. *Very gradually*, add the vinegar followed by the olive oil. It is vital that you dribble these last two items in slowly. Use a spatula to get it all out of the blender goblet into your storage container. Keep for up to a week in the fridge.

Aïoli

When I feel I need to be decidedly decadent, I raid the aïoli jar in the fridge and make a pig of myself, spreading it on anything and everything to hand – digestive biscuits, wholemeal bread, raw carrots – and feel very much better afterwards for giving in to such wicked temptation! A few hours later I am constantly cleaning my teeth, sucking mints and munching bad-breath tablets.

Aïoli is a sort of garlic mayonnaise, but the method is so much simpler – all done in the food processor. It is wicked, but wonderful. OK, maybe six large cloves of garlic are too much for you but, dare I tell you, at home I use *eight*! Try it first with five cloves and then add more if you so desire.

It is super piped into hollowed-out cherry tomatoes and goes well with most grilled fish and a number of other recipes throughout the book. It's also wonderful with crudités as a dip. You can beat in liquidised cooked red peppers or chillies, or a little tomato paste and herbs for a change.

Makes just over 1 pint (600 ml)

2 egg yolks
2 teaspoons Dijon mustard
6 large garlic cloves, skinned and
   chopped
2 tablespoons fresh lemon juice

freshly ground black pepper
a pinch of salt
1 pint (600 ml) olive oil (or oil of
   choice)

Combine everything but the oil in your food processor. Dribble in the oil gradually, with the machine whizzing away, until it is all absorbed. That's all!

French Dressings

I have come to the very firm conclusion that the most important thing needed when making French dressings is your *finger* and your own *personal palate*.

At home I have two large glass jars with thick cork tops (bought in a kitchen shop as storage jars) which, filled with French dressing, are kept tightly shut on the kitchen work surface. When I need to use some, I simply shake the jar or stir its contents vigorously with a fork or small whisk. When each jar gets low, the remaining contents are put into the liquidiser, the jar is washed thoroughly and then play can commence again, giving me plenty of time to use my finger for tasting. I have found that I can go away for my winter break and come back eight weeks later and take up where I left off by simply putting my own personal dressing back into the machine to emulsify (the oil usually splits in the cold winter kitchen) and start my witch's brew once more.

The *basic* French dressing is simply made from the ingredients below, but you can play around with it to your own satisfaction, perhaps preparing it in batches so that you have *several* jars of different dressings for different purposes.

Makes 1¼ pints (750 ml)

⅛ to ¼ pint (75–150 ml) wine vinegar of choice

1 pint (600 ml) oil to suit pocket and palate

1 teaspoon dry English mustard powder

1 teaspoon soft brown sugar

1 tablespoon fresh lemon juice

a pinch each of salt and freshly ground *white* pepper

Put all the ingredients into the blender or liquidiser and switch the machine on to high speed. In seconds an emulsion mixture is ready for you to sample.

It may be too sharp, too oily or too bland – you and only you can know that. You can try adding a couple of tablespoons of runny honey if you have a sweet tooth like me. But it is the wickedly expensive walnut or hazelnut oils that change this Cinderella of French dressings into a princess! You only need add a little over a ¼ pint (150 ml) to this basic recipe for the basic nut flavour to come through to your palate at the very end. However, if the purse is light, just over ¼ pint (150 ml) smoked bacon fat (accumulated during the week from the daily grilled bacon) will make its impact on the basic recipe – while a similar quantity of duck fat (see page 148) makes for a richer dressing.

To make a dressing sharper, extra mustard may be added. Besides the basic dry English mustard powder, a French Dijon will leave its very own personal mark, as will the lovely seeds of Moutarde de Meaux.

Leftover toasted pine kernels or flaked almonds, hard-boiled eggs, a pinch of curry powder, or a touch of curry paste or tomato purée will all give you a change of flavour, and it goes without saying that any finely chopped fresh herbs will give a further added joy – but all these will reduce the shelf life of the dressing. Keep only for about 4–5 days.

If you are one of the ever-growing band (unfortunately) who abhor the good things in life – i.e. a wonderful thick, oily French dressing – a thinner product may be made by adding a little white (dry, medium or sweet according to taste) or rosé wine to the basic recipe to let it down until it appeals to you.

Root Ginger Dressing

A good salad dressing for those who like something hot and spicy, and it can also be used for painting sausages prior to barbecuing or mushroom caps before frying or baking (particularly the large ones).

Makes ½ pint (300 ml)

⅛ pint (75 ml) soy sauce

¼ pint (150 ml) olive oil

2 tablespoons white wine vinegar

2 tablespoons fresh lemon juice

1 tablespoon sesame oil

½ teaspoon salt

a pinch of freshly ground white pepper

1 teaspoon soft brown sugar

at least ½ teaspoon freshly grated peeled root ginger

Simply put everything into your liquidiser and swirl away and then *taste*. Add some more ginger if you think it needs it.

Flavoured Oils

These are easy to make and very handy to have if, like me, you are keen to have various flavours daily on your plate to tempt your palate. They can be used to dress salads, to fry off croûtons for soups or garnishes – the flavour difference is amazing – or to sauté meat or stir-fry vegetables.

All you need are a few 1 lb (450 g) screw-top jars – those which once held honey or pickle are ideal. Place the flavouring ingredient in the bottom of the jar, and simply fill it up with oil. I always use olive, but you can use any blander or cheaper oil. Allow 10 days at least of steeping for the flavour to come through, and the occasional shaking of the jar will help it all along.

The following quantities are per 1 pint (600 ml) oil, but you could also, of course, have a mixture (try garlic and ginger).

• *Garlic Oil* •

8–12 garlic cloves, peeled and lightly crushed (I use 12!).

• *Ginger Oil* •

Use 2 oz (50 g) peeled root ginger pieces.

• *Herb Oil* •

Use as much as you like of any chopped herb, or a mixture. Basil is one of my favourites, and whenever my basil plants are about to give up the ghost each year, I religiously strip off every single leaf and press them into my jars and cover them with oil. After a few weeks, the oil gives a bouncing basil flavour to remind me of the erstwhile summer. (And if you liquidise some toasted pine kernels with a clove of garlic and some of this oil, it makes a delightful spread for cold white meats.)

Aspic

Although I'm not in favour of many pre-prepared and packeted foods, the Swiss powdered aspic is very good, and saves an enormous amount of time. All you have to do to make 1 pint (600 ml) aspic is follow the manufacturers' instructions – *but*, instead of using all water as they suggest, use one-third sherry, Marsala, port or any wine to two-thirds water. This makes an amazing taste difference.

Simmer the aspic according to instructions and then leave to set. You can do this in advance and chill in the pan in the fridge. When ready to start using it, bring it out and heat very gently over a low heat until it is barely brought back to a coating consistency.

To cover the duck liver pâté twirls on page 41 is fairly simple, but generally, to build up a good coating on anything else – a salmon cutlet, tomato, egg or whatever – you should coat with the minutest amount of aspic, chill, coat again, and so on. In this (yes, I agree, rather time-consuming) way, you can build up good layers on the food. And always place the food to be coated on a cooling tray over another solid tray. Any surplus will drip through, and can be reheated and re-used.

Beurre Manié

To thicken a sauce, the juices of a stew or whatever, simply add little knobs of beurre manié – equal amounts of butter and flour mixed together. Beat it in well so that it dissolves evenly throughout the dish.

Basic Stock Syrup

2 lb (900 g) preserving or cube sugar   1 pint (600 ml) water

Place both ingredients in a large, very clean saucepan and heat gently to dissolve the sugar. When dissolved, turn up the heat and simmer for about 15 minutes. Poach your fruit in this.

For additional tang, add 2–3 tablespoons wine vinegar whilst simmering, or, for many fruits, a couple of cinnamon sticks give a rich flavour.

Butterscotch Sauce

This is a recipe Delia Smith told me about, and I now use it regularly at home and at Miller Howe to add that special – and fattening – something to a variety of desserts. It goes well with simply poached nectarines, peaches, pears or apples; with home-made ice creams, and with many farmhouse pies.

Fills 2 × 1 lb (450 g) jars

1 × 1 lb (450 g) tin golden syrup $\frac{1}{4}$ pint (150 ml) double cream
3 oz (75 g) butter   a few drops of vanilla essence
4 oz (100 g) soft brown sugar

Put the tin of syrup, opened, into a saucepan and half-fill up its sides with hot water. This makes the syrup more runny and it will come out of the tin more easily.

Pour the syrup into a large, thick-bottomed saucepan and add the butter and sugar. Heat very gently until all have melted together, stir slowly, and cook for about 10 minutes. Remove from the heat and when it has cooled a little, stir in the double cream, a little at a time, along with the vanilla essence. Stir continuously for a smooth sauce.

Use immediately, or put into clean jars and store in the fridge.

Chocolate Sauces

These can be used with a variety of desserts – particularly with cream-filled profiteroles.

Remember, anything cooked with chocolate is only as good as the basic chocolate you use (see page 19). Do not be tempted by supermarket bargains!

A simple chocolate sauce is made by bringing $\frac{1}{2}$ pint (300 ml) milk to the boil in a thick-bottomed saucepan and then beating in, a little at a time, 4 oz (100 g) grated chocolate of choice. Remove the pan from the heat and quickly and quite vigorously beat in 4 egg yolks. Leave to cool.

A far richer (and I think better) version is for you to bring together in a bowl 8 oz (225 g) grated chocolate of choice with $\frac{1}{2}$ pint (300 ml) single cream along with a couple of tablespoons of rum or brandy!

And for that different approach, use a good *white* chocolate for a sauce to accompany a dark chocolate pudding.

The Fourth Course
· MAIN · COURSES

For most people, this course is exactly that, the main event of the dinner. When planning a dinner party you should start by choosing what you want to serve for this course *first*, so that everything else can be designed around it. If you're serving a starter, a soup, and a fish course before, each of these should be light enough so that the diner still has some room for his meat and veg (the cliché is meat and *two* veg; at Miller Howe it's sometimes *seven*!) – and I've yet to meet someone who hasn't got room for a Miller Howe dessert.

You will have encountered some of the following before, but many are so representative of Miller Howe cooking that they had to be included. There are plenty of new recipes though, along with clever variations and ideas for both poultry and meats. Most recipes are suitable for using as the main course at a dinner party – some roasts are spectacular enough to display to your guests before carving as we do in the dining-room at Miller Howe – and many can be taken cold on a picnic, or cooked on the barbecue (see pages 177–82 for some basic ideas on outdoor or moveable feasts).

If you like to emulate the Miller Howe style, serve the meat centrally on a heated plate, and surround with up to six vegetables. This may *sound* too much, but each portion of vegetable is just a taste really – one small potato, about six tiny French beans, a spoonful of a vegetable purée etc. Pour sauce generously under, over or around the meat, and garnish imaginatively. I wish you success.

POULTRY

After lamb my favourite main course is farm chicken poached, grilled, barbecued or plain roasted. With some free-range chicken on your plate, the very first bite will make you swear immediately that you will never again settle for a frozen freak fed on fish food and phoney pellets.

As for ducks and turkeys, they must be fresh, not frozen, and once you've found a good reliable supplier of both, encourage him for all you're worth!

• Carving Poultry •

If you have trussed a chicken (as in my roast chicken recipe), first remove the strings, and then transfer the bird to your wooden carving board with legs towards you. Put the carving fork into the left leg in order to stabilise the chicken and then insert your knife into the lower side of the left breast in order to draw the leg away from the main carcass. Your knife should slowly slide down towards the hip joint at the same time as the fork is bending the whole leg away from the body of the bird. Cut through this small ball-like joint smartly and put the full leg to one side. Greedy folk like me only get four portions to a bird and serve the whole leg as one portion, but if you wish to be more genteel – and economical – cut through this knee joint thus giving two portions – thigh and drumstick – from each leg.

Turn the bird round now so that the wings are towards you. The centre bone is clearly visible and, putting your knife point in at the end furthest away from you, come forwards and down, feeling your way along the rib cage, until you completely remove the breast and wing. Once again, being a greedy toad, this represents one whole portion for me, but of course the wing can be taken off along with a little of the breast, and the breast can be sliced in half lengthwise. Turn the chicken round and repeat the whole process on the other side.

Turkey can be carved in the same way – but you'll get considerably more than four portions, of course!

When carving a duck I only get four portions as well. To do this, the bird is put on to the carving board, legs towards you, breast up. Using the clear middle breast bone as a guide, cut the bird clean in half. This is made easier if you hold your knife at a 45 degree angle and start at the end furthest away from you. Use your hands to remove the rib cage and then lay each half, skin side upwards, on your work surface and simply separate the end of each breast from the top of each thigh.

Roast Chicken

I never stuff the inside of a chicken, but cook the stuffing in a separate container. In this recipe, however, a 'stuffing' is thrust between flesh and skin before roasting: whether butter based or not, it means the flesh is always much more flavourful and the meat more moist. Some cookery writers say it also means you needn't baste the bird as often, but I religiously baste every 10–15 minutes as I like my birds nice and brown with fairly crisp skin.

I like to truss a chicken prepared in this way as it keeps the filling very much in place, and if I'm doing two chickens at one time in one tin, helps to keep them firm and compact. At one time, a special long kitchen needle threaded with strong kitchen string was always used to truss a chicken – in fact I remember it being part of the only catering exam I ever took as a trainee manager – but this isn't really necessary these days.

Stuff the bird first. The stuffings can be various: try mushroom pâté or cheese and herb pâté (see pages 40 and 39), or one of the flavoured butters on page 108 (tarragon and curried are perhaps the most interesting for chicken). To get this stuffing between the skin and flesh, take hold of the bottom of the chicken in your non-working hand – if right-handed you hold with your left! With the neck opening facing you, probe with your middle fingers in between the skin and the flesh as if you were starting to pull on a pair of silk gloves. Your hand will soon go gently and carefully over the breasts and around the thighs, separating the skin from the flesh. Do go gently, as you don't want to break the skin. When the skin has come away from flesh as far as it will go, stand the bird on its bottom. Take some of your chosen stuffing and smoothly press it down over the thighs and work upwards towards the breast and the neck cavity.

Have ready a fairly strong kitchen string (thin mediocre stuff will only cut your fingers when pulled, or snap when you give it a tug to bring the bird together). Push the ends of the drumsticks back into the backside cavity, plump up the breast and tuck the wings right underneath the chicken. Place the chicken, breast upwards, and neck towards you, and carefully place the centre loop of your string under the parson's nose. Bring it a few inches towards you so as you can bring both ends up and across and, when pulling, hold the ends of the drumsticks tight across the opening. Press both ends of the string round the underside of the ends of the drumsticks – this, if you could see it, would be like a figure-of-eight – then bring each string towards you underneath the leg and tie in a bow at the neck cavity.

Roast a 3 lb (1.4 kg) chicken for 1½ hours at 350°F/180°C/Gas 4; for a larger chicken of up to 3½ lb (1.5 kg), roast for the same length of time, but with the oven preheated to 400°F/200°C/Gas 6. Baste as already stated, every 10–15 minutes. Remove from the oven and allow to rest for a little while before you start carving.

Breast of Chicken

Chicken breasts are almost tailor-made for an individual portion. I like to buy them on the bone – the fleshy breast can easily be removed, and the bones make a wonderful stock, but try to retain the wing bone. The breasts can be stuffed first – see below for some ideas – or cooked plain and *then* decorated for additional flavour.

I used to cook chicken breasts in foil packets in the oven – with some wine, butter and seasoning added – or poach them in stock. Now, however, I have discovered the magic of food film. There have recently been some worries about the use of film in cooking, but a special kind available from Lakeland Plastics in Windermere is considered safe.

Season the chicken breasts well and then place on a piece of film. Fold it over and swing the ends around as if you were wrapping a sweet. Place the transparent chicken parcels on a wire cooling tray in a roasting tin and, just as you are about to cook (in the preheated oven at 350°F/180°C/Gas 4), pour in enough boiling water to come up to just below the level of the cooling tray. Put in the oven and bake for 30 minutes. When ready to serve, simply cut open one end of the film parcel, and the cooked and succulent breast can be pushed out on to the plate.

• *Stuffings for Breast of Chicken* •

Some cheese and herb pâté or mushroom pâté (see pages 39 and 40) – needless to say – are good, and you can try some of the rolled sole stuffings on page 120. You could chop up some brandy-soaked dried apricots and mix them with ground almonds. Walnut butter (see page 109), with a little added diced red pepper, is a good chicken stuffing. Cream cheese with added diced apples, walnuts and celery tastes delicious as does minced belly pork mixed with some grated fresh root ginger and the juice and grated rind of a lime.

• *Garnishes for Breast of Chicken* •

Hollandaise or any of its variations, and béarnaise go well with cooked chicken breasts. Don't forget about the possibilities of a fruit purée sauce under the chicken – choose one to complement your other flavourings or garnishes – or go to town and decorate it lavishly. The photograph between pages 112 and 113 is quite modest; I like to go even further!

You need some home-made potato crisps (see page 107), a small amount of creamed potato in a piping bag, gherkin fans (see page 102), or thin strips of pepper, stuffed olives and parsley sprigs.

Place the chicken breast, fillet side down, on the plate and coat with the sauce you have chosen – a little hollandaise or béarnaise – and then, up towards the wing, pipe a small twirl of creamed potato. This should be large enough to take two crisps, one on either side to resemble butterfly wings. In the middle of this potato twirl, place the unfanned end of the gherkin fan; fan it out across the bare bulk of

Roast loin of pork with crackling, served with baby corn,
mangetouts, parsnip purée and toasted pine kernels,
stir-fried grated carrot, courgettes and a wedge of our delicious
new carrot and potato cake.

*A slice of our new triple fillet roast — beef, pork and
lamb fillets encased in bacon — served here with rich brown sauce,
baby corn, courgettes with toasted almonds and a
fanned roast potato.*

A huge bowlful of seasonal salad is the perfect accompaniment
● *to a simple but delicious salmon escalope with a Noilly Prat and* ●
chive cream sauce.

*One of our packed lunch lockers filled with a selection of goodies,
among them slices of stuffed red pepper, melon, terrine and quiche,
smoked salmon sandwiches, strawberries and cream, with a few
chocolates for the sweet of tooth.*

the breast. Put the half olive on top of the potato twirl and the sprig of parsley coming up towards the wing. If you have cutlet frills (and they can be obtained from a good kitchen shop), put one of these over the thin projecting wing bone end which will enable your diners to pick up even the juiciest of bits to finish off the dish. Very theatrical and perhaps a little OTT – but it does look good!

——Breast of Chicken in Calvados Cream——

On my periodic visits to Normandy, whenever I see this traditional dish on a menu for the first time, I immediately order it – and I always think it is better than mine. Don't be put off by that touch of honesty: it's probably because of their very special rough Calvados or their local apples – or perhaps my own sentimentality, as I do so enjoy regional dishes eaten in their own regions.

It can be pre-prepared in the morning, and then just finished off prior to serving.

Serves 6

2 tablespoons oil
2 oz (50 g) butter
6 chicken breasts
salt
freshly ground black pepper
$\frac{1}{4}$ pint (150 ml) Calvados
$\frac{1}{2}$ pint (300 ml) dry or sweet cider, to taste

3 small dessert apples (I like Orange Pippins)
$\frac{1}{4}$ pint (150 ml) double cream

Garnish
sprigs of watercress

Preheat the oven to 350°F/180°C/Gas 4.

In a small frying pan large enough to take two chicken breasts at a time, heat the oil and then melt the butter. Season the chicken breasts with salt and pepper and seal well in this spitting combination.

Transfer to a casserole dish that will take the six breasts flat in one layer.

Heat through the Calvados in a small saucepan and then, holding the pan at an angle (if you have an open gas hob), ignite the liqueur and pour it immediately over the chicken. (If using an electric hob this tricky task will need to be done with a match!) When the flames have subsided, pour the cider over the chicken, cover, and cook in the oven for 20 minutes. Remove and leave to cool until required.

Meanwhile, peel, core and slice the apples and fry in the oil and butter remaining in the pan until they are slightly brown. Remove using a slotted spoon. This too can be done in the morning.

When you want to serve the chicken, preheat the oven again to 350°F/180°C/ Gas 4. Warm the chicken through for 20 minutes and then remove. Put the chicken breasts on a plate and keep warm, covered, along with the apple slices, in a warming drawer.

Put the casserole and its alcoholic contents over a high heat and add the double cream. Boil away until thick – this should only take about 4 minutes. Serve the chicken breasts on individual plates, pour the sauce over them, and garnish with cooked apple slices and some watercress.

Baby Poussins in Dark Ale

This is a good dish for a dinner or supper party as it needs to be prepared at least a day before, and it is relatively inexpensive. Don't be put off by looks: one portion of about 12–14 oz (350–400 g) does appear large, but by the time the meat has fallen off the bones each guest will just be 'nicely' fed!

Serves 6

2 tablespoons oil
3 oz (75 g) butter
6 poussins, about 12 oz (350 g) each, well trussed
1 large onion, peeled and thinly sliced
3 garlic cloves, crushed to a paste with 1 teaspoon salt
1 dessertspoon malt vinegar
freshly ground black pepper

3 tablespoons demerara sugar
½ teaspoon ground ginger
3 tablespoons plain flour, sieved
1 pint (600 ml) dark or brown ale
4 teaspoons freshly chopped herbs

To garnish
1 bunch watercress

Preheat the oven to 350°F/180°C/Gas 4.

Heat the oil in a frying pan and then melt 2 oz (50 g) of the butter. The frying pan should be large enough to hold two poussins. Seal two at a time on all sides and transfer to a casserole dish large enough to take all six birds.

Add the finely sliced onions and the crushed garlic to the oil and butter left in the pan, along with the vinegar, pepper, sugar and ginger. Cook for a few minutes and then add the flour. Stir well and pour in the ale, a little at a time, beating with a wire whisk. Cook until the gravy has thickened, a few minutes. Pass the gravy through a sieve over the poussins in the casserole, then sprinkle on the herbs. Put the casserole on top of the stove and bring back to the boil. Cover, then cook in the preheated oven for 25 minutes. Remove, leave to cool, then store in the fridge for at least 24 hours.

When you wish to serve, preheat the oven again to the same temperature. Remove the poussins from the casserole and warm the gravy on the hob, dropping in a few knobs of the remaining butter. Beat briskly to give the sauce a slight sheen. Replace the poussins, spoon the sauce over them, put the lid back on and warm through in the oven for 20 minutes. Serve, one poussin per plate, with some sauce over the top, and garnished with generous sprigs of watercress.

—Farm Chicken Cooked in Red Wine—

This is delicious served with some buttery mashed potatoes.

Serves 4 generously

1 fresh farm chicken, about 3 lb (1.4 kg) in weight
plain flour
salt
freshly ground black pepper
3 tablespoons olive oil
3 oz (75 g) butter
6 oz (175 g) smoked bacon, rinded and diced
8 fresh garlic cloves, peeled and soaked in some milk

12 small button onions, peeled
5 tablespoons brandy
4 oz (100 g) mushroom caps, trimmed
3 tablespoons freshly chopped herbs of choice
¾ bottle inexpensive red wine
1 oz (25 g) beurre manié (optional, see page 139)

Garnish
croûton rounds (see page 72)

Portion the chicken with a sharp knife, removing the wings first, then the legs – which can be cut in two through the 'knee' joint. Take off the breasts, cutting them into two portions as well. You will now have ten pieces of chicken. Coat them liberally in seasoned flour.

Heat the olive oil in a frying pan, and then add and melt the butter. Fry the diced bacon until it turns brown and crisp, then add four of the garlic cloves, crushed with a little salt, as well as the whole onions. Cook until golden then, using a slotted spoon, remove everything to your large casserole.

Seal the floured chicken pieces in the fat left in the pan, along with the remaining whole garlic cloves. The chicken pieces should sizzle all the time – but they won't do this if the pan is too crowded, or if the fat isn't hot enough. Transfer the chicken pieces and garlic cloves, using the slotted spoon again, to the casserole, and liberally scatter the contents with more flour from a sieve.

Heat the brandy in a small saucepan (if you have a gas hob, flame it), and pour over the contents of the casserole. Add the mushroom caps, the herbs, some pepper and the wine, put over a high heat and bring back to the boil. Cover as tightly as possible, transfer to the preheated oven, and cook for 30 minutes. Remove the lid and gently stir the ingredients, then lower the heat to 250°F/120°C/Gas ½, and cook for a further hour.

Serve immediately if you like – thickening the liquid with some beurre manié if necessary – but in my opinion the casserole should be left to go cold and then reheated the next day. The taste is infinitely better. Serve with some croûton rounds cooked in the fat left in the frying pan.

—*Roast Duck on Calvados Purée*— *with Green Peppercorn Sauce*

Cook the stuffing separately alongside the duck for the last 30–40 minutes of the cooking time, and heat the gravy through with the peppercorns at the last moment. And *never* waste the duck fat – it's wonderful for frying potatoes, and can be used to make the duck liver pâté on page 40.

Serves 4

1 fresh plump duck, at least 3¼ lb
   (1.5 kg) in weight
1 carrot
½ onion, peeled
a thyme and parsley sprig
sea salt
freshly ground black pepper

To serve
Calvados apple purée (see page 133)
rich brown sauce with green
   peppercorns (see page 130)
stuffing (see page 150)

Wipe the duck inside and out, and then dry the outside as well as you can to ensure a crisp skin. You could hang it in an airy place for 24 hours like the Chinese do for their Peking duck (put some newspaper underneath, and keep animals away), and some experts even go so far as to dry the skin with a hairdryer! (Hair drying instead of air drying perhaps!) Preheat the oven to 475°F/240°C/Gas 9.

Place the carrot, onion and herbs inside the duck and season inside generously. Place the bird on a wire cooling tray inside a foil-lined roasting tin. Simply put the tin into the preheated oven and bake for 1½ hours. Note I say 'bake', not 'roast', for the secret of crisp-skinned duck is to remove the copious fat that forms – and this must be done *every 15 minutes* during the cooking time. (Always close the oven door immediately, so that the temperature stays constant.)

Serve the portioned duck (see page 142) on a dessertspoon of Calvados apple purée, with a green peppercorn enriched sauce. Arrange a portion of stuffing at the side – in a savoury pastry tartlet if you like.

—*Muslin-Roasted Turkey*—

I've always cooked my turkey this way, and it always turns out wonderfully with a crisp skin, and a nutty, buttery, moist flesh. A necessity is a double thickness of butter muslin measuring 30 inches (75 cm) square. This average sized oven-ready turkey will suit an average family – and there will be plenty left over to enjoy cold with the macadamia nut delight following.

1 oven-ready fresh turkey, about
   12–14 lb (5.5–6.3 kg) in weight
2 large carrots
1 large onion

1 apple, quartered
1½ lb (675 g) salted butter
parsley stalks

Preheat the oven to 350°F/180°C/Gas 4, and place the turkey, breast upwards, in the centre of the doubled muslin.

Peel the carrots and the onion, and put the peelings and onion skin into the bottom of your large turkey roasting tin. Put the carrots, onions and quartered apple inside the rib cage of the bird, along with 8 oz (225 g) of the butter. Chop the parsley stalks roughly and combine them with the remaining butter. Smear this liberally all over the breast and legs of the bird.

Draw the top left corner of the muslin up over the turkey breast and secure it at the bottom right; the bottom left corner up over the breast, securing at top right. Use wooden cocktail sticks to hold it all together. Put the muslin-wrapped turkey into the roasting tin on top of the peelings, and then into the preheated oven. Leave for 4 hours, basting half-way through the cooking time over the muslin.

When the bird is cooked, remove from the oven, peel off the muslin and leave for a few minutes before carving. Serve with all the traditional trimmings, including some turkey stuffing (see page 150) using the liver. A nice touch would be to warm some cranberries through; heat some red wine and orange juice, thicken the juices with some arrowroot, then fold in the cranberries and serve some per portion in a tiny savoury pastry tartlet.

Warm Macadamia Nut Delight

One of the best things about roasting a turkey in my way is all the beautiful rich tasty dripping you have left over. Some of this can be used when you serve the white and dark meat cold for a scratch meal a day or two after the main event. This is a sort of savoury scramble, but it's delicious with cold turkey. Add some finely diced pineapple or red pepper as well if you like.

2 oz (50 g) turkey dripping
4 oz (100 g) onion, peeled and finely chopped
2 apples, cored and finely chopped
4 celery sticks, trimmed and finely chopped

4 oz (100 g) macadamia nuts, toasted and coarsely chopped
2 eggs
$\frac{1}{4}$ pint (150 ml) double cream

Melt the turkey dripping and fry the chopped onion gently until soft. Fold in the apple and celery and stir-fry for a few minutes before adding the toasted nuts.

Lightly beat the eggs with the cream and pour into the mixture. Stir-fry until set, just like your conventional scrambled eggs. Serve *warm* spoonfuls with the cold turkey.

Pig that I am, I personally like to par-cook the eggs in the mixture and then put in 2–3 tablespoons of that lovely rich jelly now settled at the bottom of the jar of dripping. This makes it all rather runny.

Poultry Stuffing

I never cook a stuffing inside the bird. I like to put it in a 1 lb (450 g) loaf tin, and I cook it for the last 30–40 minutes of the cooking time alongside the bird. You can serve it in spoonfuls or in slices or, to make it look even more spectacular, spooned into a tiny savoury pastry tartlet. You don't have to follow this recipe exactly – stuffings are for improvisation and demand creativity. You can add anything you fancy – cheese, ground almonds, garlic, pine kernels, leftover spinach purée. Diced orange segments or diced apples are nice in a stuffing for chicken or duck, and diced celery, walnuts and apple are delicious with turkey.

Fills a 1 lb (450 g) loaf tin

1 medium onion, finely chopped
2 oz (50 g) butter
the liver of the bird, plus extra chicken, duck or turkey livers to bring the weight up to 4 oz (100 g), finely chopped
4 oz (100 g) breadcrumbs

4 oz (100 g) sausagemeat
1–2 tablespoons freshly chopped herbs (marjoram is *the* stuffing herb)
salt
freshly ground black pepper

Fry the onion in the butter until brown and then add the livers. Mix in the breadcrumbs, sausagemeat, herbs and a little salt and pepper until you reach a good consistency. Put into the loaf tin and bake in the oven for 30–40 minutes.

MEAT

I will put my head on the block – or my body in the firing line – by categorically stating that meat is without any doubt the finest food available. I find it sad that a very minor part of society – about $1\frac{1}{2}$ per cent – avidly avoid meat and spend most of their time endeavouring to persuade the other $98\frac{1}{2}$ per cent to do likewise. The fanatic anti-flesh folk I have encountered all look to me as if they could do with a bloody good plate of mince and cooked liver to bring sparkle to their cheeks, colour to their pasty complexions, lustre to their scurfy hair and a smoothness to their dried-out skin. Quite apart from giving them a sense of *joy*! The slaughtering of animals both ritually and as food has been going on since Adam met Eve and has nearly always been part of a celebratory process – so why on earth we should be told it is not normal to eat animals is beyond my limited comprehension.

It is supposed to be possible to judge meat accurately by its appearance in the butcher's shop. I can't altogether agree with this as I personally think that you have to shop around for a butcher you can trust implicitly: one who hangs his meat well and who, given sufficient warning, will provide you with a joint to your liking which will cook tasty and tender. It is *no use* deciding on Saturday morning that you want a good leg of pork for tomorrow's lunch – unless you know your butcher well and *trust* that his meat is good. Although young bright red meat might visually appeal to some shoppers on the butchers' slabs, avoid it like the plague.

At Miller Howe we have an advantage over the average domestic household as we have one enormous walk-in cold room put aside purely and simply for hanging and storing uncooked meats. We buy whole sirloins on the bone, whole pork loins and legs, and whole carcasses of Lakeland lamb. (Never once during the horrible Chernobyl radiation scare in early 1986 did one single guest raise this question when confronted with lamb at Miller Howe: they probably knew that I never ever buy young spring lamb – it simply doesn't have the taste and flavour of the older well-hung beast.) Beef is hung for up to 28 days until, yes, it does look rather dark and off-putting at the two ends, but these are discarded. The lambs are never actually cut up until they have been hanging for 21 days, and pork is kept for up to 14 days. Any joints left over when the hotel closes each year – after this hanging period – are transferred to the freezer. Provided the joint is taken out the night before at least, put into the fridge and then allowed to come round gently to room temperature, it is none the worse. These are super then for pre-season staff luncheons!

I am wary of giving positive cooking times for joints as so much depends on the actual cut and age etc, but the following rough guide should be of use.

• Rough Guide to Roasting Meat •

Obviously there are two ways of roasting meat – quick and slow. I always go for the quick each time and tend to see that it is medium to well done when finished – particularly as the meat is always very well hung in the first instance.

Meat	Quick roasting	Slow roasting
	425°F/220°C/Gas 7 for 30 minutes then 350°F/180°C/Gas 4	325°F/160°C/Gas 3
Beef	20 minutes per 1 lb (450 g) plus 20 minutes	30 minutes per 1 lb (450 g) plus 30 minutes
Lamb	25 minutes per 1 lb (450 g) plus 25 minutes	40 minutes per 1 lb (450 g) plus 40 minutes
Pork	35 minutes per 1 lb (450 g) plus 35 minutes	Not suitable
Veal	Not suitable	45 minutes per 1 lb (450 g) plus 45 minutes

• Braising Meat •

Casseroles are relatively easy to cook provided you seal the meat correctly first. I also think they should be made the day before and then slowly reheated as this gives more flavour. No matter what meat you are planning to casserole, the pieces have first to be quickly sealed to keep all the tasty tenderising juices *inside*; the mistake most people make is plonking 1 lb (450 g) of meat or more into one pan at the same time. You should use *two* small pans or, if you only have one pan, you will simply have to take the time to painstakingly do a little at a time. First heat the oil and then add an equal amount of soft butter. When it begins to foam drop in no more than six cubes of meat. A sizzling noise will start but, more importantly, so it should continue. If you plonk too much meat in initially, the 'singing' will cease, the temperature of the fat will drop drastically, and the juices will start to run from the meat. I always stir-fry with a wooden spoon and then remove with a slotted metal spoon to the casserole. Make sure the fat is sizzling again before you put in your next lot of meat.

When all the ingredients have been browned, add your stock and any other ingredients. Bring everything back to the boil on top of the stove, cover and then cook in the low oven as specified in your recipe. Look at the contents from time to time to check that they're not drying out too much.

• Grilling Meat •

I can only grill meats after they have been marinated (see pages 181–2, and several of the following recipes), and the same applies to barbecuing meats. This way they are cooked well *but* are still relatively moist. So often I have fancied a simple grilled chop in a restaurant which, when it appeared, looked succulent but was like cardboard when cut into. Have faith – one can marinate for up to 5 days in wine etc!

Allow most grills up to 40 minutes to reach their maximum temperature before putting the pan underneath, and before placing your meats under the red-hot grill, always paint them with a little more oil of choice. Always use tongs to handle the meat – never a large fork, as this will pierce into the flesh and let the delicious, mouth-watering juices escape. When the outside of both sides has been sealed in the fierce heat, turn the grill down a little and continue to grill until the meat is done.

Barbecuing follows the same principles really: you need the heat as fierce as possible, and so you must wait until the flames have died down and the coals are white-hot instead of red-hot.

• Carving Meat •

Put a leg of lamb, rounded skin side uppermost, on your work surface. If you're right-handed, the small shank bone end, or knuckle, should be to your left as you will take hold of this first. About 2 inches (5 cm) from the shank bone, cut into the meat at a slant, from top right to lower left, until you hit the bone. Depending on how thick or thin you like your meat (I prefer mine carved thinly), take your knife a little to the right and slice through again giving a flick to the left as you reach the bone and your first slice will come off. Do this all along right up to the hip bone and then turn the joint over and remove meat from the underneath.

The French way – so cleverly demonstrated by Anne Willan of the La Varenne school of cooking in Paris – is totally different, and very good indeed if you want to present the leg of lamb already carved to your guests and then simply serve out the slices at table. The leg is laid skin side uppermost and you cut along from the hip bone towards the shank bone *parallel* to the bone. Each slice is removed as carved and then these are built up again on to the bone and taken like that to the table. I was always taught that it just was not done to carve against the grain – but it works, I assure you.

Rolled sirloin of beef or boned loins of pork, veal or lamb are simplicity to carve. After leaving the meat to rest, and having removed all the strings, the meat can be sliced through as simply as you would a cucumber.

A loin on the bone can be sliced through into chops or cutlets (a little prior attention from the butcher will help).

Beef Cooked with Fresh Herbs and Red Wine

Serves 6–8

1 piece sirloin, about 3½–4 lb
  (1.5–1.75 kg) in weight when off the
  bone (keep the bones)
8 garlic cloves, peeled and halved
1 tablespoon curry powder
salt
freshly ground black pepper
3 tablespoons olive oil
½ pint (300 ml) red wine
1 onion, peeled and chopped

2 carrots, scrubbed and chopped
2 celery sticks, trimmed and chopped
2 tablespoons brandy or port
½ oz (15 g) beurre manié (optional, see
  page 139)

Garnish
freshly chopped herbs

Preheat oven to 375°F/190°C/Gas 5.

Make sixteen evenly divided incisions into the skin of the meat, and into these press the halved garlic cloves. Spread curry powder evenly over the fat along with the salt and pepper.

Put the olive oil in a roasting tin on top of the stove, and heat. Seal the joint all over in this, basting it well. Push the bones from the joint underneath the meat and place the tin in the preheated oven. Cook for 30 minutes, then remove. Add the wine, chopped onion, carrot and celery to the tin, and return to the oven. Cook for a further hour, basting frequently, or until cooked to your liking.

Turn off the oven, wrap the joint loosely in foil and return to the warm oven. Strain the juices from the tin into a saucepan, and add the brandy or port. Simmer until reduced by half and, if you like a thick sauce, simply thicken with the beurre manié. If you are going to carve the sirloin in sight of your guests, it looks splendid with the fat sprinkled with a very very generous amount of freshly chopped herbs.

Whole Fillet of Beef Poached in Consommé

This is ideal for a picnic or supper dish and done at least the day before, it's deliciously moist and flavoursome served at home with a simple salad.

Serves 4–6

1 beef fillet, about 1½ lb (675 g) in weight
8–12 garlic cloves, peeled (optional)
1 tablespoon olive oil
1 oz (25 g) butter

1 × 15 oz (425 g) can condensed consommé
4 tablespoons cooking sherry
a generous pinch of curry powder

Preheat the oven to 400°F/200°C/Gas 6, and make sure that the fillet will squash into one of your loaf tins.

Lay the fillet flat on your work surface, bringing the tail over at the end in order to make an evenly shaped thick sausage. Make as many small incisions into the fillet as will take up the amount of garlic you plan to use (if using), and firmly force the cloves into the gaps.

Seal the fillet in a mixture of foaming oil and butter, and transfer to the loaf tin. Bring the consommé, sherry and curry powder to the boil together, and pour over the fillet. You won't be able to fit it all in; pour only to within ½ inch (1.25 cm) of the top. Cover firmly with foil and place in the preheated oven. Bake for a maximum of 30 minutes, taking it out every 10 minutes to top up with the still heated consommé mixture. The fillet will be pink after 20 minutes, medium after 25, and without any trace of blood after half an hour.

Take out of the oven and leave to cool. When cold put in the fridge and take on your picnic in the mould. The jelly will be slightly set, providing a lovely moisture to the meat. Slice it thickly or thinly and fan out on the plates. Serve with horseradish cream or a strong mustardy French dressing. If you're at home, it's delicious with a herbed hollandaise.

Fillet of Beef Puff Pastry with Mushroom Pâté

I know there is a much more traditional and classical way of describing this dish, but as I abhor French menus (quite apart from the fact that at grammar school I barely got beyond the *plume de ma tante* stage), this is the way this tempting dish is called at Miller Howe.

Serves 6

1 fillet of beef, weighing about 1½ lb
  (675 g), well trimmed
1 tablespoon olive oil
1 oz (25 g) butter

½ recipe quantity rough puff pastry (see
  page 57)
4 oz (100 g) mushroom pâté (see page
  40)
glaze of beaten egg and milk

A fillet is usually very thick at one end and then goes down to a diminished circle of a tail so this little end should be brought slightly back over the meat to form a complete round large sausage. This tail end can be stuck in initially with a wooden cocktail stick. Pat the fillet dry with kitchen paper.

Heat the olive oil and butter together in a frying pan, then seal the fillet well on all sides over a high heat – the oil and butter in the pan should whistle to you all the time! Remove the fillet and pat dry again, removing all the fat.

Roll out the puff pastry (do read the instructions well, remembering especially the bit about rolling in the right direction) until it is at least 2 inches (5 cm) longer than the actual fillet and wide enough at each side so that it will wrap around the whole fillet. In the middle of this spread half the mushroom pâté. Place the sealed fillet on this and cover with the balance of the mushroom pâté. Remove the cocktail stick!

From the four corners of the pastry cut in at an angle of 45 degrees to the top corners of the fillet and then paint the pastry edges with the glaze. Bring the two end pieces up over the top part of the meat and then the two side pieces. enclosing the fillet quite tightly. Press all edges to seal completely. Roll the fillet over so that the good side is now looking at you. If you have any odd bits of pastry left these can be cut out and glazed on to the top as decorations. Glaze the whole 'sausage' and leave to chill well.

When you wish to cook, preheat the oven to 425°F/220°C/Gas 7 and bake for 35–45 minutes. Leave to rest for 10 minutes and then slice through and serve with a herbed hollandaise (see page 126) or rich brown sauce (see page 130).

Fillet Steak Stuffed with Mushroom Pâté and Fried Garlic

I must admit that I don't normally choose fillet steaks: although they are invariably nice and tender, they lack taste compared to a well-hung rump or sirloin. Buying the whole sirloin of beef on the bone, as we do at Miller Howe, the fillets are carefully cut out and frozen enabling us occasionally to serve our version of the classic *boeuf en croûte* (see previous recipe). However, to ring the changes, I once decided to do the fillet steak portions in the following way, and all sixty-eight diners on the first occasion gave them the thumbs-up signal when I went round the tables. And I must admit I heartily devoured mine along with the rest of the staff at staff supper time. It's a good dish for a dinner party as it is all prepared way in advance.

Be as generous or as mean as you like when cutting the fillet into steaks. A 5–6 oz (150–175 g) steak is quite adequate!

Per person

1 whole garlic clove
milk
oil
butter
1 fillet steak
1 tablespoon mushroom pâté (see page 40)
1 rasher streaky smoked bacon, rinded

1 round 3 inch (7.5 cm) croûton (see page 72)
béarnaise or rich brown sauce (see pages 128 and 130)

Garnish (optional)
2–3 turned, cooked mushrooms

Top and tail the clove of garlic and peel it. Leave to soak for a few hours in a little milk, then strain, dry and brown in a little oil and butter.

Remove any strips of gristle and fat from each fillet steak and then make a neat incision in one side. Open up a small gap into which you can press the mushroom pâté and the whole clove of fried garlic.

Place each bacon rasher flat on your wooden work board and stretch and flatten it with a small knife. Wrap it right round the fillet steak and fix it in place with two wooden cocktail sticks pushed through to form a cross.

Seal the steaks – no more than two at a time – on both sides in the frying pan with a little more butter and oil. Remove and place on a baking tray. All this can be done well in advance.

When you want to cook and serve, preheat the oven to 475°F/240°C/Gas 9. Cook the steaks for only 15 minutes, slipping the croûtons and mushrooms (if using) in for the last 5 minutes or so. Have a pair of pliers handy as these make short work of removing the cocktail sticks. Place the steak on top of the warmed croûton, top with the mushrooms if using, and serve with a sauce of choice.

Fillets of Beef, Lamb and Pork Roasted in Bacon

This is very good indeed served hot with a rich brown sauce or hollandaise (see pages 130 and 126), but is superb cold as picnic fare, as long as you take along a wooden board and a sharp knife for slicing. You need an obliging butcher before you contemplate this dish as he has to sort out the little lamb fillets which are so sweet and succulent.

Serves 4 generously, or 6 meanly!

1 lb (450 g) good smoked bacon, rinded
1 fillet of beef, weighing about 1½ lb (675 g) and measuring approximately 10 inches (25 cm), well trimmed

1 full pork fillet, usually weighing about 8 oz (225 g) and measuring just over 8 inches (20 cm) in length
2 little lamb fillets, about 3–4 oz (75–100 g) each

Preheat the oven to 425°F/220°C/Gas 7.

Draw an imaginary line down your work surface and, using this as the 'middle', arrange the slices of bacon, thin ends to the centre and fat ends to the outside. Place the beef fillet along this middle line. If the tail end is *very* thin, simply lap this over to give you a fairly even-sized sausage-shaped fillet. Along the top of this, place the pork fillet and then along the side of this the two lamb fillets. You want to have a fairly even sausage shape from the four pieces of meat. The thick ends of the bacon are then brought up and over, making a lattice-like container. Stud the whole thing with about 30 wooden cocktail sticks to keep it in shape.

Place in a roasting tin and roast in the preheated oven for about 45–60 minutes. Remove, place on a warmed serving plate, and remove the cocktail sticks. Carve, and serve the interesting slices, thick or thin, with a sauce of choice and a selection of vegetables.

Steak Tartare

I will always remember the look of horror on the face of a new member of staff when confronted with this dish in a local restaurant. At the end of each season, the kitchen staff are taken out to a local hostelry for a 'Dutch' party, and on this particular occasion the Porthole was the venue. The six of us were hell-bent on a good night out and consumed a bottle of wine while studying the delightful menu. Young Richard decided to go for steak tartare. In a polite and quiet aside, I asked, 'You do know what it is, don't you?' to be heatedly told, 'Of course I do!' Not true, readers, as when his eyes fell on the plate of minced raw steak, they grew to the size of the egg yolk beautifully placed in the well in the centre of the steak! I couldn't resist saying, 'You knew what it was, so what's the problem – get on and eat it.' And eat it he did, but with such anguish.

It is not a dish that is served at Miller Howe, but at least once a year I serve it at home, using up a few tail ends of fillet from the hotel, and it is also extremely nice spooned on to small round croûtons for pre-dinner canapés.

Per main course portion

5 oz (150 g) tail end of beef fillet, all
  gristle and fat meticulously removed
2 anchovy fillets
a pinch of salt
1 egg yolk
1 teaspoon prepared mustard of choice
4 teaspoons good olive oil
1 teaspoon red wine vinegar
a liberal dash of Worcestershire sauce (in
  fact I like a *lot*)

a meagre dash of Tabasco (watch it, 'it
  ain't half hot')
1 dessertspoon cooking brandy
1 tablespoon small fine capers
1 tablespoon finely chopped parsley
final seasoning to taste (some put a little
  tomato paste in, others crushed garlic)

Mince the fillet steak finely and put to one side. Pound the anchovy fillets to a paste
with the salt in a pestle and mortar. Combine the egg yolk with the mustard, oil,
vinegar, sauces and brandy, and mix into the meat with the pounded anchovies.
Good restaurants do all this in front of your very eyes – which is why it's often quite
expensive – and when it's done, a sample morsel should be handed to you in a half
egg shell for tasting and for comments. (I invariably need more Worcestershire
sauce.) Fold in the capers and parsley, season to taste, and serve on a simple green
salad lightly dressed with walnut oil.

Roast Loin of Veal with Bacon Bits and Leek Sauce

Serves 6

2 tablespoons olive oil
2 oz (50 g) butter
3 lb (1.4 kg) loin of veal, boned and
  rolled
3 leeks, trimmed and diced

$\frac{1}{4}$ pint (150 ml) Noilly Prat
6 rashers smoked bacon, rinded and
  diced
$\frac{1}{4}$ pint (150 ml) double cream

Preheat the oven to 375°F/190°C/Gas 5.

In a small roasting tin on top of the stove heat the oil and then melt the butter.
Heat until spitting, and seal the loin all over evenly. Put the tin with the meat into
the preheated oven and cook, uncovered, for 30 minutes, basting occasionally.

Take out of the oven and scatter the diced leeks underneath the loin along with
the Noilly Prat. Return the tin to the oven and cook for a further 45 minutes,
basting frequently. Turn off the oven, remove the veal and wrap it in a loose
covering of foil. Return to the oven.

Meanwhile, fry the bacon dice until crisp, then strain off fat (use this for further
frying). Add double cream to the leeks in the veal roasting tin and simply bring up
to the boil.

To serve, slice the veal, cover individual portions with sauce, and sprinkle with
bacon bits.

Escalopes of Veal, Turkey or Chicken

If there are just four for your dinner party, it is an easy task to prepare and cook escalopes. They cook so quickly – virtually only 5 minutes each is needed – so if you use two frying pans which can take two escalopes at a time, it will take 5 minutes, not too long in the middle of an intimate party. Time to serve the next wine and to chat and maybe stir-fry a few vegetables too!

Escalopes can be bought prepared but it is cheaper – and sometimes I think better – to prepare them yourself. The slices should be cut at an angle *across* the grain with a very sharp, thin, stainless steel knife as this will produce a larger slice. A good portion should weigh from 5–6 oz (150–175 g). If you want to use a chicken breast or fillet of veal, cut into thicker pieces weighing about 5 oz (150 g) each, and then slice two-thirds of the way through them. Open them up like a book to form one piece (which you will pound down and out). If you are using small pieces of chicken or veal, flatten them out carefully, individually, and then overlap them and pound them together. When they are cooked, they will look just like one large piece, believe me. Trim the escalopes of all sinews and fat.

To pound and flatten the escalopes, lay them out on your sturdy work surface. I use as a pounder the flat end of a thick rolling pin, and it should be quite damp as this stops the meat splitting. You must always pound *flat*: if your pounder is at an angle you can tear the meat. Personally I like to place the escalopes between oiled sheets of cling film but purists say the oil flavour can come through.

Some people query the breading of this type of food. Well, it is essential to protect the thin slivers of lean meat from drying out during the actual cooking. And any old breadcrumbs *will not do*. Always use fresh, brown or white as you fancy – the savoury breadcrumbs on page 106 are delicious.

I usually arrange three lipped baking trays with sieved seasoned flour in the first, lightly beaten egg in the second and breadcrumbs in the third. Lift up your escalope and gently and lightly coat each side first with flour, then egg and finally breadcrumbs. Transfer immediately to good squares of greaseproof paper, and pile them up. This can be done earlier in the morning, but they are never the same if done too far in advance.

Fry in equal parts of hot oil and butter in the two frying pans and serve immediately.

Traditionally olives wrapped in anchovies are used as a garnish for veal escalopes. Place them on a slice of lemon. For turkey or chicken escalopes, I use strips of tongue wrapped round a seeded grape.

Roast Leg of Lamb with Coriander

Everybody still likes to be served the leg of Lakeland lamb baked with herbs in hay – done every week at Miller Howe when autumn arrives – but coriander goes so well with lamb that this is almost as popular.

Serves 8

1 leg of lamb, about 6–7 lb (about 3 kg) in weight, trimmed of surplus fat
4 oz (100 g) soft butter
4 tablespoons coriander seeds, coarsely crushed
2 teaspoons sea salt
freshly ground black pepper

onion skins, carrot peelings and parsley stalks

To serve
rich brown sauce (see page 130)
watercress

Preheat the oven to 450°F/230°C/Gas 8, and criss-cross the top skin of the leg with a sharp knife to make small diamonds. Rub the soft butter all over, and then dab the crushed coriander seeds down into this. Sprinkle the salt and a good generous grinding of pepper over the leg.

Put the onion skins, carrot peelings and parsley stalks on the base of the roasting tin, and lay the leg down on these, fat side up. Put into the preheated oven and cook for 2 hours, basting every 30 minutes. After this time, your meat will be devoid of blood, very flavoursome, and with a lovely crisp skin. Serve with rich brown sauce, garnished with sprigs of watercress.

Barnsley Chops

A Barnsley chop is my very favourite grilled meat. I am always tickled pink by the comprehensive menu at the RAC Club in Pall Mall; it is painstakingly written in French – with a very faint line saying 'English translation available on request' – apart from, leaping out at you, the simple words, 'Grilled Barnsley Chops'! These are double chops, cut through the whole loin, often with the kidney attached. Good for a barbecue.

Serves 6

6 double lamp chops, about 1¼ inches (3 cm) thick

Marinade
2½ fl oz (75 ml) each of white wine, lemon juice, olive oil and Noilly Prat
2 tablespoons runny honey

2 tablespoons each of fresh rosemary leaves and finely chopped mint

Any good day — rarer than ever recently — has me setting up the table on the patio at Brantlea, and lighting the barbecue: I serve marinated sirloin steaks, chicken breasts and kebabs, along with minty, buttery new potatoes and an enormous seasonal salad.

*A spectacular way in which to present a fresh fruit salad
for a summer buffet party — in a sculpted watermelon basket.
Don't forget to use the luscious red flesh in the salad.*

Lemon chiffon pie can be made in a square or round tin,
but always decorate it attractively — here with piped whipped cream,
lemon and lime wedges and mint leaves, and a strawberry
in the middle.

*A pyramid of choux pastry puffs makes a breathtaking
centrepiece for a buffet party: build up the tiers with whipped cream
(and a discreet use of wooden cocktail sticks), and decorate colourfully
with strawberries and mint leaves.*

Trim the chops well, and mix the marinade ingredients together. Leave the chops in the marinade for 4–5 days, turning daily.

When you wish to cook, turn the grill up to its very highest and grill the chops for about 4–6 minutes on each side, according to taste. Use tongs to turn them over. Serve with something like mashed swede and baked potato rings (see page 168).

Marinated Loin of Lamb with Redcurrant and Caper Sauce

We never cook spring lamb at Miller Howe as I am always disappointed with the flavour. But come the late summer and early autumn this is what I like to do with maturer loins (some might call it mutton!). Ask your butcher to take the well-hung loin off the bone, but keep the bones to make a sauce.

Serves 6

1 loin of lamb, 2 lb (900 g) in weight off
   the bone

Marinade
3 tablespoons French mustard
1 tablespoon dried rosemary
1 tablespoon olive oil
1 tablespoon soy sauce
a pinch of ground ginger
1 garlic clove, peeled and crushed

Sauce
rich brown sauce (see page 130)
redcurrant jelly
a few capers

To serve
6 × 3 inch (7.5 cm) croûtons (see page
   72)
freshly chopped parsley or mint

Trim the meat well and spread it out flat in a dish. Bring together the marinade ingredients in a liquidiser; it will be a thick orange-brown sauce which has to be taken out with the help of a spatula. Coat this all over the meat side of the loin, cover the dish with cling film and leave in the fridge for at least 3 days – up to 5 is better. Keep turning and wiping the marinade well in, at least twice a day.

Meanwhile, make the rich brown basic sauce.

When you wish to cook the 'tournedos', preheat the oven to 475°F/240°C/Gas 9. Take the loin out of the marinade, tuck in the two outer end bits and roll the loin up tight into the shape of a sausage. Cut into six thick 'tournedos' steaks, securing them tightly with two cocktail sticks stuck through like a cross. Place on a baking tray and roast in the preheated oven for a maximum of 10 minutes, turning them over after 4 minutes. Remove the cocktail sticks.

Meanwhile, heat the basic sauce through, adding some redcurrant jelly and capers to taste at the last minute. Warm the croûtons through briefly then dip one side in melted redcurrant jelly and then into the finely chopped parsley or mint. Serve the individual tournedos on a decorated croûton with the sauce.

Roast Loin of Pork
Cooked on the Bone

Most people crave for roast pork with crisp crackling skin, and this is easily obtained only if the full loin of pork has been well hung (for up to 2 weeks by your butcher), and has never seen the inside of a freezer.

Serves 6–8

1 piece loin of pork on the bone, about
   3½ lb (1.5 kg) in weight
onion skins, parsley stalks and carrot
   peelings

salt
freshly ground black pepper

This weight of joint will give eight good-sized pork chops. Get your butcher to 'nick' the chop bones through slightly and to score the skin well. If he hasn't done the latter, a Stanley knife from a good ironmonger does the job. Preheat the oven well to 450°F/230°C/Gas 8.

   Put the onion skins and other vegetable trimmings into the base of your roasting tin, and place the pork on top, skin upwards. Sprinkle salt and a little freshly ground black pepper on the skin. Roast, without basting, and the pork will be done to a turn in an hour.

   To serve, cut into chops, and place each on individual plates, on a portion of warmed Calvados apple purée (see page 133), if you like, instead of serving with a conventional apple sauce.

Braised Pork Chops with Tomato
and Mustard Cream Sauce

This dish is easy, delicious and rich. Start preparing it well in advance – for from 2–4 days – as the meat has to be well marinated. Never throw away the marinade in which the meat is cooked – use it to enhance a soup.

Serves 6

6 pork chops, trimmed, about 1 inch
   (2.5 cm) thick
salt
freshly ground black pepper
1 bottle dry white wine
3 tablespoons olive oil
2 oz (50 g) butter
6 fresh sage leaves

To serve
tomato and mustard cream sauce (see
   page 128)
6 gherkin fans (see page 102)

Put the pork chops in one layer on the base of a casserole and sprinkle liberally with salt and pepper. Cover with the white wine and leave for up to 4 days in the fridge.

Preheat the oven to 300°F/150°C/Gas 2. Take the chops out of the marinade and dry well. Heat the oil in a large frying pan and then melt the butter. Seal the chops, two at a time, on both sides before returning to the wine in the casserole. Add the sage, cover, and place the casserole in the preheated oven. Bake for about 2 hours. Take the lid off, turn the oven up to 350°F/180°C/Gas 4 and cook for a further 30 minutes.

Remove the sage from the chops, and serve them up, drained, on individual heated plates. Coat with the warmed sauce and garnish with the gherkin fan.

Braised Pork Chops with Dill and Turmeric Sauce

This recipe is almost exactly the same as the one above, except that, of course, it has a different sauce. Marinate, seal and braise the chops exactly as in the previous recipe, but omitting the sage. When they are done, remove the chops from the casserole, wrap loosely in foil and return to the warm oven.

Transfer the juices from the casserole to a saucepan and simmer swiftly, uncovered, until reduced by half. Beat in $\frac{1}{4}$ pint (150 ml) double cream, 2 tablespoons freshly chopped dill and 1 tablespoon turmeric. Warm through and serve with the chops.

·Miller Howe· Vegetables and Salads

Having recently written a whole book on vegetables (my *Feast of Vegetables*, published in 1985), it would be silly to repeat here all the recipes printed in that. Therefore I'm just going to give you *ideas*, the basics of Miller Howe thinking about vegetables, plus a few new recipes which have come along since then. The same is true of the salad section where I give a virtual listing of the ingredients which can be used in salads.

VEGETABLES

At Miller Howe I still try to mix various flavourings and textures with vegetables, and as it is comparatively easy there to cook everything off at the last minute (one person alone is responsible for this task), each main course goes out into the restaurant on the plain white plates surrounded by six small portions of different fresh seasonal vegetables and one kind of potato. At home I used to think it clever to pre-cook vegetables and use a Hostess trolley to keep them warm, but having realised how simple it is to cook diced root vegetables, to reheat purées and to deep-fry coated prepared vegetables – all virtually as you are about to arrange the main course on the plates – my entertaining pattern at home has now become more Miller Howeish with vegetables. There's no reason, therefore, why your own approach to vegetables shouldn't be like that as well!

Fresh, however, is a must with vegetables, and 'seasonal' should be your guideline. Just as a Christmas strawberry never tastes the same as those flavourful English ones we enjoy in June, so a vegetable that is patently *out* of season will never be as good – or as cheap! Our sense of seasons, of course, has been knocked haywire by all the imports – but always use your eye and your judgement, picking out your own individual items whenever possible. Avoid all those vegetables that are packed in plastic bags; not only do they sweat, thereby losing a lot of their goodness, but there could be the odd bad one lurking in the middle.

As a general rule, *small* is usually best. Smaller vegetables are younger, therefore tastier and more tender, and of course they'll cook more quickly. If the vegetables are larger, they should be cut into even-sized pieces so that they will all cook evenly. You can also cut them into different shapes – dice, strips, turned chunks, chips or balls cut with a Parisian scoop. This can make vegetables look very much more interesting. Grated vegetables – done on an old-fashioned metal grater, not in a machine – take only seconds to cook, and it is these that most appeal to me these days when entertaining.

Try not to prepare *too* far in advance: this would help a lot when entertaining, I know, but a lot of goodness escapes when vegetables are cut.

To accompany a main course, you usually need 6 oz (175 g) of *prepared* vegetables. You can work out your own permutations from that but, just to clarify, if you plan to serve three vegetables, you will need 2 oz (50 g) of each vegetable per person. And do remember that as far as both health and flavour are concerned, *under*cooked is better than *over*cooked, so apply that rule to all your vegetable cooking from now on, and your family and dinner-party guests will all benefit and appreciate.

• *Boiled and Steamed Vegetables* •

For both you need lots of simmering salted water. Plunge the vegetable pieces to be boiled into the water and time from when the water comes back to the boil again. In general, batches of vegetable pieces, of 1 lb (450 g) in total, will cook crisp in 4 minutes, firm in 5, and soft in 6. It's really more of a blanching in most cases than what we understand as boiling. Drain well and serve immediately, or warm through with some plain or flavoured butter. Delicious baby carrots with the little green top ends still on (this gives colour and a contrast in texture) can be boiled crisp in minutes, drained and then tossed in hot butter with a little sugar. Older maincrop carrots, sliced, can also be par-boiled then 'glazed' in butter and a little sugar with many flavourings added – ground caraway seeds and lemon, thyme, marjoram, fresh lime juice, ground coriander (from your mill), ginger and a sprinkling of Pernod (one of my more successful recent discoveries). Those very thin imported French beans (commonly referred to these days as Kenyan Frenchies!) can be cooked crisp in 2 minutes; after refreshing (and perhaps leaving aside for a while), they can be heated through in seasoned butter (with extra freshly ground black pepper) in another couple of minutes.

Many vegetables can be served with a sauce as appropriate – hollandaise, béarnaise, cheese, mustard and most cream sauces. Broccoli florets, for instance, are delicious with a little hollandaise.

Steamed vegetables should be placed in a colander *over* the simmering salted water, and in general steaming takes slightly longer than boiling as the heat is neither so direct nor so intense. Serve as above.

• *Puréed Vegetables* •

Purées are very useful, and they can be made the day before and then simply heated through for about 15–20 minutes in a double saucepan or a bain-marie on top of the hob. Cook 1 lb (450 g) evenly sliced vegetable in simmering salted water until soft, then drain. Dry out well over the heat with 1 oz (25 g) butter, then liquidise with $\frac{1}{4}$

pint (150 ml) single cream. Pass through a sieve into your container, and cover with a butter paper.

You can add seasonings to individual purées: ground ginger is good with carrot, curry powder with celeriac, nutmeg with parsnips, horseradish or honey with swede, lots of black pepper with turnip, and ground hazelnuts add bulk and flavour to a broad bean purée, for instance. Decorate purées on the plates with things like toasted pine kernels, diced red pepper, chopped or sliced nuts, chopped herbs, crispy bacon bits (see page 99), desiccated coconut and lemon twirls (see page 100).

Other vegetables that can be puréed are peas, parsnips, asparagus, Brussels sprouts, cauliflower and, of course, potato. Spinach purée, used several times as a garnish or sauce throughout the book, is prepared rather differently. Wash and stalk 3 lb (1.4 kg) spinach leaves and tear up into small pieces. Cook in 2 oz (50 g) butter until soft and 'shrunken' (about 8 minutes), then pass through a sieve. Cook the purée in another 2 oz (50 g) butter for about 5 minutes. Add salt, freshly ground pepper and grated nutmeg to taste. This too can be prepared earlier in the day, and takes 12–15 minutes to reheat in a double saucepan, bowl over simmering water or bain-marie.

• *Stir-Fried Vegetables* •

This is easy and quick, and all you basically need are one or two frying pans. As the roast is resting – or your guests are, between courses – you can stir-fry prepared vegetables in less than 5 minutes. Use a good oil and some butter – 1 tablespoon oil and 1 oz (25 g) butter for a 9 inch (22.5 cm) pan; 2 tablespoons oil to 1½ oz (40 g) butter for an 11 inch (27.5 cm) pan; and 3 tablespoons oil to 2 oz (50 g) butter for a 12 inch (30 cm) pan. Experiment with different oils and butters: a virgin olive is wonderful, but try stir-frying in walnut or hazelnut oils, or one of the oils you can 'make' at home, the garlic, ginger and herb oils mentioned on page 138. And a flavoured butter (see page 108) could be used instead of plain. A favourite mixture of mine for stir-frying is sesame oil and raspberry vinegar – ½ pint (300 ml) sesame oil to 2 tablespoons raspberry vinegar. And don't forget about those old favourites, the bacon and duck fats left over and stored from your grilling and roasting respectively.

Tiny courgettes – wiped, topped and tailed and scored three times – can be stir-fried whole in about 3 minutes: the scored edges 'catch' to give a buttery, nigh burned flavour. Scored slices can be stir-fried in about the same time, flavoured with a little Marsala, and topped with toasted flaked almonds. Tiny broccoli florets are delicious quickly stir-fried in sesame oil or bacon fat, as are cauliflower florets, and you could finish these off with a generous grinding of coriander from your mill. Small mangetouts can be topped, tailed and left in the fridge in a bowl of ice earlier on in the day; drained, they can be stir-fried crisp and warm in a mixture of oil and butter in 2–3 minutes. My cabbage recipes are usually baked, but if you like cabbage crisp (as I do), it too can be stir-fried in a few minutes: try frying it with a ground mixture of juniper berries and garlic, with lemon juice and rind and fresh mint, or fried in bacon fat with chopped sweet gherkin.

It is the grated stir-fried vegetables that I like most though. Always wipe or peel the veg first as appropriate and grate into bowls (or store in polythene bags in the fridge if you want to prepare them earlier in the day). The following go well together:

beetroot	orange rind and juice and walnut oil
carrots	fresh lemon or orange juice and walnut oil (try adding some grated radishes too)
celeriac	a touch of yoghurt and horseradish (adding chopped walnuts and sultanas as a final garnish), or walnut oil and chopped walnuts as garnish
courgettes	rind and juice of lemon, lime or orange
kohlrabi	chopped preserved ginger
potato	bacon fat with diced baked bacon
turnip	a touch of white wine and ground caraway seeds

• *Deep-Fried Vegetables* •

These too can be prepared in the morning, and once the deep-fryer is preheated to 360°F/182°C, they take minutes to cook brown and crisp.

Most, however, need some sort of coating to protect them from the high temperature of deep-frying. You need to soak them in milk or, occasionally, beaten egg, then coat with seasoned or curried flour. For the latter, use roughly 1 teaspoon curry powder to 4 tablespoons flour – but you can experiment with proportions to find what you like. Some vegetables can be coated in a batter.

Aubergine chips (after salting to get rid of sour juices) can be battered and deep-fried, as can courgette chips or circles, and onion rings; carrot chips, marrow balls, kohlrabi matchsticks, and scored courgette slices can be soaked in milk then tossed in seasoned flour. The curried flour coating is delicious for salsify and celery strips, but my own particular favourite is leek rings. Top and tail leeks and remove outer leaves, then slice through at an angle to give an *oval* rather than a circle. Leave to soak in milk then drain, toss in curried flour and deep-fry. They are extraordinarily flavoursome.

• *Roast Vegetables* •

Parsnips can be cubed and roasted in dripping at 400°F/200°C/Gas 6 for 15 minutes, but it is mainly potatoes that we roast brown and crisp. Our fanned roast potatoes are particularly popular: cut into medium potatoes several times like a cockscomb, but keeping the bottom uncut. Separate the cuts slightly using a wooden cocktail stick, and then paint inside the cut edges with walnut oil. Roast as usual for about an hour at 375°F/190°C/Gas 5. They are quite delicious.

Potatoes Baked with Cream, Hazelnuts and Cheese

This is an old favourite – a very fattening one too – but lent a magnificently different taste by the addition of ground hazelnuts.

Serves 6

about 1½ lb (675 g) potatoes, peeled
sea salt
½ pint (300 ml) double cream

about 2 tablespoons ground hazelnuts
2–3 oz (50–75 g) Cheddar cheese, grated
chopped parsley

Choose smallish potatoes, or 'turn' them so that all the potatoes are of the same size, roughly 2½ inches (6 cm) in length. Cover with cold water and bring to the boil with the salt. Simmer for 5 minutes only then drain well. Place in a casserole dish, and pour in the cream mixed with the ground hazelnuts. The cream should come half-way up the sides of the potatoes. Cover the top of the potatoes and cream with the grated cheese.

Bake in the preheated oven at 375°F/190°C/Gas 5 for about 45 minutes. Remove from the oven and sprinkle lavishly with parsley.

Baked Potato Rings

Whenever faced with a Lancashire hotpot I (like you!) tend to save the really well-done top potato slices for myself, but this recipe will enable all your guests to enjoy this luxury.

Serves about 6

6 medium potatoes, peeled
butter
1 egg

salt
freshly ground black pepper

Slice the peeled potatoes very, very thinly through to form circles rather than ovals. Place the circles into a bowl of ice-cold water and leave for an hour.

Generously paint baking tray(s) with melted butter, drain the potato circles and dry well on kitchen paper. Arrange overlapping circles into small rings, to your required size. Using a 1 inch (2.5 cm) paint brush, coat the circles liberally and, more important still, *evenly*, with a mixture of the egg beaten with 2 oz (50 g) melted seasoned butter, and leave to one side.

When you wish to cook them, preheat the oven well to 375°F/190°C/Gas 5, and put the trays in. The potato rings will take 15–20 minutes to come out lovely and brown. If you use a fish slice which goes under them sharply, it is a relatively simple task to get the rings off the tray; if necessary a gentle push with a finger will slide them off the slice and on to the plate.

Highly Herbed Carrot and Potato Cake

This is a new and delicious vegetable cake recipe. If sliced into small enough wedges, it looks good served with a variety of other vegetables with a main course.

Serves 8–12

butter
1 lb (450 g) potatoes, peeled
salt
freshly ground black pepper
6 oz (175 g) onion, peeled and finely chopped

1 tablespoon olive oil
8 oz (225 g) carrots, grated
2 level tablespoons finely chopped mixed fresh herbs

Butter an 8 inch (20 cm) loose-bottomed flan tin, and preheat the oven to 375°F/190°C/Gas 5.

Slice the potatoes crosswise extremely thinly, and spread half the slices over the greased base of the flan. Season well with salt and pepper. Fry the onion in a mixture of 1 oz (25 g) butter and the oil until golden, then combine with the grated carrots and chopped herbs. Press this mixture down on to the potatoes and season again. Place a further topping of thinly sliced potatoes on top of the carrot mixture, and brush with melted butter.

Bake in the preheated oven for 30 minutes. Test to see if the potatoes are cooked with the sharp end of a knife. Remove sides from the flan tin and return the cake to the oven for a further 5 minutes. Simply slice as you would a sponge cake and move to serving plates using a palette knife.

Savoury Aubergine Slice

Another new vegetable dish – and it's simplicity itself.

Serves 6

1 medium aubergine, wiped
salt
$\frac{1}{2}$ pint (300 ml) tomato juice

3 oz (75 g) savoury breadcrumbs (see page 106)

Slice the aubergine widthwise into $\frac{1}{4}$ inch (6 mm) circles, and arrange in one layer on a wire cooling tray. Sprinkle with salt, cover loosely and leave to stand for an hour. Turn the slices over and repeat the process so that all the bitter juices run out. Dry off well with kitchen paper.

Poach the slices in the tomato juice for 10 minutes until they are softening and beginning to take up the colour of the juice. Leave in the juice to go cold.

When you wish to serve the aubergine, preheat the oven to 350°F/180°C/Gas 4. Using a slotted spoon remove the slices to a buttered baking tray and lay flat in one layer. Top each slice with savoury breadcrumbs and warm through for 15 minutes.

SEASONAL SALADS

These dishes served at Miller Howe sound, when reading the dinner menu, dull to say the least. But once confronted with them as a starter to a meal, and having devoured the tasty morsels, guests tend to offer more complimentary comments than is the norm. They are relatively inexpensive to prepare, but very labour intensive. However, when preparing them at home, the mere fact that practically everything can be done the day before and stored in the fridge, then simply 'brought together' at the last minute makes them top of my list for parties.

Outrageously daring as I am at times, I now seriously attempt to stun the palate with a galaxy of tastes and textures – and it works. Quite apart from the wonderful green and varied salad leaves now readily available at most of the upmarket supermarkets, fruit, nuts, bacon, vegetables, pâtés, chutneys, duck skin, pork crackling, chicken and duck livers, leftover chicken or game can all be used to good effect. Various dressings – served both hot and cold – can also delight the palate (see pages 136–7). You could tease the palate even further by using two different dressings on one salad.

These salads look best in the Miller Howe fashion served either on small side plates, individual wooden salad bowls, old-fashioned fruit or pudding bowls, or small glass dishes. But at home you could, of course, make up one large salad from which your guests can help themselves. Use a large flattish dish rather than a deep bowl for the best effect, and serve either as a starter, or as an accompaniment to the main course. Whatever you use as the container, the effect is heightened if you provide a plate to go under it, perhaps with a doyley, but always decorated with a fern leaf or some greenery from the garden, plus a small flower. Remember, if you've got it, flaunt it! And have a look at the photograph opposite page 49 to see what I mean.

I have not given a recipe as such, as it all depends on what is available seasonally or locally, but I hope that the following listing of potential ingredients will stir your imagination and whet your appetite. All salads are made in the same way, rather like a flower arrangement, with the basic structure first, followed by the decorative or 'filling-in' elements.

First wipe the container or containers with the oil of your choice – the good olive oil you will use in your dressing, or a nut oil – and then rub a skinned and halved clove of garlic around the inside, on top of the oil. Grind on a little black pepper and/or coriander, and be pretty generous with chopped seasonal fresh herbs (*never* dried ones). Tear your basic salad leaves up and scatter round the base. You can then use a twirl of cheese and herb pâté (see page 39) as the centre to hold the apple wedges, French beans or whatever, to build up a very small pyramid of goodies. No real artistic flair is necessary, but I think you will be surprised and pleased with the result – both visually and gastronomically.

• Salad Leaves •

These should form the base of your salad, and you can choose from any of the wondrous variety available nowadays. There are many lettuces – Cos, round,

Webbs, iceberg or crispheart or the colourful oakleaf – and Chinese leaves. Don't forget about spinach and sorrel leaves which make delicious salad greens (but don't use *too* many of the sorrel as they are bitter in quantity). Use endive leaves, white chicory or leaves of the red chicory known as radiccio. Watercress could be a base, or a decoration, as could mustard and cress or beansprouts. If you can get hold of some of the more unusual greens such as lamb's lettuce (corn salad), rocket or purslane, they make delicious salads – as do the more mundane leaves of young dandelions.

• *Apple Wedges* •

Rarely does a guest at Miller Howe recognise the apple marinade, so quite apart from anything else, this is a good start to a meal as it gets your guests guessing! Finely grate the rind of 2 limes into your dish and then add the juice. With a damp cloth wipe the apple(s) – preferably Granny Smiths – clean, and then cut through the core into four. Remove and discard the cores and seeds, slice the flesh thinly, leaving the lovely green skin on, and marinate for a few hours –a day even – in the pure lime juice, covered with cling film.

• *Asparagus* •

Simply use the flower heads of young asparagus (the stems will make an excellent soup or lovely sauce). Tip the heads into a saucepan of lightly salted boiling water to which you have added a tablespoon of olive oil, and bring back to the boil. Simmer for 3–4 minutes only – I prefer them to be crisp and crunchy. Tip into a strainer and refresh underneath running cold water, and then put out on to a triple thickness of kitchen paper to dry. Paint with fresh lemon juice, French dressing or an oil of your personal choice, and leave covered with cling film.

• *Avocado* •

Half an avocado roughly chopped and left to marinate in a French dressing will scatter sufficiently round eight salads to give just the merest sensation of this delicious fruit.

• *Bananas, Dried* •

I use these mostly in my own home-made muesli (see page 32), but they can be crushed with a rolling pin and sprinkled on to a salad, again providing just that something different. (They're even better sprinkled over a minced meat dish. Italians will groan, but I have even scattered dried bananas over my English version of spaghetti Bolognese.)

• *Beans* •

Dried beans make good additions to the best mixed seasonal salads – and they add protein too. You can soak and then boil any dried bean – I like red kidney beans best, mainly for their colour – but you can also use canned, although they must be drained of their canning juices and well washed and dried before use.

• *Broccoli and Cauliflower Florets* •

Provided you take the time and have the patience to cut the broccoli and cauliflower off the stems (use them in stocks or soups), and then into individual flowers no larger than your fingernails, the effort will be worthwhile. However, they need to be blanched, and I always add a tablespoon of vinegar to the boiling water to impart a tangy flavour – my favourite for both these vegetables (but watch out, it's strong and lethal) is raspberry vinegar.

• *Cape Gooseberries* •

Rather spasmodic deliveries make these an all too rare treat, but they're magnificent in a salad. They're usually coated with a fondant for traditional petits-fours, but I can't for the life of me get the ruddy fondant to stick on! Simply break open the pointed tip of the dry skin casing and peel this back to reveal a glowing round orange fruit. Serve like this, as if it is bursting out of its casing.

• *Carrot and Chopped Ginger* •

Peel the carrots then grate them on the finest grater so the carrot looks like balls of cottonwool rather than chips of wood! Marinate with very finely chopped preserved ginger and ginger syrup.

• *Celery* •

Very finely chopped celery and ground caraway seeds go well together and are unusual. You could also cut celery chunks into twirls (see page 104) for decorating your salads.

• *Cheese* •

Besides using cheese and herb pâté as a central anchor, you can add finely grated strong hard cheeses to contribute both a kick and richness (not for me the cottage cheese with its watery lumps so fashionable on diet-conscious platters).

• *Cherries, Paired* •

Now if you think this is really going overboard, then I must contradict you! Fresh cherries are superb when in season but to serve them to your guests in pairs linked by their stalk immediately makes your guests want to start in and eat them!

• *Coconut, Desiccated* •

Toast this in the oven and sprinkle sparingly on to a salad.

• Cold Meats •

The odd slice of any leftover meats – particularly pork, veal or chicken – can be finely diced and incorporated into your dish.

• Croûtons •

For texture alone these are a *must* in a salad (see page 97), but vary the flavourings by frying in curried or herb butter, or in garlic or ginger oil (see pages 109 and 138). Warm them through if you like prior to scattering on the dish.

• Cucumber •

Not for me a simple sliced cucumber, with or without its skin. I wipe the skin clean with a cloth and then coarsely grate the vegetable on an old-fashioned kitchen grater and combine it with the merest dollop of horseradish cream and a generous grinding of black pepper. Do make sure, however, when you put the gratings into your salad that you try to separate the clinging shreds. Don't have them just in a dollop.

• Currants, Black, Red or White •

I prefer to simply scatter 'branches' of these on top of the salad just before taking to the table, but if you do want to go to the trouble to take them off their stalks, use a silver fork (goodness knows why).

• Duck and Pork Skin •

I occasionally portion a duck using the meat from the legs minced in terrines and then either frying or baking the breasts with the skin removed. In this way I have lots of duck skin over which, when cut into small diamonds and either baked in the oven or fried (if the latter, you have to drain off the fat constantly otherwise the skin gets soggy), can be served hot or cold sprinkled on salads.

Crisp pork crackling can be portioned out likewise in croûton-sized pieces.

• Eggs •

When you wish to serve boiled eggs in this seasonal salad, it is best to cook them – for 8–10 minutes after the cold water comes to the boil – and leave them to go quite cold in a bowl of iced water. Shell them, cut lengthwise in half and put the yolks and whites into separate bowls. Although it is a tedious and fiddly job, the yolks and white should then be grated on a fine grater and scattered over the salad separately – otherwise the white and yellow seem to 'blend' together if the whole eggs are done roughly.

Quails' eggs are the very devil to shell, so I have resorted to poaching them. This takes virtually no time at all, and lets you actually see when the yolks are cooked but still lovely and soft! An egg poacher pan with the little 'saucers' normally used for hen eggs will be fine. Get the water boiling in the base and put the merest touch of butter into each saucer. Break the eggs, one at a time, into each saucer and by the time you have broken open the fourth the first will just about be ready. Slide them out carefully on to a tray lined with kitchen paper and leave to dry a little.

• *Fennel* •

Trim the bulbs and chop very finely. Use any feathery herb from the top of the bulb.

• *French Beans* •

Use the thin 'Kenyan Frenchies'. Top and tail them first. I usually pick up a dozen in my hand, levelling the ends on the flat top of my work surface, then cut the ends off with a pair of kitchen scissors; I then repeat the exercise on the other end of the beans. This makes an irksome task relatively easy, and is much more economical too. Plunge the beans into boiling salted water, bring back to the boil and cook for 4 minutes. Refresh and drain, and leave for up to 24 hours to marinate in garlic oil (see page 138).

• *Herb Flowers* •

Quite apart from being perfectly delicious to eat, adding yet another flavour to the salad, herb flowers look so good nestling among the dozen or so other ingredients. Marjoram, chive, borage and sage flowers are but four possibilities.

• *Lemon and Orange Rind* •

To add more tang I occasionally put the merest touch of shredded rind on top of the oil used to rub the salad dish or container. This is then covered with the basic salad greens. Remember you are endeavouring to titillate the palate.

• *Lychees and Water Chestnuts* •

Lychees come fresh on the market at various times of the year, but they're both available canned. One of each for every guest – finely chopped – make a remarkable combination not only in flavour but, more important still, in texture. The coarse, chewy, snappy water chestnut is nigh sensual when eaten with the soft silky flesh of the lychee.

• *Mangetouts* •

Serve uncooked. If you can get lovely small ones the size of your little finger, top and tail them and try to take the stringy thread off the edges; then force one side open slightly, and pipe in some cheese and herb pâté (see page 39). If they are on the older side – in other words bigger than your thumb and not having the lovely bright green colour – top, tail and string and then shred very finely. Leave in a tray or tin and add some ice cubes; cover with cling film and chill. Dry well prior to putting into the salad.

• *Mushrooms, Gingered* •

Use only the tiny baby button mushroom caps (the stalks can be fried in bacon fat for breakfast, or used in soup or mushroom pâté). Quickly sauté them in ginger oil (see page 138), and then dry well on kitchen paper and leave to go cold.

• *Nuts* •

A larger and larger choice is now available in health-food and other specialist shops. Any are good used discreetly in a salad but try also the curried nuts on page 77.

• *Orange Segments* •

See page 101 for details of how to do these. They are tasty, refreshing and enhance any salad.

• *Pine Kernels* •

These are obtained from health-food shops and gourmet counters and, although they may seem expensive, they are used so sparingly and weigh so light that they are a good investment. They should, in my opinion, always be toasted first, as this actually brings out the flavour. When you have your oven on for something else at 350°F/180°C/Gas 4, simply scatter a handful of the kernels on a baking tray and put in the oven for about 10 minutes. Bring them out, leave to go cold, and then keep in a screw-top jar or container. Quite apart from being of use in salads they are delicious on several vegetable purées (parsnip in particular), and are very nibblish with drinks before dinner (especially if mixed with crispy bacon bits, see page 99).

• *Pineapple Dice* •

Slice pineapple very, very finely and then chop into minute dice. You don't have to use a lot to provide that certain 'hint' of flavouring to your salad.

• *Radishes* •

A couple of radish flowers or one alone in the middle (see page 103) gives a salad a centre point, but if you finely slice or chop radishes, the flecks of red and white flesh add colour and interest.

• *Raspberries and Strawberries* •

Four raspberries put N, S, E and W on the completed salad are delicious, quite apart from adding a singing colour. Alpine or wild strawberries can be used in the same way. Ordinary strawberries should be sliced into four, with the stalks left on, and then used as above.

• *Salami* •

Finely grate chunks of salami by hand on a kitchen grater then spread out on a tray to dry (use the warming oven of your cooker or airing cupboard for about 8 hours). The oily spicy taste will intrigue when the pieces are sprinkled around the salad.

• *Sesame Seeds* •

Sesame seeds 'toasted' – as the pine kernels – can be sprinkled around the salad when everything else has been arranged, and add interest for the eye and for the palate.

• *Spring Onions* •

The green stems may be wiped and then cut very very finely with kitchen scissors. The white bulb can simply be sliced through as finely as possible. It might help if you push the outside prong of a fork through the bulb at the root end to hold it steady and save nicking your fingers. Spring onion twirls are good as well.

• *Tomatoes* •

If you can get hold of the new cherry tomatoes, leave the stalks on and simply serve whole. You might be able to find an even newer strain called grape tomatoes; then you are lucky indeed for these little clusters will bring gasps of pleasure from your guests. Otherwise slice or serve vandyked halves.

Soured cream apple pecan pie is a delicious new pudding,
and the puff pastry cream cornets — here with whipped cream,
kiwi slices and strawberries — are as popular for afternoon
tea as for dessert.

A honey wheatmeal pancake — which can also be served as a starter
— is here served as a pudding with whipped cream, strawberries, cucumber
and mint leaves, with a burned icing sugar pattern on top.

Guests staying at Miller Howe have almost been bribing me
● *to get the recipe for this chocolate orange gâteau — it's the richest* ●
and most delicious of all my chocolate recipes!

A trio of Miller Howe puddings:
top left, *a glass bowl holding three mousses;*
top right, *caramelised apple hazelnut cake;*
and bottom, *St Clement's icebox pudding.*

Miller Howe
· Picnic Lunches and ·
Occasional Barbecues

Because we serve a good rib-sticking breakfast and a five-course dinner, we tend not to serve lunch at Miller Howe. (It also allows us to get on with all the other things running a hotel and restaurant entail.) However, we do offer a packed lunch which our guests can picnic off somewhere on the fells – or perhaps in their cars if the Lakeland weather is doing its usual! In fact the packed lunches are ideal fodder for travelling, whether by car or train – moveable feasts, rather than a conventional picnic.

We have had barbecues at the hotel on special occasions, but they're more a feature of my home life, whether at Brantlea beside the conservatory, or on the new barbecue patio at the Farm.

——— PACKED LUNCHES ———

Although I say it myself, we get numerous compliments about these, and it does make me blush a little because they are certainly not haute cuisine but mainly simple fare left over from previous meals helped along with salads etc. We use special 'lockers' or boxes which have handy divisions and compartments to contain the goodies. The whole thing is hinged and the object of the exercise is that they open out to be held on the knees (I never find this 100 per cent successful but it's possible!). The photograph opposite page 145 should give you an idea of what they're like – and do please note that none of the food is wrapped as it should be before being packed. Packets of food wrapped in cling film don't look very exciting in photographs!

When we travel to do cooking demonstrations, we invariably take a couple of lunch boxes and feel very superior sitting in the car park of a service station by the side of the motorway. And once when five of us were going down to London to do our annual cooking stint at the Athenaeum Hotel, I decided to take packed lunches rather than suffer the indignities of the then British Rail dining car (much improved of late, I must admit). We felt as if we were part of feeding time at the zoo, as fellow travellers passing along the corridor were stopping and staring with ever-widening eyes!

Apart from the cold meats and salads, which do need particular care, practically everything we serve in these lunch lockers at Miller Howe can be done at home, wrapped in cling film and packed into a plastic bag or a small cardboard box to provide nourishment and pleasure on any journey or picnic. At Miller Howe we tend to serve a selection of things – starters, main courses and puddings – with a piece of fruit and some sweets. Just because you're on the move, it doesn't mean that you can't eat well. The whole idea – and part of the pleasure of the whole occasion – is that the picnic or lunch should be one endless opening up of surprise packages, each one being exciting and delicious.

Triangular sandwiches of smoked salmon or gravadlax and brown bread with a quarter slice of very thin lemon on top make a pleasant starter, and you could also pack a small wedge of melon. Don't simply leave the wedge as it is, but carefully use your sharp knife to separate the flesh from the skin and then cut it through again into nice easily managed wedges. Re-form and once again wrap in cling film. Avocado dipped in lemon juice and then wrapped in Parma ham is good as well. Any leftover pâtés can be piped into choux eclairs or profiteroles, or they go particularly well on a portion of the Cheddar cheese wedges (see page 78). Wedges of cold quiche are good as are slices of a terrine or stuffed red pepper. If you know you are going to need a packed lunch, cook some extra sausages, mushrooms and bacon at breakfast the day before and then, when they're cold, stick them on cocktail sticks to make simple starter kebabs.

Sandwiches are typical fare for moveable feasts, but do always prepare *interesting* ones. Use thinly sliced brown bread and lots of butter (flavoured if you like, see page 108). Try some of the following combinations: prawn and avocado with a lemon dressing; pork with apple sauce and chutney; beef with horseradish and grated celeriac; canned salmon mashed well, seasoned and then layered with thin cucumber slices; good old canned corned beef is delicious enhanced with a good chutney (or mashed baked beans if your store cupboard is devoid of chutney); breast of chicken thickly sliced and coated with cold hollandaise or lightly curried mayonnaise; skinned tomato slices sprinkled with a little caster sugar and then topped with finely chopped celery and fennel; small avocado wedges alternated with fresh pear wedges and orange segments in the merest coating of French dressing. There must be something in your fridge or store cupboard that you can mix together to provide something different. Being a pig I am partial to condensed milk with mashed banana in a sandwich – turn your nose up if you like, but do try it! (Even better if a few raisins or sultanas plumped up in cooking brandy are included as well.)

Personally I prefer sandwiches to be mushy rather than dry, so I always wrap them when prepared in the outer leaves of lettuce and then in cling film. And, I am sorry to say, I always, but always, cut the crusts off.

For a main course for a picnic or lunch box, I would serve cold meats and salads. Try to choose *moist* meats – the beef fillet poached in consommé and a cold chicken breast, cooked and stuffed with something like cheese and herb pâté (see pages 154 and 144) are ideal. I have often taken casseroled meats on a picnic because I know they will be tender, tasty and moist – but the merest smear of redcurrant jelly on a slice of lamb is acceptable, likewise spreading a little apple sauce on pork. Take plates – china or plastic – already arranged with the food, and covered tightly with cling film. Keep them upright. Many of the roast dishes can be taken whole and sliced at the picnic.

For the salad part of the meal, you can take salad ingredients in a plastic bag, and a French dressing in a little screw-topped jar, and put them together at the meal time. Other fancies of mine are root vegetables grated, and whole radishes dipped in a little French dressing and then sea salt. Marinated French beans and mushrooms are good as once again they are slightly wet. And I always take on *my* travels a little home-made aïoli into which to dip things like carrot sticks, strips of pepper or tiny cauliflower florets. I steal those horrendous little milk tubs served in mass-catering establishments to go with your tea or coffee, and empty them to use for my aïoli, covered in cling film.

But I can't wait to get through all this to get on to the puds. Cold sticky toffee pudding (see page 199) is my firm favourite, sliced and filled with cream. It's not sliced the way you think, however. I get my piece of the pudding looking like a slice of fruit cake and cut it in half *lengthwise* so that I can smear lots of whipped cream on and make a sandwich. Individual sponge cakes filled with jam and cream are luscious, and so are rock cakes, shortbread, small individual creamed meringues, tartlets with strawberries and cream, mini puff pastry cornets with mincemeat or jam and cream, leftover farmhouse pie with a spoonful of butterscotch sauce, etc, etc. Use cling film to wrap all these yet again.

A few sweets sweeten me up nicely. Remember, however, to include some wet wipes (or whatever they're called) to clean your sticky hands and do not, whatever you do, pack single- or double-ply napkins. Lash out on the more expensive three-ply or take along a large packet of men's paper tissues. When travelling and eating in the car, I also take an old-fashioned corded travelling toilet bag with a very wet facecloth in it.

And what to drink on your picnic? Because of the drinking and driving laws, we normally take a large flask of soup or coffee. The latter is laced with a very little rum, but heightened with some grated fresh nutmeg. But of course you can take some wine with you – half or quarter bottles are handy.

Ratatouille in French Bread

An ideal – and delicious – 'sandwich' to take on a picnic. Prepare the bread and ratatouille in advance, but bring together just before you set off, and wrap tightly in a double thickness of foil. Take a carving knife and board with you, so that you can portion it out at your destination.

You could also use buttery scrambled eggs as a filling for the French bread – liven it up perhaps with some smoked salmon pieces or red pepper dice.

Serves 6

1 long French loaf
good olive oil
8 oz (225 g) aubergine, wiped
salt
1½ lb (675 g) tomatoes, skinned, seeded
   and roughly chopped
1 teaspoon sugar
6 garlic cloves, peeled

4 tablespoons hazelnut or walnut oil
8 oz (225 g) onions, peeled and finely
   chopped
12 oz (350 g) red peppers, trimmed and
   cut into thin strips
6 oz (175 g) green peppers, as above
8 oz (225 g) baby courgettes, topped,
   tailed and sliced

Slice the French loaf through the middle horizontally and scoop out as much bread as possible with a tablespoon (use the bread for savoury breadcrumbs). Paint the insides of the loaf with olive oil and then bake in an oven preheated to 375°F/190°C/Gas 5 – cut sides upwards – for 20 minutes until quite crisp. Leave to go cold.

Meanwhile make the ratatouille. Cut the aubergine into strips and sprinkle with salt. Leave to drain. Sprinkle the tomatoes with the sugar, and crush the garlic to a paste with 1 teaspoon salt.

Heat half the walnut or hazelnut oil and 2 tablespoons olive oil in a large frying pan and fry the garlic and onion until golden. Add the balance of the walnut oil plus 2 more tablespoons of olive to the pan along with the rinsed and drained aubergine strips and the pepper strips. Cook for 10 minutes over a medium heat, stirring from time to time. Add the tomatoes and sliced courgettes and cook for a further 10 minutes. Leave to go cold.

Put the ratatouille into a colander to strain off the liquid (use in a soup), and then pack into the cold hollowed halves of the French loaf. Wrap tightly in doubled foil.

BARBECUES

As I say in the meat introduction in the main courses chapter, I would never dream of grilling or barbecuing meat until it has been well marinated – for up to 5 days! This means that anything you want to barbecue – be it boned whole shoulders of lamb or legs, meat cut up for kebabs, steaks, chops, chicken breasts, pieces and drumsticks – are all marinated in something delicious for *at least* 24 hours before barbecuing. The only things I like at barbecues that I *don't* marinate beforehand are sausages – and the salmon pieces on page 117.

A flavoured yoghurt can do wonders for many meats, but you can combine anything (within reason) to add flavour. Try one of the following.

Marinade 1

This is a spicy recipe, good for lamb kebabs. Blend all in a liquidiser. Marinate 3 lb (1.4 kg) of boned shoulder cut into 1 inch (2.5 cm) cubes for at least 3 days. It will serve six, if you intersperse the lamb cubes with onion wedges and dried apricots (marinate these too).

$\frac{1}{2}$ pint (300 ml) red wine
$\frac{1}{4}$ pint (150 ml) red wine vinegar
juice and grated rind of 2 lemons
2 garlic cloves, peeled and chopped
2 tablespoons each of ground coriander,
   ground ginger and soft brown sugar
1 tablespoon each of chilli powder and
   turmeric

$\frac{1}{2}$ tablespoon freshly ground black
   pepper
2 teaspoons salt
1 teaspoon mustard seeds
$\frac{1}{2}$ teaspoon ground cardamom
$\frac{1}{4}$ teaspoon cayenne pepper

Marinade 2

This is good for sirloin steaks. Whizz all ingredients together and pour over four large or six smaller steaks. Leave for at least 3 days.

1 medium onion, finely chopped
2 garlic cloves, peeled and chopped
4 tablespoons each of bottled tomato
   sauce and olive oil
1 tablespoon each of wine vinegar and
   Worcestershire sauce

1 teaspoon soft brown sugar
$\frac{1}{4}$ teaspoon salt
lots of freshly ground black pepper

Marinade 3

This is wonderful for chicken breasts. Whizz all round in the liquidiser then pour over four to six breasts. Leave for at least 36 hours, turning over every 8 hours or so.

$\frac{1}{4}$ pint (150 ml) each of white wine vinegar and olive oil
$\frac{1}{2}$ tablespoon Worcestershire sauce
2 teaspoons cayenne pepper

1 teaspoon each of salt and paprika
$\frac{1}{2}$ teaspoon dry English mustard powder
2 garlic cloves, peeled and chopped

★   ★   ★

While the meats are marinating, you can prepare all the other ingredients for your barbecue meal – various vegetable salads (potato salads are ideal), or a huge bowl of seasonal salad (see page 170). Flavoured butters are good to have on hand for barbecued meats – choose from the variety on page 109 – and you could use one to make garlic (or other) bread that can be wrapped in foil, baked in the oven and then kept warm by the side of the barbecue coals. Starters if you want them can be prepared in advance, as can a pudding. Not *everything* needs to be barbecued!

Never, ever start to cook anything until the charcoal has turned to white-hot ash – and do remember that, as you're cooking and eating outdoors, everyone will be quite hungry!

The Fifth Course
·DESSERTS·

This is the only course of a Miller Howe dinner at which there is any choice, and I always think it must be difficult for guests to choose what to have: I know *I'm* always torn between about three gloriously sweet and fattening concoctions (if there are any left by the time I eat)!

The pudding or dessert is the finale of a meal, so it must be something worthy of remembrance, something that will linger on the taste buds of your guests and make them want to taste it again (maybe you don't want your guests to return, but I certainly do!). I don't expect you to prepare a selection of puds – we usually have five or six on offer, along with local cheese and home-made biscuits – but do try to choose something that will blend with the rest of the meal: a simple dessert to follow a rich main course; a substantial farmhouse pie if the rest of the meal has been light; a hot confection if the majority of the rest of the meal has been cold.

The glory of most of my puddings is that they can be prepared in advance, which means that you can concentrate on the other courses on the evening itself, only having to remember to take cold puddings out of the fridge in time, and to decorate them prettily at the last minute. Whipped cream twirls are classic, but consider flowers, doyleys and ferns; cocoa powder; icing sugar; grated orange rind or strips; chocolate leaves or gratings (and piped chocolate shapes: use your thinnest nozzle, pipe on to greaseproof paper and chill); chopped nuts; fresh fruit, whole, sliced or diced; and desiccated coconut.

If you know a guest hasn't a sweet tooth, do try to offer a cheese or cheeses and home-made biscuits (they show you care) – and to pamper everyone else, offer a truffle or a piece of Turkish delight with the coffee. *Now* you can relax!

Farmhouse Pastry Fruit Pies

This pastry has been subtly altered from the recipe I gave in *Entertaining with Tovey*, and it's the better for the change. The fillings are the same – it was difficult to better them – but you can also use half the pastry recipe, baked blind, for farmhouse pastry tarts *without* a lid as in some of the following new recipes. Freeze the remaining pastry, or make *two* open tarts at a time!

This pastry recipe gives sufficient pastry for two tarts or one full pie with a base and lid and decorations on the top if you use an 8–11 inch (20–27.5 cm) loose-bottomed, fluted flan tin. Each pie or tart will divide into eight to twelve portions. And do have a look at the pastry 'rules' on pages 48–50, they should help.

12 oz (350 g) self-raising flour
4 oz (100 g) Jordan's jungle oats
12 oz (350 g) soft butter, broken into
   walnut-sized pieces

4 oz (100 g) icing sugar
finely grated rind of 2 oranges
3 egg yolks, lightly beaten

I like to use a 14 inch (35 cm) plastic bowl which is more or less a perfect half circle as this means the butter and flour mixture will not get caught in any crevices.

Sieve the flour into the bowl and mix in the oats. Add the soft butter pieces, spreading them all over the dry mixture.

Standing quite relaxed, hold your hands spread out in front of you, palms upwards and with left- and right-hand fingers opposite each other. Slowly go down into the mixture and lift up as much as you are able without the fingers closing up on one another. As you lift up, just keep on flicking your thumbs across the outline of your four fingers. (No, this is not a lesson on a new form of crocheting!) The action at all times is methodical and you might try doing it to a slow waltz rhythm. On ONE, your hands come together in front of you in the bowl and lift up some of the mixture; on TWO and THREE, your thumbs flick from pinkie to forefinger, letting the mixture drop back into the bowl. It is imperative that in no way do you forcefully *squeeze* the butter into the flour, or else you will certainly get a heavier pastry.

Once the butter has been roughly absorbed – it is important that you do not overwork it – it will get rather wet and sticky to the touch. Fold in the icing sugar along with the orange rind.

Zig-zag the lightly beaten egg yolks over the mixture, and then, holding the bowl firmly at the edges with both hands, shake it vigorously, tossing the mixture up and down and around. You will be amazed at how soon the dough comes together.

Divide the dough into two parts, and bring together into two ball shapes *very, very gently*. Wrap individually in foil and leave overnight (at least) to chill.

The next day, following Note 8 on page 49, allow the pastry to come back to its previous texture before rolling out one of the balls of dough. Line the flan tin, and put back into the fridge to chill for at least 30 minutes, while you preheat the oven to 325°F/160°C/Gas 3. Bake the case blind as outlined on page 50 for 30–35 minutes.

• *Filling and Topping a Farmhouse Pie* •

Many fillings – a selection of which I give below – are quite liquid so I always sprinkle Farola or semolina on the cooked base before adding any filling. I also add a sprinkling *after* the filling has gone in. This soaks up the liquid a bit, but doesn't alter the flavours. Fill the pie generously, and sweeten to taste with demerara sugar.

Roll the second ball of dough out gently on a floured board and run a palette knife underneath to ensure it is not stuck to the board. Manoeuvre over the rolling pin, lift up and place over the filled pie. Don't chop off all the smaller overhanging pieces, but ease them up gently on to the inside rim of the fluted flan case. Press your thumb in to seal all the way round. Use any leftover pieces to decorate the top of the pie with roses and leaves etc.

Chill the pie again before baking, and preheat the oven to 400°F/200°C/Gas 6. Bake at that temperature for 20 minutes, then reduce the heat to 350°F/180°C/Gas 4 and bake for a further 25–35 minutes. If it's browning too much, cover loosely with foil.

• *Apple and Orange* •

Peel, core and slice 6 Granny Smith apples, part-cook and cool them, then arrange in the blind-baked case. Peel and segment 2 oranges (see page 101) and arrange the segments on top of the apples.

• *Apple and Raspberry* •

Peel, core and slice 6 Granny Smith apples, part-cook and cool them, then arrange in the blind-baked case. Scatter 4 oz (100 g) fresh raspberries over the top.

• *Banana, Walnut and Ginger* •

Skin and slice about 8 bananas, and pile the slices into the blind-baked case. Add 2 preserved pieces of ginger, chopped, and 18 chopped walnuts.

• *Gooseberry and Juniper* •

Top and tail 1½ lb (675 g) gooseberries and place them in the blind-baked case. Grind 8 juniper berries in a mortar and pestle with some brown sugar, and sprinkle on top of the gooseberries.

• *Black Cherry and Rum* •

Drain 2 × 10 oz (275 g) cans of pitted black cherries. Place cherries in the blind-baked case and sprinkle generously with 2 tablespoons dark rum.

• *Pear and Stilton* •

Peel, core and slice 5 pears and arrange in the blind-baked case. Sprinkle the top with 2 oz (50 g) crumbled Stilton.

• *Spiced Apple* •

Peel, core and slice 6 Granny Smith apples, part-cook and cool them, then arrange in the blind-baked case. Sprinkle with about ½ teaspoon each of ground cinnamon and grated nutmeg (or 1 teaspoon allspice), plus a few whole cloves if you like.

• *Spiced Apricot* •

Poach about 24 fresh apricots lightly in stock syrup to cover (see page 139) with 1 tablespoon white wine vinegar. Drain well and arrange in the flan case. Sprinkle with about ½ teaspoon each of nutmeg, cinnamon and ginger, and 1 tablespoon white wine vinegar.

Soured Cream Apple Pecan Pie

A delicious new pudding made at least once a week at Miller Howe, and it seems to be going down rather well! It can be served hot or cold, but is far nicer warm.

Serves 12 good or 8 enormous portions!

1 × 10 inch (25 cm) farmhouse pastry fluted flan case, baked blind (see page 184)

Filling
2 lb (900 g) Granny Smith or English dessert apples
2 eggs
4 oz (100 g) demerara sugar
2 oz (50 g) self-raising flour
½ pint (300 ml) soured cream

Topping
1 oz (25 g) self-raising flour
1 oz (25 g) demerara sugar
4 oz (100 g) pecan nuts (you could use walnuts, but they are slightly bitter; add a little more sugar), finely chopped
3 oz (75 g) soft butter
a pinch each of ground nutmeg, ginger and cinnamon

Preheat the oven to 350°F/180°C/Gas 4.

Peel and core the apples, and then slice them very thinly into a bowl. Beat the eggs, sugar and flour into the soured cream. Put a fanned-out circle of apples on the base of the cooked flan case and spoon over some of the cream mixture. Continue building up until all the apple slices and cream are used. Bake in the preheated oven for 40 minutes.

Meanwhile, mix the topping ingredients in your food processor. When the 40 minutes are up, remove the pie from the oven and scatter the topping over the apple filling. Turn the oven up to 400°F/200°C/Gas 6 and bake for 15 more minutes. If you are serving it hot, allow it to rest for 15 minutes first. If you are serving it cold, decorate it further with whipped cream, apple slices (dipped in lemon juice) and pecans as in the photograph opposite page 176, if you like.

Tart Lemon Tart

I rather like this sweet as it truly is tart, and so, if served without some cream, is a palate cleanser. However, I must admit that cream is served with it at Miller Howe, occasionally even ice cream!

Serves 8

1 × 8 inch (20 cm) farmhouse pastry flan case, baked blind (see page 184)

Filling
2 lemons, quartered
½ pint (300 ml) dry white wine
8 oz (225 g) cube sugar
3 eggs

Preheat the oven to 350°F/180°C/Gas 4.

Poach the lemon quarters in the white wine with the sugar for 15 minutes.

Remove pips, and put the lemons in your food processor along with the syrupy wine mixture. Turn on to whizz at top speed, and add the eggs, one at a time, to blend thoroughly.

Pour the lemon custard through a coarse sieve into the blind–baked pastry case and bake in the preheated oven for about 30 minutes.

Key Lime Pie

Most Miami restaurants sport this pud, writing rapturously about it on their otherwise limited menus, and more often than not I have found it to be very indifferent. Bobby, the head chef at Miller Howe, came up with this version after we had returned from a week's cooking in Miami – and me having had a long face six nights in a row turning my nose up at the dish. This is a winner – sharply sweet and very, very moreish.

Serves 8

1 × 10 inch (25 cm) farmhouse pastry
   flan case, baked blind (see page 184)

Filling
3 eggs, separated
1 × 14 oz (400 g) can condensed milk
juice and finely grated rind of 4 limes
$\frac{1}{4}$ teaspoon cream of tartar

Preheat the oven to 350°F/180°C/Gas 4.

Beat the egg yolks in a bowl and combine them well with the condensed milk. Fold in the lime rind and juice. Beat the egg whites until stiff with the cream of tartar, and then fold into the condensed milk mixture.

Spread into the blind–baked flan case and bake for 15 minutes only. Leave to cool and set.

Hot Cinnamon Pear Honey Slice

Serves 8

1 × 10 inch (25 cm) farmhouse pastry
   flan case, baked blind (see page 184)

Filling
2 ripe pears, peeled, quartered and cored

juice of 1 lemon
3 egg yolks
$\frac{1}{4}$ pint (150 ml) double cream
2 tablespoons honey
1 teaspoon ground cinnamon

Preheat oven to 375°F/190°C/Gas 5.

Slice each quarter pear two-thirds of the way through like a cock's comb, keeping the narrower end uncut. Place the pears in the flan case, uncut ends towards the middle of the flan, and spread out evenly over the base of the flan.

Beat all the other ingredients together and pour over the pears. Bake in the preheated oven for 40 minutes. Allow to cool a little prior to serving, with whipped cream.

Hot Cheesecake Slice with Raspberry Pernod Purée

By 'hot', I mean a cooked cheesecake rather than one made with gelatine. I prefer this served lukewarm with a hot purée.

Serves 8

1 × 8 inch (20 cm) farmhouse pastry fluted flan case, baked blind (see page 184)

Raspberry and Pernod purée
2 tablespoons Pernod
2 tablespoons soft brown sugar
4 oz (100 g) raspberries

Filling
4 tablespoons double cream
8 oz (225 g) good cream cheese
4 oz (100 g) caster sugar
2 eggs, separated, plus 1 egg yolk
½ oz (15 g) cornflour
2 oz (50 g) sultanas
4 tablespoons Frangelico

Preheat the oven to 350°F/180°C/Gas 4.

To make the filling, beat the cream into the cream cheese, adding the sugar a little at a time to obtain a light fluffy mixture. Beat the 3 egg yolks and cornflour together and then, little by little, add to the cream cheese mixture. Fold in the sultanas and Frangelico.

In a separate bowl, beat the 2 egg whites to a peak and then fold into the other mixture. Spoon into the blind-baked flan case and bake in the preheated oven for 10 minutes. Reduce the heat to 300°F/150°C/Gas 2 and cook for a further 40 minutes. Test to see if it's cooked by putting the sharp end of a knife into the middle: it should come out clean.

Remove from the oven and leave for about 10 minutes while you liquidise the Pernod, sugar and raspberries together. Serve the cheesecake in wedges with a little of the resultant sieved purée (hot if you like).

Pastry Desserts

Farmhouse fruit pies fall into a category of their own, but the choux and rough puff pastries in the Starter section (see pages 55 and 57) can also be made for desserts.

Puff pastry can be made into cornets to be filled with a variety of sweet fillings. Whipped double cream is the basic, but this can be flavoured with a spirit, sugar or a fruit purée (add some finely chopped fruit as well). You can put a blob of jam in the tip of the cornet first. Many of the mousses on page 190 can be piped in, and I often fill cornets at Christmas time with mincemeat; with lots of cream, they're much nicer than conventional mince pies – although I regret the brandy butter!

Mille-feuilles – or simple slices of puff pastry built up on top of each other – can be filled similarly. Try some of the thick vanilla custard on page 211 too.

Choux pastry makes wonderful desserts – and the most famous of these are profiteroles and eclairs, both of which demand creamy fillings and a chocolate sauce (see some of my ideas on this on page 140). Instead of simple whipped cream, add a flavouring: one of those mentioned above; or, for a coffee cream, mix 1 pint (600 ml) double cream with 2 tablespoons Camp coffee and 3 tablespoons soft brown sugar; or, for a hazelnut cream, add some ground hazelnuts. A banana filling is delicious too: whizz some very ripe bananas in your blender with a couple of tablespoons dark rum and some soft brown sugar.

Or, you can really go to town with a profiterole or choux puff pyramid, a spectacular dish for a buffet party (see photograph opposite page 161). Make sure, however, that you have quite a few helpers in the kitchen, as the pyramid takes some time and care to dismantle.

Fill the profiteroles with a filling of choice, and have ready lots of extra whipped double cream. Pipe a thin layer of double cream over the base of a dish – an old-fashioned tiered glass cake dish is super – and put your first layer of filled balls on this. Build up in layers, using cream and wooden cocktail sticks to make the pyramid form. Where you have gaps you simply fill these with whipped cream twirls. Stick strawberries into these creamy gaps, peak point down, so that the lovely green stalk adds a bit of colour, as well as lots of crisp mint leaves.

In the winter when strawberries are scarce, little coloured balls for the Christmas tree can be used – but they will get a bit creamy!

Honey Wheatmeal Pancakes

These are a more cakey version of the basic pancake in the starter section. I like to prepare them when summer soft fruits are in profusion for dessert, but they can be served as a starter with a pâté such as cheese and herb inside, and fanned avocado, with something like a tarragon cream and a savoury salad. Many savoury fillings are possible – use your imagination! They store extremely well in the freezer (as do the basic pancakes), and also hold well for a few days in an airtight tin. I find it best to make them in a mixer, but you can, of course, mix and beat by hand – it just takes longer.

Makes about 18 × 5 inch (12.5 cm) pancakes

4 eggs, separated	*To serve*
2 tablespoons runny honey	double cream, whipped
2 oz (50 g) caster sugar	filling (see below)
2 oz (50 g) wheatmeal flour	vanilla or icing sugar
1 tablespoon cornflour	
a pinch of ground nutmeg or ginger, if liked	

Make sure the mixer bowl is very hot, and the easiest way of doing this is to fill it to the rim with boiling water from the kettle. Put the whisk in as well, and leave for 3–4 minutes before emptying and drying. Preheat the oven to 425°F/220°C/Gas 7.

Place the egg yolks in the bowl, beat rapidly for at least 5 minutes and then, little by little, still beating, dribble in the honey. The longer you beat the lighter your pancake will be. Transfer the mixture to another large bowl and wash the mixer bowl. Cool it and then beat the egg whites in it as you would for meringues, slowly adding the sugar a little at a time, until stiff. Fold the egg whites carefully into the yolk mixture. Mix the flour, cornflour and nutmeg or ginger (if using) together, then fold half of this into the mixture, followed by the other half.

Cover at least two baking trays with good greaseproof paper and on to each tray spread no more than three rounds (a good heaped tablespoon will be sufficient for each pancake). Bake for 10–12 minutes. Remove from the oven and, as they are cooling, slide a palette knife under each pancake and place on a wire cooling tray.

When you wish to serve, turn them upside down and pipe whipped double cream over one half. Add the chosen filling (see below), cover with more cream on top, and fold over to give you a half-moon shape. For a wonderful decorative effect, dredge the top with vanilla or icing sugar, and then sear with a red-hot poker (hold it over the gas flame) in a pattern, as in the photograph on the jacket.

• *Fillings* •

sliced strawberries with cucumber slices and mint leaves
caramelised apples (see page 199) with fresh apple slices
gooseberries and toasted macadamia nuts
Calvados apple purée (see page 133)
red, black and white currants
raspberries coated with soft brown sugar
mincemeat and ice cream
pineapple pieces with preserved ginger (use some of the syrup when whipping the
    double cream)
pipped cherries with toasted desiccated coconut
banana slices with soft brown sugar, and dark rum to flavour the cream

Mousses

Mousses are a lovely way to finish a dinner party as they are neither rich nor heavy – and they can be made the evening before, a boon when entertaining. I always make them in individual dishes which look so much nicer, especially if put on a small plate with a doyley and a fern and flower from your garden. But you can make them up decoratively in one single pretty dish. I was fortunate enough to find three old-fashioned sweet storage bowls in a junk shop and they come in useful when entertaining a crowd of people rather than just a handful of close friends. Three different mousse mixings can be made and layered into your dish. For the photograph opposite page 177, I used chocolate raspberry, crème de menthe and orange mousses, a colourful combination which tasted lovely too. Mind you, I always shudder at what the dish looks like after people have plunged the serving spoon in and out. But an idea anyway.

This recipe will give you enough to fill from ten to twelve 3 inch (7.5 cm) ramekins. (It might be ten the first time you make it, but as you become more confident and therefore more competent, twelve will be the end result.) Firstly, though, you've got to learn how to deal with gelatine.

• *Gelatine* •

When some people read that gelatine is required in a recipe they swiftly turn over the page as they have had so many failures in the past: their end result has been stringy like witches' hair, so hard it wouldn't wobble if an elephant stood on it, or soft and gooey. And there are so many varying methods of instruction too. Some recipes say the gelatine should be put in a tea cup with the liquid, then placed in a pan of boiling water and stirred round; I find this unacceptable as it is unpleasant and uncomfortable trying to stir something partly submerged in boiling water. Others say put the gelatine in a saucepan and add the liquid – but if the heat is too strong, the minute particles of gelatine simply cling to the bottom of the saucepan. So do bear with me for a few moments while I explain the *successful* way of working with gelatine!

Always use powdered gelatine, and buy it in the $\frac{1}{2}$ oz (15 g) sachets (a tricky quantity to weigh accurately on a home scale). Practically every recipe will need 5 tablespoons of liquid to bring the crystals round.

Whenever you need to use gelatine, always but always start off the recipe by preparing it in advance. This simply means emptying the sachet into a small saucepan, then adding the desired liquid *all in one go*. Do *not* measure out tablespoon by tablespoon. Gently swirl the small saucepan round until the fine particles dissolve and resemble a rather tacky mess. Put to one side and forget about it until you need to fold the gelatine into your mixture towards the end of the recipe.

At this stage you have to put the saucepan on the *very lowest* heat possible, and to ensure this, constantly remove the saucepan from the heat and let the pan rest on the palm of your hand. If you go OUCH you deserve the shock as the heat is far too high! If this is so, the small particles of gelatine will stick to the base of the saucepan and in no way will they then blend into your mixture as required; the liquid content can also evaporate.

The next step is pouring the gelatine into the mixture. This must always be done through a very fine sieve. I have an old metal coffee strainer which I use only for gelatine *but*, before doing so, I always gently warm it; if I were to put lukewarm dissolved gelatine through a cold sieve on a cold day, a lot of the gelatine would simply stick to the strainer. (Of course, if you're using a fine plastic strainer, you shouldn't warm it – you'd end up with one large hole!)

When the gelatine liquid has been poured into your mixture, do not be scared about the folding in. I always like to use a long-handled spoon which I keep turning in figures-of-eight, bringing the bottom mixture up over to the top. You cannot *over*fold, but you can *under*fold, resulting in some parts of your pudding being runny and others hard.

Dishes with gelatine usually require 6–8 hours in the fridge to be ready for serving. They are fine for about 48 hours, but after that I feel they go a little rubbery. I am also absolutely against freezing any dish that has gelatine in it – although this is only my personal fad.

• *The Mousse* •

½ oz (15 g) gelatine plus 5 tablespoons
   liquid according to recipe
approximately 5–6 fl oz (150–175 ml)
   liquid or other flavouring, according
   to recipe

3 eggs, plus 2 egg yolks
2 oz (50 g) caster sugar, sieved
½ pint (300 ml) double cream

Heat your Kenwood bowl and beater (I usually simply fill the bowl with boiling water, put the beater in, and leave for a few minutes before draining and drying well). Place the ramekins on a tray and sprinkle some extra liqueur or booze needed for the particular recipe into the base of each.

Prepare the gelatine as outlined above.

Put the eggs and egg yolks into the warmed Kenwood bowl and beat away on the highest speed for at least 8 minutes (make yourself a mug of tea or coffee) then go over to the mixture, and little by little sprinkle in the caster sugar. You cannot go too slowly with this but you *can* do it too quickly, adding too much at once. Just pause and think for a moment. You have spent 8 minutes letting your eggs alone build up into a light fluffy mixture – and the more volume you achieve at this stage the more portions you will eventually get and the lighter your pud will be. Should you boldly throw in the sugar in two stages you will tend to flatten this fluffy mix and it will never regain its lightness. Add the sugar tablespoon by tablespoon at the most.

The double cream should then be lightly whipped, but *do* take care with the whipping. If you whip it too far and too thick, until of piping texture, the fluffy eggs will soon flop when combined with the cream. Whip until the cream is roughly of the same texture as the eggs – soft peak – then fold in the flavouring.

Although I know it means one more piece of washing up, I always turn the egg mixture out from the Kenwood bowl into a large 14 inch (35 cm) plastic bowl; this makes it easier for the whipped cream and flavouring to be folded in lightly.

The gelatine should be brought round as described above, and then added swiftly through the sieve. Fold it in with sharp determined moves. Pour the mixture into a jug with a good pouring lip and then into your individual ramekins. If you don't have ramekins, wine or cocktail glasses would do. Put in the fridge, covered, to set, which will take about 8 hours. *Never* freeze.

• *Calvados Apple Mousse* •

Use 3 tablespoons Calvados and 2 tablespoons water to reconstitute the gelatine. Peel, core and slice 2 large Granny Smith apples and cook with a little brown sugar and a knob of butter until fallen. When cooled, pass through a nylon sieve with 2 tablespoons Calvados and fold into the cream. Fold together the cream and basic mousse mixture, followed by the gelatine. As it starts to set, fold in a finely diced Granny Smith apple.

• *Chocolate Raspberry Mousse* •

Use 3 tablespoons Kirsch and 2 tablespoons water to reconstitute the gelatine. Melt 6 oz (175 g) chocolate with 4 tablespoons brandy. When it has

*A table set for afternoon tea on the Miller Howe terrace
with a visual feast of Windermere in the background.
The edible feast includes cream-filled brandy snaps and fairy cakes,
and chocolate-topped profiteroles.*

A beautiful sunset over Lake Windermere – this is the splendid view enjoyed from the dining room at Miller Howe.

cooled, fold into the cream and then into the basic mousse mixture followed by the gelatine. As it starts to set, fold in 6 oz (175 g) whole fresh raspberries.

• Coconut Mousse •

Use 5 tablespoons canned coconut milk to reconstitute the gelatine. Use $\frac{3}{4}$ pint (450 ml) double cream instead of $\frac{1}{2}$ pint (300 ml) and fold in 3 level tablespoons toasted desiccated coconut. Fold this cream into the basic mousse mixture, followed by the gelatine.

• Coffee, Ginger and Rum Mousse •

Use 3 tablespoons rum and 2 tablespoons Camp coffee to reconstitute the gelatine. Use $\frac{3}{4}$ pint (450 ml) double cream instead of $\frac{1}{2}$ pint (300 ml), and fold in 2 large preserved ginger rounds, finely chopped. Fold this cream into the basic mousse mixture, followed by the gelatine.

• Coffee and Pernod Mousse •

Use 3 tablespoons Pernod and 2 tablespoons water to reconstitute the gelatine. Use $\frac{3}{4}$ pint (450 ml) double cream instead of $\frac{1}{2}$ pint (300 ml), and add 3 tablespoons Camp coffee to this when whipping. Fold this cream into the basic mousse mixture, followed by the gelatine.

• Crème de Menthe Mint Crisp Mousse •

Use 3 tablespoons crème de menthe and 2 tablespoons water to reconstitute the gelatine. Use $\frac{3}{4}$ pint (450 ml) double cream instead of $\frac{1}{2}$ pint (300 ml), and beat in 2 tablespoons crème de menthe.

Fold this into the basic mousse mixture, followed by the gelatine. Pour some of the mousse mix into the ramekins, followed by some finely chopped mint crisp bars. Top up with mousse.

• Gin and Lime Mousse •

Use 3 tablespoons gin and 2 tablespoons fresh lime juice to reconstitute the gelatine. Use $\frac{3}{4}$ pint (450 ml) double cream instead of $\frac{1}{2}$ pint (300 ml). Fold the cream into the basic mousse mixture, followed by the gelatine.

• Grapefruit and Pernod Mousse •

Use 3 tablespoons Pernod and 2 tablespoons water to reconstitute the gelatine. Add 1 can defrosted concentrated grapefruit juice ($6\frac{3}{4}$ oz or 178 ml) to the cream, and place a segment of fresh grapefruit on the base of each ramekin. Fold the cream into the basic mousse mixture, followed by the gelatine.

• Hazelnut, Coffee and Banana Mousse •

Use 3 tablespoons Camp coffee and 2 tablespoons water to reconstitute the gelatine. Add 4 oz (100 g) mashed bananas and 3 oz (75 g) ground hazelnuts to the cream. Fold this into the basic mousse mixture, followed by the gelatine.

• Mango and Lime Mousse •

Use 3 tablespoons *fresh* squeezed lime juice and 2 tablespoons Rose's bottled lime juice to reconstitute the gelatine. Add 6 fl oz (175 ml) mango purée to the cream. Fold cream into the basic mousse mixture, followed by the gelatine.

• Mint Mousse •

Use 3 tablespoons gin and 2 table-spoons water to reconstitute the gel-atine. Use $\frac{3}{4}$ pint (450 ml) double cream instead of $\frac{1}{2}$ pint (300 ml), and fold in at least 18 finely chopped mint leaves. Fold this cream into the basic mousse mixture, followed by the gelatine.

• Orange Mousse •

Use 3 tablespoons orange curaçao and 2 tablespoons water to reconstitute the gelatine. Add 1 can defrosted con-centrated orange juice ($6\frac{3}{4}$ oz or 178 ml) with the finely grated rind of 1 orange to the cream. Fold the cream into the basic mousse mixture, followed by the gelatine.

• Orange and Mint Mousse •

Make as in the orange mousse above, but add 3 level tablespoons finely chop-ped mint to the cream, along with the orange juice and rind. Put fresh orange segments in the base of each ramekin. Fold the cream into the basic mousse mixture, followed by the gelatine.

• Passionfruit Mousse •

Use 3 tablespoons Kirsch and 2 table-spoons water to reconstitute the gel-atine. Fold the cream into the basic mousse mixture followed by the gel-atine, and *then* fold in $\frac{1}{4}$ pint (150 ml) passionfruit seeds and flesh.

• Pawpaw and Ginger Mousse •

Use 3 tablespoons Crabbie's green ginger wine and 2 tablespoons water to reconstitute the gelatine. Add $\frac{1}{4}$ pint (150 ml) puréed pawpaw flesh to the cream. Fold this cream into the basic mousse mixture, followed by the gelatine.

• Strawberry or Raspberry Mousse •

Use 3 tablespoons Kirsch and 2 table-spoons water to reconstitute the gel-atine. Liquidise 8 oz (225 g) of either fruit with 2 tablespoons icing sugar and 2 tablespoons brandy. Reduce this on the stove down to just over $\frac{1}{4}$ pint (150 ml). When cool, add to the cream, then fold this into the basic mousse mixture, followed by the gelatine.

Miller Howe Cheesecakes

I love cheesecakes and, judging by the speed at which they disappear whenever we have them on the Miller Howe menu, our guests do too! The basic recipe given below is the same as I've always used, but I want you to use your imagination and invent new ways of presenting it and blending different ingredients. Once you have the hang of this basic method – and of the use of gelatine: do read the instructions carefully on page 191 – you can adapt and create by yourself. Most of the mousse variations on the preceding page, for instance, can be adapted for cheesecakes.

This recipe will make one cheesecake that will fill a 10 inch (25 cm) loose-bottomed cake tin, and which will serve eight to ten portions.

1 × 10 oz (275 g) packet plain or
   chocolate digestive biscuits
2 oz (50 g) butter, melted

Cheesecake
½ oz (15 g) gelatine plus 5 tablespoons
   liquid, see individual recipes

3 eggs, separated
9 oz (250 g) good cream cheese
2 oz (50 g) caster sugar
½ pint (300 ml) double cream
flavouring, see individual recipes

Line your cake tin with greaseproof paper, and preheat the oven to 350°F/ 180°C/Gas 4.

Put the biscuits – plain or chocolate, just as you fancy – into your liquidiser in batches and reduce to crumbs. You could also break them up on to some greaseproof paper, top with more paper, and roll them into crumbs. Or you could put the biscuits into a polythene bag and roll them into crumbs. Turn the crumbs into a bowl and fold in the melted butter. Line the base of the paper-lined tin with this crumb mixture. Use your hands to smooth it down, then bake in the preheated oven for about 20 minutes. Leave to cool.

To make the cheesecake, prepare the gelatine as outlined on page 191, using the liquid specified in the individual recipes. Put to one side while you lightly beat the egg yolks. Beat these into the cream cheese with the sugar followed by the double cream. Add the relevant flavourings (see the individual recipes), fold in the stiffly-beaten egg whites, then fold in the reconstituted gelatine carefully. Pour the mixture on to the cooled biscuit base – there is often a flavouring added at this stage – then place in the fridge to set. Top with a topping if appropriate.

• *Banana Rum Cheesecake* •

Use 3 tablespoons Negrita rum and 2 tablespoons water to reconstitute the gelatine. Mash enough bananas to a pulp to give you 5 oz (150 g) in weight (use a silver fork), and beat this into the basic cheesecake mixture. Line the biscuit base with half the mixing. Place further sliced bananas through the middle of the cheesecake, and top with the remaining cheesecake mixture.

• *Bilberry Cheesecake* •

Use 3 tablespoons gin and 2 tablespoons water to reconstitute the gelatine. Drain a 10 oz (275 g) can of Polish bilberries, keeping the juice. Line the biscuit base with half the bilberries, and top with the cheesecake mixture. Chill to set. Reduce the liquid

from the bilberries by half, and, if necessary, thicken with a pinch of arrowroot. Combine this with the other half of the bilberries and decorate the top of the cheesecake when it is thoroughly set.

• *Cheese, Apple and Celery Cheesecake* •

This unusual cheesecake is occasionally served as a starter at Miller Howe – when I get twelve portions rather than the eight for a pudding – and it is often prepared for packed lunches. I personally like it accompanied by some home-made tomato provençale or sauce (see page 132) or with a dollop of home-made chutney.

Use 2 tablespoons cooking brandy and 3 tablespoons water to reconstitute the gelatine. Finely peel, core and dice 2

Granny Smith apples, and sprinkle with the juice and finely grated rind of 1 lemon. Finely dice 2 good celery sticks, and finely grate 4 oz (100 g) strong Cheddar cheese. Fold the apple and celery dice, the lemon juice and rind, and the cheese into the basic cheesecake mixture with 1 teaspoon salt. Leave to chill and set. You could also add, if you like, for a really unusual flavour, a teaspoon of horseradish cream and a tablespoon of chopped chives.

• Coffee, Rum and Pecan Cheesecake •

Use 3 tablespoons Negrita rum and 2 tablespoons water to reconstitute the gelatine. Add 2 tablespoons Camp coffee to the basic cheesecake mix. Line the cooled crumb base with about 2 tablespoons chopped pecan nuts, and then put half the cheesecake mixing on top. When nearly set, add a further layer of pecan nuts, and top with the balance of the cheesecake.

• Coffee, Whiskey and Walnut Cheesecake •

Use 3 tablespoons Irish whiskey and 2 tablespoons water to reconstitute the gelatine. Add 2 tablespoons Camp coffee to the basic cheesecake mixture, and line the cooled crumb base with about 2 tablespoons chopped walnuts. Put half the cheesecake mixture on top, then a further layer of walnuts. Top with the balance of the cheesecake.

• Lemon Cheesecake •

Use 5 tablespoons fresh lemon juice to reconstitute the gelatine. Fold the juice and finely grated rind of 2 lemons into the basic cheesecake mixture. You could also make an orange or lime cheesecake in the same way (using 3 tablespoons gin and 2 tablespoons water for the gelatine): use the juice and rind of 2 oranges (top with toasted macadamia nuts); the juice and rind of 1 lime.

• Strawberry Cheesecake •

Use 3 tablespoons Kirsch and 2 tablespoons water to reconstitute the gelatine. Liquidise 8 oz (225 g) strawberries with 1 tablespoon cooking brandy and 1 tablespoon icing sugar and add to the basic cheesecake mixture. Line the cooled biscuit base with extra whole strawberries, and fill with half the cheesecake mixture. As it sets, spread further sliced strawberries on top, and then cover with the remaining cheesecake mixture. You could also make a raspberry cheesecake in the same way.

Long Island Cheesecake

A good American friend, when eating the Miller Howe cheesecake for the first time, remarked, 'Good, I like it', at which I beamed and said nothing, acting sort of coy. She immediately went on to say, however, 'But mine beats it!' I can't say that I unreservedly agree – but it *is* wickedly different, and I love it, especially when served with lots of new season raspberries.

You need an old-fashioned, square or round, solid 10 inch (25 cm) cake tin. If you were to use a loose-bottomed tin the mixture could so easily run out; in fact, as an added precaution, line the base and sides with lightly oiled greaseproof paper.

Serves 8–12

8 oz (225 g) chocolate digestive biscuits
  (or plain or ginger)
2 oz (50 g) butter, melted

Filling
12 oz (350 g) good cream cheese

4 oz (100 g) caster sugar
6 eggs, beaten
½ pint (300 ml) double cream, lightly
  whipped
juice and finely grated rind of 2 lemons

Preheat the oven to 325°F/160°C/Gas 3.

Liquidise the biscuits in your machine or in one of the other ways described for the Miller Howe cheesecake. Combine in a bowl with the melted butter and then spread on to the base and just up the sides of your prepared tin. Use your hands to spread it evenly. Bake for about 15–20 minutes in the preheated oven, then leave to cool.

Combine the cream cheese and sugar until light and fluffy (using an electric hand-beater), about 3–4 minutes. Add the beaten eggs a little at a time. Fold in the lightly whipped cream along with the lemon juice and rind, and pour into the prepared crumb base.

Put the cake tin in a deep roasting tin and half-fill the latter with warm water. Bake for 1 hour in the preheated oven. The cake should be firm in the centre and nicely browned; a skewer inserted in the middle should come out clean.

Remove from the oven and set to one side until cool. Refrigerate to chill overnight. Serve in wedges with raspberries or with some strawberry Pernod purée (see page 130).

Chocolate Rum Cheese Tart

Use a spring-sided 10 inch (25 cm) cake tin for this cheesecake tart, and line it first with some lightly greased greaseproof paper.

Serves 8

12 oz (350 g) chocolate digestive biscuits
4 oz (100 g) butter, melted

Filling
4 eggs
1 lb (450 g) cream cheese

2 oz (50 g) caster sugar
8 oz (225 g) good chocolate, broken into
  pieces
4 tablespoons rum
½ pint (300 ml) double cream, lightly
  whipped

Preheat the oven to 300°F/150°C/Gas 2.

Crush the biscuits to make them into crumbs as described on page 195. Mix with the melted butter and use to line the base – and a little up the sides – of the cake tin.

Beat the eggs, cream cheese and sugar together in a bowl. Melt the chocolate pieces with the rum in a double saucepan (or a bowl over simmering water), then, as it is cooling, fold into the cheese mixture along with the whipped cream.

Pour into the biscuit base and bake in the preheated oven for 1½–1¾ hours. Remove from the oven and leave to cool and set.

Lemon Chiffon Pie

This recipe goes against the basic rules for gelatine that I went to such elaborate lengths on page 191 to explain. It has to be started the day before and then made the following morning for serving that evening – but the final dish will hold for a further 24 hours. If there is any left after this time it can still be eaten (by the family), but is not as light and chiffony as it should be!

Serves 12

1 × 10 oz (275 g) packet digestive biscuits, crushed

2 oz (50 g) butter, melted

Filling

½ oz (15 g) powdered gelatine

12 tablespoons dry white wine

6 eggs, separated

8 oz (225 g) caster sugar, sieved

8 tablespoons fresh lemon juice

½ teaspoon cream of tartar

Have ready a 10 inch (25 cm) square or round, loose-bottomed cake tin, and preheat the oven to 350°F/180°C/Gas 4.

Mix the crushed biscuits with the melted butter, and use to line the base of the tin. Besides putting a very thin layer on the base, the biscuit crumbs should be worked as far up the sides as you can. Carefully put a ball of crushed foil in the tin – this is to hold the crumbs on to the sides – and bake in the preheated oven for about 30 minutes. Leave it to cool, and don't remove the foil until just before you put the filling in. All this should be done the day before.

Prepare the gelatine in the usual way and leave to one side. I *know* the liquid quantity is far, far more than the norm, but pour the whole lot of the wine on to the gelatine in one fell swoop! Beat the egg yolks in a warmed Kenwood bowl for 8–10 minutes until they are lovely and light and very fluffy, then little by little beat in only 4 oz (100 g) of the caster sugar.

Warm the lemon juice in a small saucepan and when all the initial sugar is beaten into the egg yolk mixture, dribble the lemon juice in while the beater is bashing away on top speed. Reconstitute the gelatine, pass through a sieve on to this mixture, and fold in well. Transfer to a large round plastic bowl and leave to one side in a cold place, or in the sink with iced water around it, until it begins to partly set.

Wash out your Kenwood bowl and wipe dry. Put the egg whites in and beat until the soft peak stage, then beat in the cream of tartar. Little by little, add the remaining caster sugar. Fold the egg yolk and egg white mixtures together.

Remove foil from the tin, pour the mixture in, and leave to set for up to 4 hours. Decorate it with whipped and piped cream as in the photograph between pages 160 and 161, with lemon and lime wedges, strawberries and mint leaves.

Sticky Toffee Pudding

This is a very popular Miller Howe pudding – I think it's the 'sticky' that attracts most! Serve it with butterscotch sauce (see page 139) or lots of double cream!

Serves 12

4 oz (100 g) soft butter
6 6z (175 g) soft brown sugar
4 eggs, lightly beaten
8 oz (225 g) self-raising flour
1 teaspoon bicarbonate of soda

2 tablespoons Camp coffee
8 oz (225 g) stoned dates, finely chopped
$\frac{1}{2}$ pint (300 ml) boiling water

Line a 9 inch (22.5 cm) square or round loose-bottomed cake tin with a double thickness of greaseproof paper, and preheat the oven to 350°F/180°C/Gas 4.

Cream the butter and sugar together and little by little beat in the eggs. Fold in the self-raising flour. Mix the bicarbonate of soda and Camp coffee together and pour over the dates in a bowl, followed by the boiling water. Mix, cool a little, then pour on to the creamed mixture. Bring together using a long-handled spoon and the result will be a very runny mixture.

Pour into the prepared tin, place the tin on a baking tray, and bake for $1\frac{1}{2}$ hours in the preheated oven until springy to the touch.

Caramelised Apple Hazelnut Cake

This can be served hot with a simple custard for an ideal family pudding, but it can also be used cold, cut in slices, for afternoon tea. Decorate it if you like with twirls of cream topped with hazelnuts, and apple slices dipped in lemon juice as in the photograph opposite page 177. The caramelised apples themselves can be used in countless other ways.

Serves 12

4 oz (100 g) soft butter
5 oz (150 g) caster sugar
3 eggs, beaten
3 oz (75 g) ground hazelnuts
5 oz (150 g) self-raising flour

Caramelised apples
4 oz (100 g) soft butter
4 oz (100 g) soft brown sugar
6 large Granny Smith apples, peeled,
    cored and sliced

Line a 10 inch (25 cm) round sponge cake tin with greaseproof paper and preheat the oven to 350°F/180°C/Gas 4.

For the caramelised apples, melt the butter with the sugar and stir and cook until well blended. Stir in the apple slices until well coated, cook for a few minutes, then leave to cool.

For the cake, beat the butter until creamy with the sugar, then add the beaten egg little by little. Fold in the ground hazelnuts, self-raising flour and caramelised apples. Place in the tin and bake in the preheated oven for 25 minutes.

Rich Chocolate Log

For this super pudding – which should be made the day before you plan to serve it – you need a tin approximately 11 × 8 inches (27.5 × 20 cm), like a lipped Swiss roll tin. On the day itself you simply fill and roll the log and, in fact, at this stage it can be wrapped in greaseproof paper and a double thickness of foil and frozen. Allow it to come round in a warm kitchen for about 2 hours before slicing and serving.

Instead of the rich filling specified here, you could simply fill with double cream whipped up with some appropriate booze and soft brown sugar.

Serves 8–12

butter
5 oz (150 g) good rich dark chocolate,
   broken into pieces
3 tablespoons brandy or rum, according
   to taste
5 medium eggs, separated
5 oz (150 g) caster sugar
icing sugar

Filling
½ oz (15 g) cornflour
4 oz (100 g) caster sugar
½ pint (300 ml) single cream
2 egg yolks
a touch of brandy or rum (as above)
grated rind of 2 oranges (optional)
8 oz (225 g) rich chocolate, coarsely
   grated

Line the tin with good greaseproof paper and butter the inside. Preheat the oven to 350°F/180°C/Gas 4.

In a double saucepan – or a Christmas pudding type bowl over a pan of simmering water – melt the chocolate gently with the chosen booze. In a heated Kenwood bowl beat the egg yolks until light in colour and fluffy in texture and then, tablespoon by tablespoon, slowly add the caster sugar, beating it in well. Turn this mixture out into a large mixing bowl. Wash and dry the Kenwood bowl and beaters and then whisk the egg whites until of a meringue or soft peak texture.

Meanwhile combine the melted, slightly cooled chocolate with the egg yolks. Do this by holding a long-handled spoon at the end and very loosely making figures-of-eight to combine the two mixtures. It is absolutely no use holding the spoon as if you were about to clout somebody about the ears!

When the egg whites are the correct texture, fold two-thirds of them into the chocolate mixture and continue to beat the remainder on a slow speed – otherwise they will fall back slightly. Then fold in this balance, making sure there are no balls of egg white floating around.

Put the mixture into the lined tin and spread evenly and gently, using a large palette knife. Bake in the preheated oven for 15–20 minutes; the end of a sharp knife should come out clean if it is ready. Remove from the oven and while still hot, place a dry tea towel gently down on the top of the log – which will be rather brittle. On top of this put another tea towel that has been soaked in cold water and well wrung out. As this dampness starts to affect the dry tea towel, the log will lightly steam and the crisp top will sink back. Leave in a cool place overnight.

When you wish to turn the log out, flatten the four corners of the greaseproof paper lining and remove the tea towels. Sprinkle icing sugar generously over the top – which will be dark brown and slightly soft – and cover with a sheet of greaseproof paper and a double thickness of foil. Invert on to your work surface. Take care when removing the greaseproof paper lining. I usually do this in 2 inch (5 cm) strips, holding the initially torn bit between fingers and thumb of one hand, and placing my other hand flat on top of the paper. Draw the strip up from the log over the back of your fingers. It sounds complicated, but what I am wanting to prevent you doing is tugging at the paper too roughly, which will bring the log up and perhaps split it in two.

When all the paper has been carefully removed, make the filling. Mix the cornflour with the sugar and put in a saucepan with the cream and egg yolks. Simmer until the mixture coats the back of your spoon. Add the booze and the orange rind if using, and then the grated chocolate, a little at a time, until you have a lovely dark brown sauce. When nearly cold, spread carefully on the top of the cake.

To roll, take hold of the foil nearest you, and pull it up at an angle of 90 degrees. Ease the log away from you and it will roll up beautifully. Sprinkle with a little more icing sugar if you like, and cut into the requisite number of slices.

Chocolate Apricot Delight

Fills 8 × 3 inch (7.5 cm) ramekins

4 oz (100 g) good chocolate, broken into pieces
2 tablespoons brandy
2 oz (50 g) icing sugar
3 oz (75 g) soft butter
3 eggs, separated

1 oz (25 g) cocoa powder (*not* drinking chocolate)
¼ pint (150 ml) double cream, lightly whipped
2 oz (50 g) dried apricots, marinated for 24 hours in 4 tablespoons brandy, then minced

Melt the chocolate pieces with the brandy in a Christmas pudding type bowl over a pan of simmering water. Beat in the icing sugar and then beat in the soft butter, a little at a time. Remove from the heat and beat in the lightly beaten egg yolks, a little at a time, along with the cocoa. Fold in the cream and marinated minced apricots.

Beat the egg whites to a soft peak with a pinch of salt and then fold them into the mixture, half at a time. Portion into the eight ramekins, and chill for 24 hours.

Chocolate Orange Gâteau

Being the chocolate freak and fanatic that I am I find it difficult to end a meal without having a pud, particularly a chocolate one! This recipe is the richest and most yummy of all my chocolate recipes, and I discovered it at the Athenaeum Hotel in Piccadilly. I have been staying there whenever I'm in London for nigh on fifteen years now, and the staff and I work there each November 'bringing a breath of the country to the bustle of the city'! I always find time to go through to the kitchen and chat to Derek Fuller – he giving me all the low-down on what is happening at the heart of things and me telling him what new dishes we have been playing around with up at Miller Howe. After a particularly trying business lunch last year I saw this new pudding on the sweet trolley and just thought I would try a small piece. After the first spoonful I immediately asked for the portion to be made up to a regular size!

Experimenting at home, I have found that adding an egg white beaten stiffly and folded in makes the pudding that much lighter than the Athenaeum's, but you can prepare it either way. It was the first time I discovered that glucose works so well with chocolate, acting as a thickening agent in a most peculiar – but sensual – way. When you turn the pudding out of your tin, sieve on some cocoa powder, *not* drinking chocolate.

The pud can be made the day before and left in the fridge, covered, but I think it is by far at its best made on the day you plan to eat it.

When fresh raspberries are around I substitute Pernod for the orange curaçao and give a slightly smaller wedge of the pudding with a generous portion of fresh rasps, and my very favourite of liqueurs, now available in this country – Frangelico – makes this pudding an experience!

Use a circular loose-bottomed cake tin or, better still, one with clip sides.

Makes 1 × 10 inch (25 cm) round gâteau, to serve 8–12

3 fl oz (85 ml) liquid glucose
juice and finely grated rind of 1 orange
2½ fl oz (70 ml) water
3 oz (75 g) caster sugar
1 lb (450 g) good chocolate, broken into
  pieces

8 tablespoons orange curaçao
¾ pint (450 ml) double cream
1 egg white

To finish
cocoa powder, sieved

Heat the glucose, orange juice and rind, water and caster sugar together gently, to melt the sugar, and then bring to the boil.

Melt the chocolate with the orange curaçao in a Christmas pudding type bowl over a pan of simmering water. Combine the glucose and chocolate mixtures, and leave to cool slightly.

Beat up the double cream until it forms soft peaks and gently fold in the cooled chocolate mixture, followed by the stiffly beaten egg white. Turn this runny mixture out into the lightly oiled tin and leave in the fridge to set. Decorate with sieved cocoa powder, and cut into wedges to serve. You can decorate the gâteau further before cutting, or each individual wedge, with twirls of cream and piped, set chocolate shapes (see the photograph between pages 176 and 177).

White Chocolate Creams

Fills 6–8 × 3 inch (7.5 cm) ramekins

6 oz (175 g) white chocolate, broken into
  pieces
4 tablespoons white rum

½ pint (300 ml) double cream
4 egg whites
4 oz (100 g) caster sugar

Put the chocolate pieces into a Christmas pudding type bowl, add the rum and melt over a pan of simmering water. Mix, then allow to cool.

Beat the double cream in one bowl to soft peak stage, and in another bowl, a stainless steel one, beat the egg whites until stiff. Little by little, beat the caster sugar into the stiff egg whites. Combine the egg whites with the double cream and then fold in the cooled chocolate.

Pour into the ramekins and *freeze*. When you want to serve, allow them to come round for 30 minutes in the fridge, then 15 minutes in the kitchen.

St Clement's Icebox Pudding

This is a new variation on an old theme, and the name comes from the combination of oranges (in the sponge) and lemons (in the cream mixture).

Serves at least 12

Sponge
3 oz (75 g) soft butter
3 oz (75 g) caster sugar
1 egg, lightly beaten
juice and finely grated rind of 2 oranges
3 oz (75 g) self-raising flour, sieved

Cream mixture
2 eggs, separated
3 oz (75 g) caster sugar, sieved
½ pint (300 ml) double cream
juice and finely grated rind of 2 lemons

Preheat the oven to 350°F/180°C/Gas 4. Well grease a terrine mould – 14 × 3 × 3 inches (35 × 7.5 × 7.5 cm) – and lightly flour it as well.

For the sponge, cream the butter with the sugar and then, little by little, beat in the egg that has been mixed with the orange rind and juice. Take care with this, so that the mixture doesn't curdle. Fold in the sieved flour and turn out into your terrine mould. Bake in the preheated oven for 30 minutes. When cool, turn out of the terrine and slice horizontally – *lengthwise* – into four slices.

For the cream, place the egg yolks in a warmed Kenwood bowl (or, easier for this small mixing, in a warmed glass bowl and use an electric hand-beater), and beat until light and fluffy. Little by little, and ever so slowly, add the sieved sugar.

Meanwhile beat the double cream to soft peak consistency and then beat in, a little at a time, the lemon juice and rind. In yet another bowl beat up the egg whites until stiff. Fold the flavoured cream into the egg-yolk mix and then, having beaten the egg whites again, until nice and stiff, fold these in too.

Put one layer of the orange sponge on the base of the terrine and top with one-third of the cream mixture. Carry on building these layers up until you finish with a sponge layer – the top one from the baking. Cover with greaseproof paper and freeze, for at least 12 hours.

About 30 minutes before you wish to serve, take the pudding out of the freezer and turn out of the terrine. Decorate it with whipped cream on the sides, and lemon slices and mint leaves on top if you like (as in the photograph opposite page 177), but it is better to slice it first and then decorate on the plate. Serve with fresh skinned orange slices or glazed orange segments (see page 209).

—Meringues and Meringue Gâteaux—

Meringues are made two or three times a week at Miller Howe as they are so popular. At home I always like to have a few in the freezer as they are a boon for unexpected teas or puddings, and they are so easy to make at the end of any cooking session in the kitchen – it takes only minutes to whip them up.

Contrary to what most cookery writers say, I prefer my whites to be straight from the fridge rather than at room temperature, and the only way to measure them is on a scale! We all know that an egg should weigh 2 oz (50 g) out of the shell, but even the Lord in all his wisdom can't make Jemima lay to order, and the sizes of free-range farm eggs do vary somewhat. The normal meringue ratio is two parts sieved caster sugar to one part of egg whites. If you blindly break eight free-range egg whites into your cold clean stainless steel bowl and then add 1 lb (450 g) sugar little by little, the end result will not turn out as good as when you *weigh* the whites. Then and only then do you get the exact proportions. Use 8 oz (225 g) of *weighed* egg whites to 1 lb (450 g) caster sugar – or any multiple of this.

Don't start adding the sugar until the egg whites have fluffed up and are at a soft peak stage (some people add a pinch of salt now, but I don't), and then add your sugar only a tablespoon at a time until three-quarters of it has been well and truly absorbed.

One night, flying back to the UK from the States, I nearly fell out of my sleeperette seat with laughter when I read in an American magazine: 'Your meringues are done when you can hold the bowl over your head and the ingredients stay in'! (Methinks the writer had shares in a hairdressing salon where hordes of meringue-makers rushed when their disasters fell on them!) However, he/she was basically correct: when the whites stay in the bowl when it is turned upside down, they are ready for the balance of the sugar to be *folded* in.

Always spoon or pipe out on to good Bakewell paper (your meringues will stick to cheap greaseproof). Using a large flat tablespoon you should get twelve meringues from this mixing; using a dessertspoon you could get nearer double that. Of course you can make even smaller meringues – for a nibble at a tea, or for a decoration for another pud perhaps. Or you can make three 10 inch (25 cm) circular gâteaux or meringue bases. Bake meringues in a preheated oven set at 200°F/100°C/the very lowest gas possible, for 3–4 hours, making sure they are really dry before taking them out.

• Meringue Variations •

So, the basic recipe, therefore, is simply two parts caster sugar to one part egg white. However, to ring the changes, in texture, colour and taste, you may use half soft brown sugar with half caster sugar, or even a quarter soft brown with a quarter demerara and half caster.

You can make hazelnut or almond meringue gâteaux in exactly the same way, but you add 4 oz (100 g) ground nuts to the basic 8 oz (225 g) egg whites and 1 lb (450 g) caster sugar. These nuts should be folded in with the last quarter of sugar.

Make the meringue mixture into three circular gâteau shapes on lined baking trays and bake in an oven preheated to 325°F/160°C/Gas 3 for 1½ hours. Turn the oven off after this time and leave the door slightly ajar (using the handle of a wooden spoon). Let the gâteaux go completely cold and dry before you freeze or store them.

• *Filling and Decorating* •

The classic filling for meringues, of course, is whipped double cream. Use this for tea-time meringues, or try some butter cream (see page 218), some caramelised apples or Calvados apple purée (see pages 199 and 133).

For gâteaux to be served as dessert, you can be a little more extravagant. Flavour the cream with some caster sugar and liqueur to taste (2 tablespoons of each) and decorate with a complementary fruit or flavouring (see below). Top with a second gâteau (saving the third for the family, or to freeze for another time, or to serve as an open meringue base). Fill and decorate only at the last minute, and cut carefully (saw is perhaps a more accurate description) with a sharp serrated knife. Each double gâteau will serve about eight to twelve people.

apricot	apricot brandy or plain brandy
banana	Crabbie's green ginger wine
cherry	gin
chestnut	brandy
chocolate	rum
coffee	crème de Cacao or Kahlua
hazelnuts	Frangelico
kiwi fruit	Kirsch
mango	lime juice and rum
orange	orange curaçao, Drambuie or Grand Marnier
passion fruit	nothing
peach	peach brandy
pineapple	Kirsch
raspberry	Framboise (*very* expensive) or brandy
strawberry	nothing, or brandy or Kirsch

Dark Rum and Lime Syllabub

Cruising in the Caribbean a few years ago, I became devoted to a rum and lime cocktail which, in that heat, was as effective as a good strong Bloody Mary. The flavour stayed with me, and I decided to make it into a rich pud to end a meal. It's also an easy pud to make when sudden guests descend on you – and its potency will certainly make the evening in one way or another!

Serves 6

¼ pint (150 ml) good dark rum
juice and finely grated rind of 4 fresh
    limes

4 oz (100 g) icing sugar
½ pint (300 ml) double cream

Mix the rum, lime rind and juice and sugar together. Start to beat the double cream, and pour in the rum mixture little by little, taking care that each addition is properly mixed in before pouring in any more.

    Simply pour into chilled glasses and serve with a good home-made biscuit.

Cheeky Crème Brûlée

I was once attacked most vociferously by a diner who was, to say the least, disgusted with this dish as she said I had cheated and it wasn't a traditional burnt Cambridge cream. I told her it wasn't labelled as such, and that I thought it grand as the crisp toffee topping cracked beautifully when hit with a teaspoon and the rich thick custard never curdled underneath. See what you think.

    Practically any fruit can be used for the optional filling – but try a couple of strawberries, raspberries, pipped grapes or exotic fruit in slices.

Fills 8 × 3 inch (7.5 cm) ramekins

4 egg yolks
2 level tablespoons caster sugar
1 pint (600 ml) runny double cream
1 vanilla pod, split

Filling (optional)
a little fruit of choice

Topping
about 8 tablespoons demerara sugar

Put the eight ramekins into a roasting tin and preheat the oven to 275°F/140°C/Gas 1.

    Mix the egg yolks and caster sugar in a bowl and beat together until pale. Bring the double cream to the boil in a pan with the split vanilla pod, then pass through a fine nylon sieve on to the yolk and sugar mixture. Beat this together well.

    Wash and dry the saucepan and return the mixture to it. Heat gently over a medium heat, stirring continuously, until the mixture begins to thicken and lightly coats the back of your wooden spoon. *Never* allow to boil.

    Pour enough hot water into the roasting tin to come half-way up the height of the ramekins, and strain the custard cream into a jug with a good pouring lip.

Divide the custard between the ramekins, putting a fruit in the bottom of each first if you like. Bake in the preheated oven for 15 minutes so that a slight skin forms on the surface of each custard. Remove from the oven and allow to cool.

Now this is where I deviate from the norm. Instead of parping about putting the ramekins into a tray of crushed ice and finishing off under the grill, I do everything separately.

Preheat the grill until it is *red, red, red hot*. Put a double thickness of foil into a baking tray and carefully pour out circles of demerara sugar the size of your ramekin top. Flash this under the hot grill until the sugar caramelises. Transfer these when cool, to the tops of the custards, using a palette knife. What could be simpler?

Better still, make a caramel sauce in a thick-bottomed saucepan from 8 oz (225 g) preserving sugar and ¼ pint (150 ml) water. Cook until it starts to thicken and brown. Pour this out on to the same foil-lined tray in quantities that will spread, using a palette knife, to the area of your custard top. Leave to cool and harden and then remove from the foil and transfer to the custard.

Frangelico Bavarois with Chocolate Leaves

By using different liqueurs, you can easily ring the changes on this recipe – try cherry brandy, orange curaçao, or crème de menthe. Serve with chocolate leaves flavoured with the appropriate booze, and with coffee biscuits (see page 220).

Fills 8 long-stemmed hock glasses

½ oz (15 g) powdered gelatine
3 tablespoons Frangelico
2 tablespoons water
4 egg yolks
4 oz (100 g) caster sugar
½ pint (300 ml) milk
½ pint (300 ml) double cream, lightly
  whipped

Chocolate leaves
rose leaves
4 oz (100 g) dark chocolate, broken into
  pieces
1 tablespoon Frangelico

Put the gelatine into a small saucepan and add the Frangelico and water in one fell swoop (see page 191 for more detailed gelatine instructions).

Place the egg yolks in your warmed Kenwood bowl and start to beat at a very high speed. Continue to do so for at least 5 minutes then add the sugar, a little at a time, taking about 12 minutes to complete this task. Bring the milk up to blood heat in a saucepan and stir in the yolk mixture. Using a wooden spoon, stir and continually cook until the mixture coats the back of your spoon.

Reconstitute the gelatine mixture and pass it through a warm sieve into the custard. Stir in well. Put the saucepan into the sink and surround with very cold water; give it a stir from time to time, until it begins to set. Quickly fold the double cream into your mixture and then pour out into the glasses (better still if they have a touch of Frangelico in the base!). Leave to set and chill, and serve decorated with chocolate leaves.

• Chocolate Leaves •

I like to use rose leaves which are slightly larger than a 50p coin. Wipe them clean. Melt the chocolate with the liqueur in a bowl over boiling water. Dip a rose leaf in and coat one side. Leave to set, then simply tear off the leaf.

Gooseberry Gin Fool

You could use the same quantity of ripe garden rhubarb for a rhubarb gin fool. Cut it up into 2 inch (5 cm) pieces first.

Serves 8–12

3 lb (1.4 kg) gooseberries, washed and trimmed
¼ pint (150 ml) gin
¼ pint (150 ml) cold water
12 oz (350 g) caster sugar

Custard
½ pint (300 ml) single cream
1 teaspoon cornflour
2 tablespoons soft brown sugar
4 egg yolks
½ pint (300 ml) double cream

Put the gooseberries into a clean saucepan with the gin, water and sugar, and cook slowly until quite soft. Pass through a sieve, or liquidise then pass through a sieve (the latter makes the sieving easier). Leave to cool.

Meanwhile, make the custard. Mix 2 tablespoons of the single cream with the cornflour and soft brown sugar in a bowl. Bring the balance of the single cream to the boil. Add it to the cornflour, mixing and beating well.

Return to the saucepan and beat in the egg yolks. Cook over a *low* heat, stirring constantly with a wooden spoon, until the custard is thick and smooth. Strain and cool.

Combine the custard with the fruit purée. Start beating up the double cream and adding the soft mixture a little at a time. Beat until it's light. Spoon into serving glasses or dishes.

Fresh Fruit Salad in a Watermelon Basket

Those lovely large watermelons make superb fruit salad holders for a buffet party – quite apart from the delicious, deep-coloured flesh making a mouth-watering addition to the salad itself. If you are going to take the trouble to do one make sure you allow yourself plenty of time and have a pot of coffee on the go to refresh you along the way. This is an *idea* for you to use, rather than a specific recipe.

The melon should be wiped with a damp cloth and then laid down on the work surface. Gently cut a sliver off the base so that it will stand quite firm without wobbling about.

You can, if you like, simply make an ordinary basket handle by cutting down twice near the middle half-way down, and then cutting along and in from either end. When these chunks are removed you can start spooning out the insides. I think, however, that my method is far nicer. Take a piece of greaseproof paper about 4 inches (10 cm) wide, and half the top to bottom circumference of the melon. Fold down the middle lengthways and then in half again. Using very sharp small scissors, cut a zig-zag pattern along the side with the open edges. Open out one of the folds, so that you have a long strip with zig-zags on both sides. Place this strip on the centre of the top of your watermelon and use as a template; either mark with a felt pen or cut directly around the zig-zags. Remember it only goes round half the melon, and saw your way into the flesh with a very sharp pointed knife. Using a felt pen again and a ruler, draw a level line all round the melon which will act as a guide when you start to insert your knife to form little Vs running round the side to side circumference of the melon. Have a look at the photograph between pages 160 and 161 which will show you *much* more clearly what is involved!

These two top 'lids' either side of the handle will soon be released and then, using a tablespoon, ease out as much flesh as you can, remembering that you want to make this into small cubes for the salad.

Fill this container with fresh fruit salad: use the watermelon itself, as well as seeded grapes, stoned cherries, raspberries, strawberries, orange segments, apple wedges soaked in white wine, pineapple pieces, mango, peach or nectarine slices. If you have to prepare the basket earlier in the day, cover it loosely with cling film and chill in the fridge. A cinnamon stock syrup (see page 139) can be reduced and folded into whipped double cream to be displayed in a serving bowl alongside. Fingers of shortbread or home-made biscuits (see Afternoon Teas) add the finishing touch.

Glazed Orange Segments

These delicious segments will serve four people if offered alone, but can do six to eight if offered as an accompaniment to another pudding – try ice cream, the St Clement's icebox pudding or the chocolate orange gâteau (see pages 203 and 201).

4 large oranges, wiped	$\frac{1}{4}$ pint (150 ml) runny honey
$\frac{1}{2}$ pint (300 ml) water	$\frac{1}{2}$ pint (300 ml) dessert wine
6 oz (175 g) granulated sugar	$\frac{1}{4}$ pint (150 ml) Grand Marnier

Remove the peel very thinly from the oranges with a scorer, trying not to cut off too much white pith. Cut the peel into tiny strips and put to one side.

Using a sharp serrated knife, carefully remove all the pith and outer membrane of the oranges to expose the flesh. Cut into segments as described on page 101. Spread these segments on a greased, lipped baking tray.

Put the water, sugar, honey and wine into a saucepan and bring to the boil. Stir until the sugar dissolves then simmer to reduce by half. Mix in the orange peel strips, and simmer for 10 minutes, stirring *often*. Stir in the Grand Marnier and pour over the orange segments on the tray. Leave to chill. To serve, remove the orange segments to individual plates, and spoon the syrup and peel over them.

Summer Fruits in Red Wine

An easy, delicious – and alcoholic – dessert. Never *boil* the fruits.

Serves 8–12

1 lb (450 g) strawberries
1 lb (450 g) cherries
8 oz (225 g) raspberries
4 oz (100 g) redcurrants
1 pint (600 ml) red wine
4 oz (100 g) caster sugar

finely grated rind of ½ lemon
2 whole cloves

To serve
whipped double cream flavoured with
    lots of caster sugar and finely chopped
    mint

Prepare all the fruits – hulling and stalking as appropriate – and place in a glass serving bowl.

Heat the remaining ingredients together until the sugar has dissolved, then bring to the boil. Leave to cool a little then pass through a sieve over the mixed fruit. Leave to go completely cold.

Serve with the flavoured whipped cream.

Yoghurt Cream Cheese with *Summer Fruits*

Start preparing the dish a day in advance so that the cheese can form overnight.

Serves 8–12

1 pint (600 ml) double cream
½ pint (300 ml) natural yoghurt

finely grated rind of 1 lemon

To make the cream cheese, beat the cream and yoghurt together and then fold in the lemon rind. Place a large sieve lined with a double thickness of muslin over a bowl. Pour the cream mixture into the lined sieve, cover with cling film, and leave overnight in the fridge. The liquid will drain into the bowl, and the cream cheese left in the sieve is ready to use.

I normally take a spoonful of the mixture and place it in the middle of my serving dish. I then scatter it liberally with soft brown sugar and top it with a tablespoon of lightly whipped cream sweetened once again with soft brown sugar. Garnish with hulled strawberries, raspberries and redcurrants scattered around the cheese. Serve with home-made lemon biscuits (see page 220).

Many other fruits can be served with the cheese – choose from the ideas below.

Quartered fresh figs liberally sprinkled with Pernod look attractive – and the taste isn't bad either.
Likewise, apple slices soaked for an hour or so in fresh lime juice interlaced with cucumber slices that have been dashed with wine vinegar – and dieters think it slimming!

Orange wedges soaked in brandy with melon balls make an interesting pattern and provide nice textures and flavours.

Black and green grapes simply cut in two with the pips removed and then soaked for a few hours in Drambuie make a boozy end to a meal. Scatter toasted pine kernels or toasted flaked almonds on as well.

And, need I add, fanned-out caramelised apples (see page 199) underneath the cheese can be coated with the cream, and they're much more sinful than they look!

Rich Custard 'Rummed' Apples

Fills 6 × 3 inch (7.5 cm) ramekins

2 oz (50 g) butter
4 oz (100 g) fresh white or brown
  breadcrumbs
½ pint (300 ml) double cream
2 eggs, plus 1 egg yolk

1 whole nutmeg, finely grated
2 oz (50 g) soft brown sugar
finely grated rind of 2 oranges
4 Granny Smith apples, peeled, cored
  and sliced

Preheat the oven to 350°F/180°C/Gas 4.

Melt the butter and fry the breadcrumbs until lightly browned. Beat together the cream, eggs and egg yolk, grated nutmeg, sugar and orange rind.

In each ramekin, put a layer of sliced apples, then breadcrumbs, and carry on building up these layers until all the apples and most of the breadcrumbs have been used. Divide the custard mixture between the ramekins. Top off with the remaining breadcrumbs (or, better still, Jordan's jungle oats), then put the ramekins into a bain-marie. Pour in enough hot water to come half-way up the ramekins and bake in the preheated oven for 40 minutes.

Serve topped with sprigs of fresh mint. The apples are still crisp, and there is a completely false flavouring of rum!

Thick Vanilla Custard

This custard is ideal for lining pastry flans which have been baked blind. The custard can then be decorated with seasonal fruits. It can also be used as the filling for puff pastry vanilla slices.

1½ oz (40 g) cornflour
1 pint (600 ml) milk
4 oz (100 g) caster sugar

2 eggs, plus 2 egg yolks, lightly beaten
½ teaspoon vanilla essence
1 oz (25 g) butter

Mix the cornflour to a smooth paste with a little of the milk and bring the balance of the milk to the boil with the caster sugar. Pour the hot milk on to the cornflour mix, beating all the time. Return to the saucepan and bring back to the boil. Remove from the heat and beat in the beaten eggs and vanilla essence, quite vigorously, a little at a time. Simmer until the custard coats the back of your wooden spoon.

Put the butter on top of this very warm custard and it will melt, stopping a skin from forming. Before the custard goes stone cold, beat in the butter.

Frangelico Truffles

If you can't get hold of Frangelico – but do persevere, it's so delicious – you can use brandy or rum instead.

Makes 24

12 oz (350 g) good dark chocolate
1 oz (25 g) unsalted butter
¼ pint (150 ml) double cream
12 tablespoons Frangelico

To finish
cocoa powder
icing sugar

Melt the chocolate and butter together in a double boiler, then leave to cool. Mix in the cream and Frangelico, and chill all together until the mixture becomes paste-like in texture.

Dust a work surface with equal parts of cocoa powder and icing sugar and roll the paste into a sausage shape. Cut off small segments and roll these into ball shapes. Put into petits-fours paper cases after evenly dusting them with cocoa and icing sugar. Chill until required – and keep for no longer than 3 days (you won't be able to anyway!).

Turkish Delight

I always like to serve a sweet of some sort with coffee at Miller Howe, and this or the truffles above are ideal – and so delicious.

1 pint (600 ml) cold water
2 oz (50 g) powdered gelatine
1 lb 10 oz (725 g) caster sugar
4 cinnamon sticks, cut in half
1 teaspoon *very strong* rose essence
 (available from chemists)

2 oz (50 g) shelled pistachio nuts, coarsely
 chopped

To finish
icing sugar

Pour the water into a deep and thick-bottomed saucepan, sprinkle the gelatine over it, and dissolve over a very low heat, stirring continually. Add the sugar and continue to stir until dissolved. Add the cinnamon sticks and then boil briskly for 10 minutes until thick and clear.

Remove from the stove and fish out the cinnamon sticks.

Add the rose essence and nuts, stir to distribute evenly, then pour into a very wet 1 inch (2.5 cm) deep tray, measuring about 12 × 10 inches (30 × 25 cm). Cover with cling film and leave to set in the fridge – about 8 hours.

Turn out on to greaseproof paper generously coated with icing sugar and cut into squares. Coat these equally generously with icing sugar.

· Miller Howe · Afternoon Teas

I have been told that it is the Miller Howe afternoon teas that most interfere with guests' long Lakeland walks – they don't want to miss tea, so they travel but a short distance from the hotel! And for us it is a pleasant 'meal' to serve: there is no frantic rush trying to see to sixty people at one go; cakes and biscuits have been made that morning and only need icing, creaming or decorating; and the laying of the trays, the brewing of the tea and serving are the essence of ease and simplicity.

Afternoon tea is traditional in Britain, and it seems to have died out a little since the last war – a great shame, as we are known as a nation of bakers, and when else can you indulge yourself in fruit and cream cakes, vanilla slices, meringues and other delicacies? In the North of England, of course, high tea is more the thing, when you not only get all the goodies of afternoon tea, but a cooked dish as well – things like scrambled eggs or poached haddock, with lots of bread and butter. This meal is served later, at about six rather than four o'clock, and is not a feature of Miller Howe – no one would have room for dinner less than three hours later! – but I do sometimes serve it at home on my days off.

Serve afternoon tea inside or, in the summer, in the garden. Go to town on your tea table – a crisp cloth, pretty china and cutlery, lots of flowers and lots of food. You can serve tiny sandwiches – thinly sliced bread generously buttered, and some delicious fillings. Cucumber and cress sandwiches are traditional, but you could try any of the fillings and toppings mentioned throughout the book. Individual cakes and biscuits should be small enough to eat in two or three bites – and if serving a creamy gâteau, it's probably better to do so on plates with pastry forks. Try to balance the meal, offering some plainer and more delicate fare to contrast with a rich chocolatey cake, for instance. When it's colder, you could serve warm items like buttered scones, muffins or teacakes. And do have a look through other sections in the book – you could make up some delicious pastries such as cream cornets or horns (see page 59), or choose one of the cakes in the desserts section.

Home-made biscuits (or cookies as they are called in the States), too, are a must for afternoon tea, and a house without a full tin tucked away in a store cupboard is, for me, a home without a fire on a cold winter's day. Quite apart from being a bit of one-upmanship should an unexpected visitor call round, they are always welcomed with joy by guests at a dinner party (whether sweet to go with a pud, or savoury to go with soup or cheese). And your guests will know you have spent *time* making them – the most wonderful thing we are able to give these days!

I must come clean and say that for several years I have been chairman of a consultancy panel for McVitie Price Biscuits and have been very much responsible for some of the new wholefood lines they have recently introduced. Their new range of St Andrew biscuits purely for the catering trade took months to develop, and I am always proud when I see them on sale at various outlets.

My store cupboard is now never without some of the McVitie range of biscuits, *but* still, for those special occasions, any of the home-made biscuits in the following section will be a joy for you to serve, and sheer delight for guests to consume. All the recipes are terribly easy if you have a Kenwood mixer, and there are few rules: one is that you must always use soft butter; another is that you must measure the ingredients very accurately; and you must in most cases allow the biscuits time to settle on the baking tray when brought out of the oven before removing to the wire cooling tray. Once you have got the idea, quite a lot of these recipes can have their flavours changed, provided you do not change the actual *amounts* involved.

Baking is one of my favourite occupations – whether biscuits or cakes – and I love setting to and scattering flour all over the carpet in my kitchen at Brantlea. It's so relaxing. My store-cupboard is replenished and from my airtight containers I can produce delights to please the most pernickety of unexpected guests. Read my notes about baking equipment on page 16, and bake away happily!

All-in-One Sponge Cake

This mixing will make two thin 8 inch (20 cm) sponges, twelve small sponges in fairy cake containers, or six medium sized sponges if baked in 3 inch (7.5 cm) ramekins.

4 oz (100 g) soft butter	1 teaspoon baking powder
4 oz (100 g) caster sugar	vanilla essence, almond essence or Camp
2 large eggs, beaten	coffee
4 oz (100 g) self-raising flour	

Prepare two sponge tins – grease and flour the sides well, and line the base with greaseproof paper. Or set paper cases in a patty tin, or butter the ramekins. Preheat the oven to 350°F/180°C/Gas 4.

Simply put everything into your Kenwood bowl and beat with the whisk until a smooth batter is formed. If you haven't a mixer, beat the butter and sugar well together until light and fluffy, then – gradually – beat in the beaten egg. Never add any more egg until the last addition has been completely taken up by the butter and sugar. Mix in the flour and baking powder and flavouring of choice – a couple of drops of either essence or a tablespoon of Camp coffee.

Divide the mixture between the prepared tins, cases or ramekins and bake in the preheated oven for 20–30 minutes (look carefully at the smaller ones, they may cook more quickly). Leave in the containers until cool.

For the larger sponges, sandwich the two together, or slice through horizontally and have two sponges of two layers or one sponge with four layers! Use whipped cream, flavoured if you like, or with soft fruit if in season, and use a butter cream (see page 218) or a simple icing on top.

214

Continental Sponge Cake

This can be made into smaller cakes as can the all-in-one sponge, and can be filled and topped similarly.

Makes 2 × 8 inch (20 cm) round sponges

3 eggs
3 oz (75 g) caster sugar
1 oz (25 g) cornflour, sieved

3 oz (75 g) self-raising flour, sieved
2 oz (50 g) butter, melted and cooled

Prepare the tins – line the bases with greaseproof paper and butter and flour the sides. Preheat the oven to 350°F/180°C/Gas 4.

Break the eggs into the warmed Kenwood bowl and beat until they are quite frothy (about 8 minutes). Little by little beat in the caster sugar. Gently fold in the sieved flours, followed by the cool melted butter.

Divide the mixture between both tins and bake in the preheated oven for 25–30 minutes. As cooling turn out on to a wire cooling tray.

Orange Sponge

This sponge should be eaten on the day it is made. Serve with whipped double cream between the layers, or with sliced poached pears to which the merest touch of ground nutmeg has been added.

Makes 2 × 8 inch (20 cm) round sponges

4 eggs, separated
4 oz (100 g) caster sugar
2 oz (50 g) cornflour, sieved

2 tablespoons plain flour, sieved
1 teaspoon baking powder, sieved
juice and finely grated rind of 1 orange

Prepare the sandwich tins by brushing with melted butter, then sprinkle in some extra flour and sugar. Preheat the oven to 375°F/190°C/Gas 5.

Beat the egg whites until stiff, and slowly add the sugar, beating all the time. Fold in the beaten egg yolks, followed by the sieved cornflour, plain flour and baking powder, and then the juice and rind of the orange.

Divide between the prepared tins and bake for 20 minutes. Turn out of the tins as the cakes are cooling.

Seedcake

4 oz (100 g) butter
4 oz (100 g) caster sugar
2 eggs, beaten
4 oz (100 g) self-raising flour, sieved
½ teaspoon baking powder

2 oz (50 g) ground almonds
2 teaspoons caraway seeds
3 tablespoons natural yoghurt
2 tablespoons Jordan's crunchy oats

Line an 8 inch (20 cm) cake tin with greaseproof paper, and preheat the oven to 350°F/180°C/Gas 4.

Cream butter and sugar together until light. Slowly beat in the eggs, a little at a time, then fold in the flour mixed with the baking powder, ground almonds and caraway seeds. Lastly fold in the yoghurt.

Spoon into the prepared tin and scatter the oats over the top. Bake in the preheated oven for an hour. Turn out when cool on to a cooling tray. It can be eaten more or less immediately, but is the better for keeping – for about 2–3 days.

Cherry Coconut Slice

Makes 3 × 1 lb (450 g) loaves

10 oz (275 g) glacé cherries
2 oz (50 g) desiccated coconut
2 oz (50 g) ground almonds
12 oz (350 g) self-raising flour, sieved
8 oz (225 g) caster sugar

a pinch of salt
8 oz (225 g) soft butter
3 eggs
¼ pint (150 ml) milk

Prepare the loaf tins by lining with greaseproof paper. Preheat the oven to 350°F/180°C/Gas 4.

Wash the cherries well in a sieve to get rid of the gooey syrup, then cut them in half. Roll them in a mixture of ground almonds and half of the coconut.

Put the flour, sugar and salt into a bowl and gently rub in the soft butter. Add the cherries and the remaining coconut mix. Beat the eggs with the milk and fold into the mixture.

Dollop out in the tins and bake in the preheated oven for 45 minutes. Remove to wire cooling trays when cool, and store in airtight tins for up to 10 days.

Raspberry Buns

Makes about 18

8 oz (225 g) butter
6 oz (175 g) sugar
3 eggs, lightly beaten

2 oz (50 g) cornflour, sieved
6 oz (175 g) self-raising flour, sieved
6 oz (175 g) fresh raspberries

Have ready about 18–20 individual sponge cup-cake cases, sitting preferably in patty tins. Preheat the oven to 350°F/180°C/Gas 4.

Cream the butter with the sugar until soft, and then add the eggs a little at a time. Gently fold in the cornflour and self-raising flour, followed by the raspberries.

Spoon into the cup cases, and bake in the preheated oven for 30 minutes. Leave to cool on a wire cooling tray.

Rock Cakes

How on earth these got their name bewilders me as they are anything but! A marvellous standby if stored in an airtight tin (for up to 2 weeks), but if you do, see the tin is hidden from the family!

Makes about 18

10 oz (275 g) self-raising flour, sieved
5 oz (150 g) soft butter, broken into pieces
4 oz (100 g) demerara sugar

4 oz (100 g) mixed dates, walnuts and cherries, chopped
2 eggs, lightly beaten
milk to bind

Line baking trays with good greaseproof paper, and preheat the oven to 350°F/180°C/Gas 4.

Put all the ingredients into a Kenwood bowl and, using the K beater on a *slow* speed, bring together, adding milk as necessary to make a dropping dough consistency.

Using 2 dessertspoons or, better still, your hands, form small balls and place them well apart on baking trays. Bake in the preheated oven for 30–40 minutes, and cool on wire cooling trays before storing.

Chocolate Fudge Sponge Frosting

This is a good topping for many cakes, among them many of the sponges, and can be used for meringue gâteaux as well.

4 oz (100 g) good dark chocolate, broken into pieces
1 tablespoon rum

¼ pint (150 ml) single cream
4 oz (100 g) caster sugar
1 oz (25 g) butter

Put the chocolate into a Christmas pudding type bowl, and place the bowl over a pan of simmering water. Melt it with the rum. Mix the melted chocolate with the single cream and sugar, put in a saucepan and stir continually over a gentle heat until the sugar has dissolved. Bring to the boil, stirring constantly, then lower the heat. Simmer away until a small ball of the mixture forms clearly in a cup of cold water – after about 15–20 minutes.

Stir in the butter and allow to stand until thick. Beat until cool. If it is too thick to spread easily, add a little more cream.

Butter Creams

These can be used for filling or topping meringues or meringue and sponge gâteaux. They're especially good as a topping (with whipped cream inside), as they hold better than double cream, and can be piped as well.

8 oz (225 g) soft unsalted butter
8 oz (225 g) icing sugar, sieved

flavouring to taste, see below

Use a Kenwood mixer or electric hand-beater, and make sure the butter is really soft. Beat the butter until light and fluffy. Now it will absorb the sugar, beaten in tablespoon by tablespoon. Add a little of the following flavourings, and use your finger to keep on tasting until you get the taste you want.

> orange, lemon or lime rind with the juice
> Camp coffee
> unsweetened chestnut purée
> rose essence
> ground hazelnuts with vanilla essence
> a few tablespoons of booze such as dark rum, cherry brandy, Frangelico etc
> toasted desiccated coconut

Shortbread

This shortbread mixing will fill a tray of 8 × 10 inches (20 × 25 cm), or make about twelve individual tartlets. If making the latter, fill with paper cases and baking beans or bits, and chill for about 30 minutes before baking.

8 oz (225 g) plain flour, sieved
4 oz (100 g) Farola
4 oz (100 g) caster sugar

8 oz (225 g) soft butter
a pinch of salt

Preheat the oven to 300°F/150°C/Gas 2.

Mix all the ingredients together, slowly, in the Kenwood. Spread it into the tray (or make into tartlets and chill), and bake in the preheated oven for about an hour.

When cooked, leave to cool, and sprinkle with vanilla sugar. Cut into fingers before it is cold.

Hazelnut Orange Biscuit Slice

This is a tarted-up shortbread!

8 oz (225 g) plain flour, sieved
2 oz (50 g) ground hazelnuts
2 oz (50 g) Farola or fine semolina

4 oz (100 g) caster sugar
8 oz (225 g) soft butter
finely grated rind of 3 oranges

Preheat oven to 300°F/150°C/Gas 2, and lightly grease, flour and sugar a tin measuring 8 × 10 inches (20 × 25 cm).

Combine all the ingredients in your Kenwood mixer, using the K beater on a slow speed. Bring together until a dough is formed.

Pat out all over the prepared tin, cover with greaseproof paper and then, using a jam jar or something similar, roll it flat and press down. Remove paper, liberally prick all over with a fork, and then chill for at least 30 minutes.

Bake in the preheated oven for 1 hour and, as it is cooling, divide into the sizes you wish.

Nutty Meringue Biscuits

Makes 24–30

4 egg whites	6 oz (175 g) caster sugar
a pinch of salt	6 oz (175 g) chopped nuts
$\frac{1}{2}$ teaspoon cream of tartar	

Cover a couple of baking trays with greaseproof paper and preheat the oven to 200°F/100°C/the very lowest possible gas.

Put the egg whites into a cold mixing bowl and beat until peaks form. Add the salt and cream of tartar. Little by little, beating on high speed, add the sugar. Finally, fold in the nuts.

Spoon on to the greaseproof-papered trays, using a dessertspoon. Bake in the preheated oven for $1\frac{1}{4}$ hours, or until the meringues are set. Remove from the oven and leave to cool. Remove from the paper and put into airtight containers. They will keep for about a couple of weeks.

Coconut Biscuits

Makes about 30

6 oz (175 g) butter	*Topping*
4 oz (100 g) caster sugar	vanilla sugar
6 oz (175 g) plain flour, sieved	
2 oz (50 g) desiccated coconut	

Cover baking trays with greaseproof paper, and preheat the oven to 375°F/190° C/Gas 5.

Combine all the ingredients in the Kenwood bowl with the K beater until a dough is formed.

Break off even-shaped balls – about the size of a marble – and place them on the baking trays. Bake in the preheated oven for 20–30 minutes, and, as they're cooling, sprinkle liberally with vanilla sugar.

Coffee Kisses

Makes 24–30

8 oz (225 g) plain flour, sieved
6 oz (175 g) soft butter
4 oz (100 g) ground almonds

2 oz (50 g) sugar
2 tablespoons Camp coffee

Line a baking tray with greaseproof paper and preheat the oven to 300°F/150°C/ Gas 2. Bring all the ingredients together in your Kenwood, using the K beater until a biscuit dough is formed.

Break off even balls – about the size of a marble – and rub to a smooth shape in the palm of your hands. Place on the tray – leaving plenty of space for them to expand – and bake for 15 minutes. Cool on the tray first, then on a wire tray.

Coffee Biscuits

To make a delightful lemon biscuit, replace the Camp coffee with the finely grated rind of 1 large lemon.

Makes about 30–36

10 oz (275 g) self-raising flour, sifted
4 oz (100 g) caster sugar

8 oz (225 g) soft butter
2 tablespoons Camp coffee

Place all the ingredients into a Kenwood bowl and mix slowly until they come together. At this stage the dough can keep in the fridge for up to a week, or can be frozen.

When you want to bake, preheat the oven to 350°F/180°C/Gas 4, and allow the dough – if it's been chilled – to come up to room temperature. Form it into small balls – about the size of a marble – and flatten on to a baking sheet, well apart, using the back of a fork dipped in cold water. Bake in the preheated oven for 10 minutes. Leave to become cold, then store in airtight containers.

Date Crunchies

6 oz (175 g) self-raising flour, sieved
6 oz (175 g) butter
6 oz (175 g) semolina
3 oz (75 g) caster sugar
8 oz (225 g) dates, stoned and chopped

1 level tablespoon runny honey
2 tablespoons rum
2 tablespoons Camp coffee
1 tablespoon lemon juice
a pinch of ground cinnamon

Grease and flour a flat Swiss roll tin, and preheat the oven to 375°F/190°C/Gas 5.

Mix all the ingredients in your Kenwood bowl, using the K beater, until you get a good dough consistency. Spread the dough into the prepared tin, and press lightly down. Chill for about 30 minutes.

Bake in the preheated oven for 30 minutes, and cut into fingers – as many as you like – just as it's cooling.

· Index ·